CHALLENGING LEVEL

The Graveyard Book
A Teaching Guide

by Mary Elizabeth

Community Strand

Printed in USA

GARLIC PRESS

Educational Materials for Teachers and Parents

899 South College Mall Road
Bloomington, IN 47401

www.garlicpress.com

Because the editions of this book differ so much in pagination, chapter numbers, rather than page numbers, are used to identify vocabulary location

Publisher: Douglas M. Rife
Cover photograph: Douglas M. Rife; styling by Elizabeth M. Podhaizer
Interior photographs: Elizabeth M. Podhaizer
Interior design: Mary Elizabeth
Cover design: Joanne Caroselli

ISBN 978-0-931993-09-1

Table of Contents

The Discovering Literature Series is designed to develop students' appreciation for literature and to improve reading comprehension. The Challenging Level focuses on reading strategies that help students construct meaning as they read, as well as make connections between and among texts. The strategies taught in each guide reflect the demands of the particular work, and material can be adapted or skipped to suit both class focus and students' developmental level, or even adapted for book club use.

Every teacher of literature faces a quandary in that the experience of literature—suspending one's disbelief and getting lost in the world of a story (aesthetic reading)—and the analysis of literature (efferent reading) cannot be carried on simultaneously. Thus, this guide is designed to be used with at least three different reading modes:

- **Aesthetic/Analytic** Students read the book through first for the experience of the story (with or without vocabulary preparation) and use the guide afterwards to work on comprehension and analysis;

- **Chapter-by-Chapter** Students read with limited preparation, but a thorough check-in on comprehension and analytic understanding after each chapter ensures comprehension is ongoing;

- **Guided Reading** Students' reading is scaffolded with, for example, a purpose for reading each chapter (e.g., using Journal and Discussion questions that do not give away major plot elements), and following up as in the other modes.

CHALLENGES AND OPPORTUNITIES IN TEACHING THE GRAVEYARD BOOK

The Four Editions

The Graveyard Book is available in print in US and UK versions, as a graphic novel, and in an audio version read by the author (and available free at http://www.mousecircus.com/videotour.aspx), which has intro music and images from the US edition showing as the "cover" of the videos. Gaiman makes some gestures, but on the whole, the audio allows students to create images in their imagination rather than having them imposed by a source. On the other hand, Gaiman's reading provides interpretation of tone and differentiates the various accents, so that students do not have to. The graphic novel version is set in all caps and uses a very small font size, but allows you to engage with students in exploring elements of visual literacy, a particularly rich exploration since eight different illustrators were involved.

Why the Edition Matters: A Book Made for Teaching Inferences

The Graveyard Book is carefully constructed by Gaiman (pronounced "Gaym'n" per the FAQs on his website) so that careful reading pays off in uncovering important information that is not explicitly stated anywhere, e.g., the location of the titular graveyard (England) and the species of being of which Silas is a member (vampire). Both the graphic novel version and the UK print edition "give away" the second point on the cover by picturing Silas in a way that leaves no culturally literate person with any doubt that he is a vampire; additionally, Vol. 2, p. 32 of the graphic novel shows him as a bat. There are clues to the setting, too, in the graphic novel: a double-decker bus in Vol. 1, p. 129 and Vol. 2 p. 32; a car with the steering wheel on the right-hand side in Vol. 2, pp. 52–53. There is no doubt, however, that the graphic novel could be well used to support students with more limited comprehension skills. The US print and digital editions avoid giving away important details, but have a different issue: the illustrations by Dave McKean are so abstract and disjointed in some cases (on p. 4, the front of the man Jack's face appears to be hanging off in the air); purposely rendered without 90° angles in some instances (on pp. 6–8, Bod's house looks frowzy and out of kilter—not what one would expect from a house that is owned by an architect); so difficult to puzzle out (on p. 100, Silas looks like a woman); and are in such disparate styles (the style of the image on p. 102 is completely different from that of the image on p. 100), that they are both distracting and confusing. You could also have students first encounter this story through the audio version, allowing them to encounter the words (spoken with an English accent) without pictures. You could also provide a US edition and encourage them to skip the pictures. In any case, choosing how you intend to present the book will help you make supportive choices about which edition is best for your purposes.

How Vocabulary Is Handled

Because of the very large number of challenging words in *The Graveyard Book* (the 5.4 grade-level equivalent reading level posted by Scholastic probably doesn't account for extensive use of colloquial British English), the small number of text divisions (eight chapters and an Interlude), and the markedly different pagination in editions, it was decided to include the bulk of vocabulary words, divided into parts of speech (nouns, verbs, adjectives, and adverbs), along with definitions and chapter of first appearance in a download from the garlicpress.com website. Ideas for introducing vocabulary are also provided. There are three reasons not to rely on print or digital dictionaries in place of teaching vocabulary: 1) it interrupts the experience of the story; 2) definitions may not match the use in the text; 3) the word may not appear (for example, Gaiman's Britishisms).

Key vocabulary is handled in three sections within this guide:

- **Special Vocabulary** (p. 20) includes 13 topics, some including a few words that will be known to students in order to give a complete picture of Gaiman's vocabulary. *This list is for your use, not for distribution.* Note that while many terms in these groups are neutral, some—such as currency terms and locales—will clearly reveal the setting of the work to culturally literature students.

  - amounts
  - art terms
  - botanical terms
  - categories of being
  - clothing
  - criminals/crimes
  - currency denominations
  - environments
  - graveyard/architectural terms
  - jobs
  - locales
  - lab equipment
  - zoology terms

- **Strategy 13: Reading Dialogue** (pp. 37.72) introduces the following five vocabulary topics, all of which are (or once were) characteristic of British speech. The list of vocabulary is in the answers.

  - Britishisms
  - British oaths
  - civilities
  - longer phrases
  - idioms

- **Strategy 15: Interpreting Allusions and References** (p. 42/78) addresses the following seven vocabulary topics.

  - celebrations
  - historic periods
  - honorifics
  - literary references
  - other aspects of culture
  - places
  - real people

THE ELEMENTS IN THIS LITERATURE GUIDE

Chapter Pages

Each Chapter Page is organized into two sections: **Journal and Discussion Topics,** and a **Chapter Summary**. The Journal and Discussion Topics can be used as prompts for entries in students' Reading Response Journals if you choose to use them, as questions for discussion to help students become deeply engaged with the literature, and/or to check comprehension. If you wish to interact with students using their journals, the dialogue will be facilitated if you periodically collect the journals and respond to students' comments. It is important for students to know beforehand whether their journals are private or public. Even if they are public, many educators believe that journals should not be corrected or graded, but only check to be sure they are being used. You may also wish to keep your own journal.

Discussion can take place between partners, in small groups, or as a whole class. Students may also wish to reflect on the discussion in their journals. Discussion starters include:

1. review of predictions made for the chapter and whether they were accurate.
2. group retelling of the chapter in which everyone participates.
3. each group member sharing:
   a. the most striking moment in the chapter for him or her;
   b. a question she or he would like to ask the author or a character; or
   c. what he or she liked most or least about the chapter.
4. analysis of how the chapter relates to the preceding material.

The Chapter Summary for each chapter is included for teacher use only, each one having enough details to refresh your memory about specific contents of each chapter. The summaries should never be used to replace reading the work of literature. Note that while the suggested questions always include a summarization idea, these questions are couched so that the summaries provided in this book will not provide adequate answers.

Strategy Pages

Strategy Pages are developed to increase students' understanding of strategies they can use to enhance their understanding of literature. A strategic approach does not eschew the teaching of skills, but takes instruction farther by helping students understand how and when to deploy their skills, that is, choose appropriate skills to employ in various literary situations. Having a strategic understanding of how meaning is made by the interaction of authors' words and readers' understanding and imagination can lead to enriched reading experiences. Because Gaiman has stated that *The Graveyard Book* grew out of *The Jungle Book* and the extensive parallels are important to understanding the work and provide a unique opportunity to explore relationships between two texts, the relevant sections of the source are included in the back of this guide, and three strategy lessons are devoted to the relationship. They are separate from the other material so that you can either look at this facet of the work after completing the book, if you choose, or skip it all together.

You may copy and distribute Strategy pages. Students can answer on the back of the page or on a separate sheet of paper. Some Strategy Page questions require ongoing attention as the students continue reading.

Tests

At the end of every second chapter, a comprehensive **Test** has been provided. Each test includes vocabulary exercises and short essay topics. You may copy and distribute these pages, which students may complete with or without access to the text, as you decide. You can also feel free to select from among the questions, rather than have students answer all of them. The third test includes the Interlude, as well as Chapters 5 and 6.

Writer's Forum Pages

Each **Writer's Forum** page presents instruction about a particular genre and directions for a particular writing task. Assignments draw on both the literature and students' own experience of the text. You can choose from these suggestions or substitute your own creative-writing ideas. Besides the six Writer's Forums in this guide, there are plenty of writing opportunities in the Journal and Discussion topics and the Tests that could be developed into full lessons, if you wish.

As you plan writing lessons, allow enough time for students to engage in the writing process:

- **Prewrite** (brainstorm and plan their work)
- **Draft** (give a shape to their ideas on paper)
- **Review** (revisit their work with an eye to improving it, on their own as well as with peers, with you, or with other reviewers)
- **Revise** (make changes that they feel will improve their draft)
- **Proofread** (check for accuracy in grammar, mechanics, and spelling)
- **Publish** (present their work to others in some way)

Theme Pages

There are several different ways to approach theme, starting with the Theme Page (p. 57). You can also set this work in the context of other works of literature that focus on community using our other literature guides in "The Community" series or other works with a community theme, for example, these works in which children have to navigate multiple communities with different cultures and expectations:

- *The Jungle Book* by Rudyard Kipling
- *Splendors and Glooms* by Laura Amy Schlitz
- *Jane Eyre* by Charlotte Brontë
- *Silas Marner* by George Eliot
- *Mansfield Park* by Jane Austen
- *Oliver Twist* by Charles Dickens
- *A Wrinkle in Time* by Madeleine L'Engle
- *Ender's Game* by Orson Scott Card

A group of books with similar themes can also throw light on Big Ideas. Big Ideas worth considering include the following:

- What are the important similarities between communities? the important differences?
- What does the community owe the individual and vice versa?
- What are different reasons for transitioning between communities, and what skills and strategies help make a smooth transition?

Answer Pages

Possible responses are given in the Answer Pages. The responses include critical analysis of the novel that you may find useful. Students' answers are expected to be more developed than the sample answers in many cases.

INTRODUCING THE LITERATURE

How you choose to introduce the literature will likely depend on the student and reading mode. For Aesthetic/Analytic reading, you may simply hand the student an edition and allow the author to unfold the world of the story in his or her own way. When students need guidance and when you are teaching analysis, you can use this guide to help students contextualize *The Graveyard Book* using Strategy 1: Beginning a Book, p. 9).

Whatever mode students are using, it is a good idea to point out that it is possible to consciously assess one's own understanding and that this process is called *metacognitive reflection*. Also point out that doing so may interrupt the experience of the story until such reflection becomes seamlessly integrated into the reader's process. You may wish to review the process by modeling with a think-aloud approach as you go through questions 3–5 in Strategy 1 (for aesthetic reading, skip over the others for now). Simply read aloud the portion of *The Graveyard Book* needed to answer the questions (or another book, if you don't want to influence students' reading), and speak aloud your thoughts as you formulate your responses, making explicit the connections and prior knowledge you are developing in your thoughts. Continue with prereading activities of your choice.

Sample Lesson Plan

It's likely that students will eventually end up reading chapter-by-chapter. If they are using the aesthetic/analytic approach, this will be their second reading of the book. At this point, all students can engage in prereading, during reading, and after reading activities geared for their abilities and needs.

Prereading Activities: Choose these activities based on how much prereading guidance students need and what can be handled after they read. Prereading activities may include both reviewing the developments of the previous chapter(s) and reviewing predictions.

During Reading: Students can read with their Reading Journals handy, if it suits their reading mode: if they are experiencing the story and don't want to be interrupted to do a journal entry, allow them to write in the journal after they read. If students need guidance as they read, you may wish to give them some of the journal and discussion topics before they read to help focus their attention. Additional journal activities they can use with every chapter include the following:

- recording questions they have about what they have read;
- recording associations they have made between this text and other texts, experiences, or situations; and
- taking notes on the images and/or feelings the text evoked.

After Reading: Students can complete the Journal and Discussion Topics, and the Writer's Forum and Strategy Pages and Test (if any). You may wish to end each discussion by having students make predictions.

NEIL GAIMAN AND THE GRAVEYARD BOOK

Born in Hampshire, UK in 1960, Neil Gaiman now lives near Minneapolis in the US. He began his writing career as a journalist, and his first published writing was biographies of Duran Duran and Douglas Adams, and early in his career, he also published a graphic novel, *Violent Cases*, a collaboration with Dave McKean who illustrated the US version of *The Graveyard Book*. His more recent works often originate as graphic novels or speculative fiction. His most widely known YA work is *Coraline* (2002), which was made into a movie in 2009. Many of his works cross genre boundaries.

The Graveyard Book has won numerous awards, and it brought Gaiman the distinction of being the first person to ever win both the Newbery Medal and the Carnegie Medal for the same book. Gaiman explains in his Newbery acceptance speech (included in the US paperback) that the book had three key influences: the "graveyard in the Sussex town in which I grew up"; an image of "my infant son, Michael—who was two …—on his tricycle, pedaling through the graveyard across the road in the sunshine, past [a] grave I once thought had belonged to a witch"; and *The Jungle Book* by Rudyard Kipling (pp. 322–323). In the FAQs on his website, he lists his favorite graveyards as "Highgate Cemetery (West), Abney Park (Stoke Newington) and Glasgow Necropolis" (http://mousecircus.com/faqs.aspx).

THE COMMON CORE STATE STANDARDS INITIATIVE

Please note that this Teaching Guide is not limited to coverage of items mentioned in the Common Core Standards: it treats all key approaches that help readers gain a deep understanding of The Graveyard Book.

The Common Core State Standards Initiative proposes educational standards that aim to "provide a consistent, clear understanding of what students are expected to learn, so teachers and parents know what they need to do to help them." As of February, 2015, 43 states, the District of Columbia, four US territories, and the Department of Defense Education Activity have adopted the Common Core Standards. The following chart shows how exercises and activities in this teaching guide align with the relevant Common Core standards. Because this guide may be used across a range of ages and grade levels, the chart refers to the key content of each standard across grades 6–12. the Common Core Standards emphasize skills and knowledge, so you may wonder why this teaching guide emphasizes *strategies* and how strategies and skills are related. A *strategy* is the knowledge of when and how to deploy your skills for the most effective results. If you have skills and don't know when and how to use them, they don't do much good. The strategy lessons in this teaching guide provide instruction in skills, contextualized with information about when and how to use them effectively.

Common Core Correlation

STANDARD	PAGE NUMBER
Reading Standards for Literature	
1. Cite textual evidence	11, 16, 24, 25, 26, 27, 33, 35, 54, 55, 57
2. Determine themes	10, 17, 31, 51, 52, 54, 55, 57
3. Analyze story development	character development,16, 28, 57; plot development, 25, 34, 45, 56; character motivation and choices, 16, 33, 44, 57; contribution of setting, 29, 48; characterization, 16, 28; tropes, 34, 43, 45, 47, 52, 53, 56; motifs, 34, 36, 52, 56, 69
4. Determine meanings of words	tone, 39, 41, 44, 58, 86; symbols, 16, 28, 29, 48 diction, 48, 65
5. Analyze structure	of poetry, 18–19; book level, 15, 17, 24, 31, 60; foreshadowing, 85; parallels, 17, 31, 35, 51, 61, 67, 85
6. Analyze point of view/narration	10, 41, 44, 58, 68, 78
7. Compare multiple versions	48, 55, 58, 59, 60, 61, 67
9. Compare/contrast texts	internal comparison, 26, 35, 43, 46, 47, 52, 53; comparison with *The Jungle Book*, 17, 31 51; comparison with a work of the student's choosing, 24, 27
Writing Standards	
1. Write arguments to support claims	11, 24, 25, 26, 27, 33, 41, 42, 54, 57
2. Write informative/explanatory texts	passim
7/8. Conduct research, gathering information from multiple sources	50, 55,
9. Draw evidence from literary texts	passim
10. Write a range of texts for various purposes/audiences	lyrics, 18; description, 30; dialogue, 39; short research report, 50; book review, 54 compare and contrast, 55
Language Standards	
4c. Consult reference sources.	dictionary 13, 38
5a. Interpret figurative language	simile and metaphor, 30, 32, 43, 67
5c. Distinguish nuances of meaning	diction, 48, 63
6 Acquire general academic and domain-specific words and phrases	20–23

Strategy 1

Beginning a Book

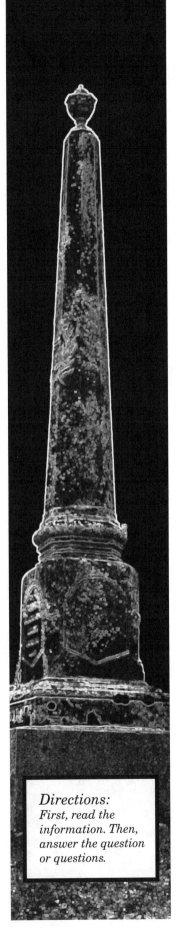

When an artist or craftworker sets about creating a work, there are a set of standard tools, techniques, and products available. The potter, for example, has different kinds of clay, glaze, and shaping tools available. The product may be a pitcher, bowl, statue, vase, lamp base, etc. The techniques used may include throwing on a pottery wheel, as well as various kinds of burnishing, incising, firing at different heats, etc. In addition, there are certain conventions, such as customary sizes and shapes for dinnerware, that the potter may choose to employ or not. The potter does not use every technique and material for every ceramic object, and his or her choices are guided by the goal, which might be the answer to a question such as, "How can I effectively communicate my vision?" The viewer observing the finished product cannot see it all at one time. Moving closer and farther away, walking around the work, attending to details, silhouettes, colors, textures, and the effect of the whole, the viewer can come to understand the pottery.

The novelist is an artist who works in words that create images, thoughts, and feelings in the reader. Like the potter, the writer may not be present when the audience experiences the product (in this case a book), but reading is, nevertheless, an act of communication in which both writer and reader play a part. The reader's understanding of the standard tools, techniques, and conventions of the writer helps the reader to understand the writer's vision. This doesn't mean that every reader has the same experience: each reader brings an individual and unique understanding to the act of reading, so different readers will have different insights and feelings. As a result, discussion between and among readers can enrich the experience of all.

Beginning a book is particularly important because readers starting a book are entering new, uncharted territory. This is true even though they may have *prior knowledge* about the author, genre, and story through having read other books by the author, having read other books in the genre, or having seen a movie or heard an audio recording of the work they are about to read. When you are starting a work of fiction, paying particular attention to the available clues can help you to enter the world of the story.

Title: It is a convention for a novel to have a title, found on the front cover, the spine, and the title page of a print edition and in the library and on the title page of an eBook. When a book is read aloud, the title is typically announced as the reading starts. The title of the book may explicitly tell what the book is about, may hint about the story, or may seem very mysterious. The author's name appears on the title page as well. Generally, the title is larger than the author's name on the cover, unless the author is so well known that his or her name is considered likely to sell books.

Cover Illustration: Many books have a picture on the cover. The writer may or may not have had a voice in what appears, so the illustration may or may not represent the writer's vision; nevertheless, it can give you some idea of characters, setting, and plot in the story.

Inside and Back Cover Blurbs: The note on the back cover of print editions is advertising, meant to give away enough of the story to pique your interest and convince you to buy the book. It doesn't necessarily reflect the writer's vision or the most meaningful view of the story. In addition, it may contain spoilers, so it is best avoided. This material is skipped

Directions:
First, read the information. Then, answer the question or questions.

when books are read aloud. It may not appear in digital editions.

Other Books By: Other books by the same author may be listed.

Copyright Page: The copyright page tells the dates of the book's publication. It can help you know whether the book is recent or older and whether it is an original version or edited, adapted, or translated.

Epigraph: An epigraph is a quotation that may set the tone for the story or suggest its theme.

Table of Contents: *The Graveyard Book,* has named chapters. Like the book title, chapter names may be revealing or oblique. When books are read aloud, it is not usual to read the table of contents, and the UK edition of *The Graveyard Book* does not include one. It's worth looking at the eBook navigation if you are reading a digital edition and there is no internal table of contents.

Inside Illustrations: Some books are illustrated throughout with drawings, paintings, photographs, etc. In whatever way they are illustrated, the illustrations and the text may have different relationships. Illustrations may duplicate what is mentioned explicitly in the text, but they often extend it, adding extra details. They may ground the reader in a specific time and place or they may imitate the style of a particular period. By their nature, illustrations always add something. *The Graveyard Book* has three different editions—US, UK, and graphic novel—each with different illustrators.

First Few Paragraphs: The first few paragraphs of the story provide the writer with the first opportunity to introduce the characters, plot, setting, and theme of the story. Read carefully to learn as much as you can about the world of the book.

1. Does the approach to beginning a book described here differ from what you usually do? If so, how?

2. What, if anything, do you already know about Gaiman (pronounced Gaym'n), his other works, or *The Graveyard Book*?

3. What is your reaction to the title of the book?

4. Describe the cover illustration on your edition. What can you gather from it?

5. When was this book was first published? How long has it been?

6. What do you think the epigraph means?

7. If your book has a table of contents, what can you tell about the story from the chapter titles? Which chapter might the cover illustration come from? How is reading different with no table of contents?

8. Read to "he began to walk up the hill," just before the line of space. Describe the writing.

9. What is the narrator like? Can you trust the narrator's perceptions? How do you know? To whom is the narrator telling the story?

10. Who seem(s) to be the most important character(s)? How can you tell?

11. Where does the story take place? Is it a real setting or a setting created by the author? What special characteristics does the setting have?

12. What more do you hope to learn about the setting and the characters?

13. What clues are there to the genre of this story?

14. What does the theme or focus of the story seem to be?

15. What do you predict will happen next in the story?

Chapter 1

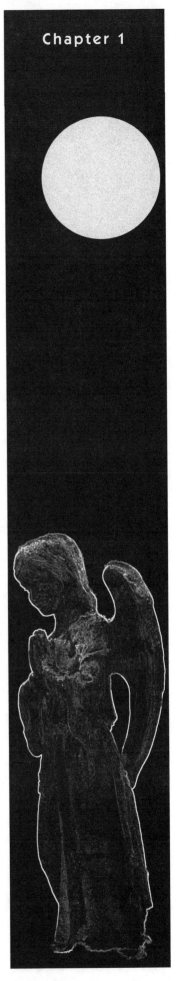

Journal and Discussion Topics

1. Now that you've read the first chapter, what do you think *The Graveyard Book* will be about? What evidence supports your conclusions?

2. Four times in this chapter, there is an extra line of space between paragraphs. What is the meaning of the space in each case? How would you characterize each of the five sections created by the breaks? What is the relation of the five sections in terms of time sequence?

3. The chapter begins and ends with Jack. What do you gather from this?

4. What differences does the narrator point out between Silas and Jack. What other differences do you see? How does Silas differ from the other inhabitants of the graveyard?

5. What is the significance of naming the baby?

6. How does Gaiman build suspense in this chapter?

7. What changes for Bod in the course of this chapter?

8. What does the reader learn about the man Jack's motives for the murders he commits and the one he fails to commit? What is left unknown?

9. How do you understand the role of the Lady in Grey?

10. What things does Mrs. Owens do that could be characterized as *motherly*?

11. What effect did the illustrations in Chapter 1 have on your understanding?

12. When in this chapter do you discover that the child in question is a boy? Why do you think it is revealed then, and not earlier?

13. Summarize the arguments about the baby. What are the different points of view presented and the rationales (if presented) for the various opinions?

Summary

The book begins with a knife and the hand that holds it, belonging to "the man Jack." Jack wipes the knife and—having already killed the parents and older child of the household—heads farther upstairs to kill the toddler, who sleeps at the top of the house. But despite initial appearances, there is no child in the crib. The man Jack, however, can smell the child, and is able to follow the child by its scent. He sheaths the knife, goes out into the foggy streets, and begins to follow the child up the hill to the graveyard at the top.

Focus switches to the child, a curious and agile child, about 18 months old, who figured out how to use his teddy bear to escape his crib after being awakened by a crash in the night. He bumps down the stairs, sucking on his pacifier (the British edition has *dummy*), losing his diaper in the process (in the graphic novel, this detail is omitted). Wearing only a nightshirt and finding the front door open, he ventures out into the night and starts up the hill.

At the top of the hill is a graveyard, and the ghost of Mrs. Betsy Owens spots the baby and calls over her husband. The baby's family—now ghosts—show up, and his Mother warns that the man approaching the graveyard and climbing over the wall is trying to harm the baby and begs Mrs. Owens to care for him, and Mr. and Mrs. Owens agree. When Mrs. Owens reaches to pick up the baby, the baby disappears from the man Jack's sight. He calls out, and Silas, allowing himself to be mistaken for the caretaker, comes and persuades the man Jack that the child he seeks is outside the graveyard and what he heard was a fox. He also is able to convince Jack to forget their conversation as he lets him out of the graveyard, and Jack goes to seek the child elsewhere.

Meanwhile, about 300 of the graveyard's 10,000 residents have begun a debate over the propriety of commiting to raise a living child. Silas is drawn into the argument and offers to be the child's guardian—because he can leave the graveyard, he can procure food for the infant. He suggests they name the child, supports Mrs. Owens in the choice of "Nobody," and—when Mrs. Owens is asked to leave the meeting—immediately undertakes to get Nobody food, while Mrs. Owens sings him a lullaby. After a very long debate, the matter is settled when the Lady in Grey appears on her horse and declares to the comunity that "The dead should have charity." The child is given the Freedom of the Graveyard, and goes to live in the Owenses' "fine little tomb." Silas visits the crime scene, and Jack, at first bemoaning his lost opportunity, then observes that he hasn't failed yet and doesn't have to report the situation to the Convocation. The chapter ends with reference to the knife, "safe and dry inside its sheath."

Strategy 2

You've probably heard of *prewriting*—the term used to designate the planning you do as you prepare to write a text—but there's no comparable term *prereading*, even though when we read we have to:

- recognize black marks on the paper as letters and words;
- process the words in groups to construct meaning and figure out how phrases, clauses, and ideas are connected;
- relate the perceived meaning to what we already know about texts in general, texts of the same genre as the one we're reading, earlier information from this particular text, etc.;
- create in our minds the world of the text;
- apply our prior knowledge of facts, experiences, other texts, ideas, feelings, sensory data, and the like to help us understand what we have read;
- try to recollect the new sequence of events that make up the plot; and
- fill gaps left by the text (no text tells absolutely everything that happened) with our own elaborations.

With so much processing going on the first time we read a book—as we discover everything about a story for the first time, we may miss some aspects. It may help you to understand this if you think about the difference between a painting—which can be seen in its entirety in an instant—and a work of fiction—which not only takes all the steps mentioned above, but also unfolds in the reader's imagination over the time that it takes him or her to read it.

One approach that can help you deal with the complexity of a first reading is to keep an eye on your reading rate and adjust it as necessary. How quickly or slowly we read may be an aspect of reading we don't think too much about: it may be automatic for us to adjust our speed to cope with different kinds of texts and reading for different purposes. But let's just stop for a moment here and identify some of the purposes and text characteristics that might lead us to intentionally slow down our reading, and if necessary, reread material or use other approaches. (For information on marking a text, see Strategy 3: Marking a Text, p. 14; for more about rereading, see Strategy 21: Rereading a Book, p. 53.)

Directions:
First, read the information. Then, answer the question or questions.

Reading Purposes	*How to Adjust*
Want/need to remember/memorize material	Slow down and reread to retain all details.
Need to correlate with other material	Slow down and mark the text with parallels and contrasts you note.
Need to prepare for a paper, class, discussion, or test	Slow down and pay more attention to details, relationships between and among parts, order of events, etc.; reread as necessary.

Reading Situation	How to Adjust
Difficult vocabulary interfering with comprehension	Pause to use context clues, built-in dictionary, glossary, or outside sources, if necessary.
Long complex or compound sentences	Slow down and note punctuation to ensure that relationships between and among grammatical elements are well understood.
Unfamiliar subject matter	Take enough time when new material is being introduced to absorb it: your grasp of new ideas/concepts/insights will then carry over into the rest of the book.
Complex subject matter	Take extra time and reread when something, by its nature, cannot be easily or clearly described.
Special formatting	Slow down to review charts, maps, graphs, and other illustrations that require more focused study and special interpretation than text.
Varying importance of material	Slow down for more important material, but increase reading rate for less important material.
Varying types of text	Poetry, by its nature, calls for a different type of reading than prose, with attention to sound, for example. Meanings may need to be teased out over a number of readings.

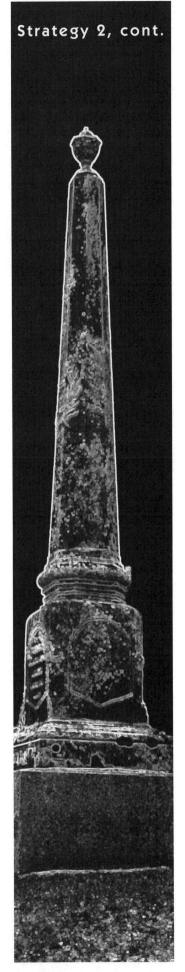

The reading process also depends on the type of text we're reading. Let's imagine texts as existing on a continuum, a range with two endpoints.

efferent (informational) texts —————————— *aesthetic (experiential) texts*

At one extreme we find **efferent texts**—texts that use words, sentences, and sounds only to convey information, after which the particular words, sentences, and sounds don't matter. It's important that you have the facts, but not important how you acquired them. If what you need to know is whether the king is alive or dead, it does not matter whether the sentence you hear is: "The king is dead" or "The king has passed away" or "The king is no longer with us." In this case, when the content of the message is conveyed, the exact wording of the message no longer matters.

At the continuum's other end, where we find **aesthetic texts**, is poetry, in which the meaning cannot be separated from the particular words, word groups, and sounds the writer chose. In poetry, the sound and sense, along with spelling and grammar and mechanics and usage, are *one* thing, and the experience of these particular choices makes the *one* thing that constitutes the poem for the reader. Information can exist apart from the way it is conveyed; a poem cannot.

In between these two outliers we find narrative fiction—much of which belongs in the category of literature. Where on the continuum a particular work of literature, or a particular part of a particular work, lies depends on how it is written. We can only discover its place by the experience itself. But a good approach to literature is to start reading it as if it were written with the care and intentionality of poetry, as if "everything counts."

1. Identify any portions of the Front Matter and Chapter 1 for which you altered your reading process and explain what you did and why.

Strategy 3   Marking a Text

Marking up a text is a good way to make a book your own. You can respond to the author and characters, give yourself helpful reminders, collect information about different parts of the book in one place, and/or record your reactions. Here are some helpful hints on what you can do with either a print or digital edition. If you are reading purely to experience the story, you might not have much (or anything) to say that you want to stop reading for, but if you are reading analytically or to write a paper, you can make your note taking more effective by creating a system.

Book As Conversation

When you read a book, you're engaging with an author who has something to say. By annotating the text, you can speak back. Questions, comments, evaluations, and even arguments are fair game. Some comments you might want to use are:

- •But what about . . . ?—for apparent contradictions
- • ! (or as many as you need)
- • TAT ("think about this")—for points that need pondering
- • WM? ("what [does this] mean?")—for points that need clarification

Memory Aids

If you know that you will need to find story events, character descriptions, thematic statements, figurative language, etc. again, you can use a variety of techniques to help you relocate what you need:

- • Use color—whether with stickies, highlighters, pens, or digital notes—to categorize your comments.
- • Close to the front of the book, make lists of page numbers/locations of items you will need to find again: important quotations, appearance of symbols, significant events.
- • Invent your own system of margin notes, using symbols to record the occurrence of repetition, symbols, connections, themes, and other important details such as key words or important quotations.

Links/Connections

Sometimes a book will call up a link to another text—a source, reference, or allusion will be known to you; a thought or quotation will connect to something someone else said or wrote. Note it: you may find the connection valuable later. (For more on identifying references and allusions, see Strategy 14, p. 44)

Writing a Paper?

When you're writing a paper, your marginal notes will be only part of what will be useful. In a print edition, flags and self-stick removable notes can be really helpful. If you are searching by chapter, marking each page that begins a chapter with a numbered flag can make locating information much easier than thumbing through every time. You can also color-code your different topics to make your task easier.

1. If you own the copy of *The Graveyard Book* that you are reading, use this opportunity to begin developing your own system of text marking. If you don't own the book, invent a system for taking notes in a separate location, in a notebook or a reading journal, for example.

Directions:
First, read the information. Then, answer the question or questions.

Strategy 4

Plot—Identifying the Overall Design of a Story

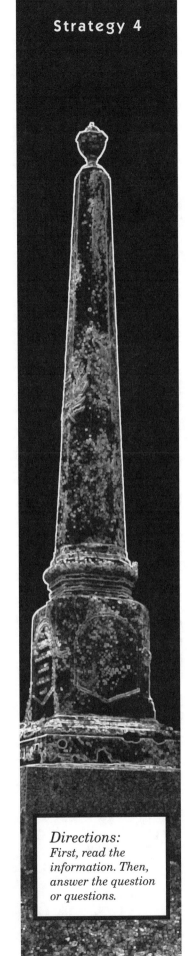

People who study and write literature have come up with several different ways of talking about plot. Literary critics often talk about a five-part structure as follows:

1. **Exposition:** introduction of essential background information, as well as characters, situations, and conflicts. Exposition may be found throughout a story, as well as at the beginning.
2. **Complication or Rising Action:** the beginning of the central conflict in the story.
3. **Crisis:** (sometimes called the **turning point**) usually the point at which the main character's action or choice determines the outcome of the conflict. Also called **climax**, or the high point of the action.
4. **Falling Action:** the time when all the pieces fall into place and the ending becomes inevitable.
5. **Resolution or Denouement:** the conflicts are resolved and the story is concluded.

Screenwriters and television script writers arrange their scripts according to a three-part division of beginning, middle, and end—a three-act structure, sometimes represented like this:

1. **Act One**—Set-up, including *exposition* (background), an *inciting incident* that sets the plot in motion, and a *reversal*, also called a plot point, which moves the action in a new direction.
2. **Act Two**—Confrontation or rising action, including a series of conflicts and ending in a second reversal or plot point.
3. **Act Three**—Resolution, including the climax and the tying up of loose ends.

Not every book will have its structure laid out so clearly, or laid out in three or five clear parts. But you can still make deductions about its structure. When you begin a book, take a moment to examine what the table of contents and chapter titles indicate about its structure. The fact that this book has an Interlude just a few pages past the halfway point suggests that it may vary from the norm. Make a mental note as you reach significant structure elements (the inciting incident, reversals, etc.), and consider whether overlaying a three-act structure yields insight into the work.

Keep in mind that writers adapt the plot structure for each particular story. They decide how much exposition should be included and where; how many conflicts there will be; what's told to the reader; and what is left for the reader to figure out.

1. As you read *The Graveyard Book*, pause at the end of each chapter and the interlude to identify how the plot structure works. When you are done, explain the structure of the story.

Directions:
First, read the information. Then, answer the question or questions.

Strategy 5

A **character** in a story is someone or something whose actions, choices, thoughts, ideas, words, interactions, and/or influence are important in developing the plot. Characters are often people, but also include other living creatures, and sometimes even non-living things. A force, such as good or evil, can operate as a character in a story.

Most stories have a single character or a small group of characters whose goal or problem is the core of the plot. This character or group of characters is called the **protagonist**. The protagonist does not have to be good, but a good protagonist may be referred to as the "hero" of the story. Readers usually identify with the protagonist and hope that the protagonist will succeed in attaining his or her goal. The character, group, or force, that opposes the protagonist is called the **antagonist**. Especially when the antagonist is a single, evil character, this character may be referred to as the **villain** (see Strategy 16, Plot—Distinguishing Types of Conflict, p. 44).

Characters, even those that aren't human, have what we may still call *personality*—a set of characteristic traits and features by which we recognize them. Personality is what helps us distinguish one tribute from another tribute. **Characterization** is the name for the techniques a writer uses to reveal the personality of characters to the reader. Characterization is achieved in a number of different ways, and the use or omission of various techniques can be revealing.

- **Words:** the character's own words and how they are said—dialect, slang, and tone—are important; what is *not* said can also be important, as well as dialogue about the character

- **Thoughts:** what's going on in the character's mind, and the character's motives, as well as others' thoughts about the character

- **Appearance:** the character's physical characteristics, clothing, and accessories (these may be symbolic; for example, Bod's loss of everything, including his diaper, suggests his vulnerability.

- **Action:** what the character does

- **Choices**: the decisions the character makes

- **Interactions:** how the character relates to others

- **Names:** often symbolic of a major character trait or role (see Strategy 11: Interpreting Names p. 35)

- **Chosen Setting:** the furnishings, etc., with which the character chooses to surround him- or herself

- **Change/Development:** the occurrence of and direction of change or development that a character undergoes

- **Illustrations:** images add a wealth of information about characters

1. What techniques are used in Chapter 1 to characterize Bod? Mrs. Owens? Bod's Mother? the man Jack? the Lady in Grey?

2. What do the images contribute to your understanding of character in Chapter 1?

3. Describe the character of Silas and tell what evidence led to your conclusions.

4. Can you identify a protagonist and antagonist in this story? Explain.

Directions:
First, read the information. Then, answer the question or questions.

Strategy 6

Drawing on a Source, Part I
"Mowgli's Brothers"

Gaiman has said repeatedly that his story draws on the *The Jungle Book* by Rudyard Kipling. To analyze an author's statement about influences, you can gather information about the sources and then compare them to the work you are reading.

First of all, we could start with the titles. Each has three words:

- the definite article, *The*,
- the name of a location/environment, *Jungle / Graveyard*
- the word *Book*

This may suggest to us that the graveyard will have a parallel function in *The Graveyard Book* to how the jungle functions in *The Jungle Book*.

And the use of a parallel name may suggest to us that there will be many other parallels. We know to expect parallels of structure (see Strategy 4: Plot—Identifying the Overall Design of a Story, p. 15), which focuses on the structure of the book, but we should also look for parallels in:

- plot events
- characters
- relationships

This does not necessarily mean that there will be one-to-one relationships in every case: there may be a mix of clear substitutions and alterations from the original to better fit the new work.

1. Read "Mowgli's Brothers" (pp. 88–95 of this teaching guide). Then reread the first chapter of *The Graveyard Book*. Explain all the parallels that you see. Consider plot, characters, and relationships. Then, consider and note the differences that strike you.

2. Name and compare the environments that each protagonist came from and went to. Which environments (the original ones or the subsequent ones) would usually be considered safer in the real world? Which environments are safer for the protagonists within the story. Explain how the reversal works.

3. Taking each chapter on its own (that is, leaving aside the rest of each book), what themes does its author develop? How do the themes of the two works compare?

4. What do you think a reader gains from reading Chapter 1 of *The Graveyard Book* with *The Jungle Book* in mind? Do you think anything is lost? Explain.

Directions:
First, read the information. Then, answer the question or questions.

Writer's Forum 1

Analyzing and Composing Lyrics

Poetry and song lyrics make meaning through the order and patterning of sound. They appeal to the senses and make the most of every sound, syllable, and word. Even though poetry and song lyrics are not exactly the same thing, because the song lyrics in *The Graveyard Book* are presented without music, analyzing them as poems is the best we can do. Knowing a little about poetic structures, rhythm and meter, and sound devices, including rhyme, will help you both to understand poems and be able to write poetry.

Verses of a traditional song, such as a lullaby, are typically each sung once. A **chorus** is a repeated element. The epigraph has a single verse.

Stanza is the name for a stand-alone division of a poem or song. A stanza with two lines is called a *couplet*, while one with four lines is called a *quatrain*. The epigraph is a four-line poem—a quatrain.

Rhyme, the use of repeated sounds, is the sound device that is most closely associated with poetry. Rhyme can be categorized by the type of sounds that are repeated and the placement of the words that rhyme. In the epigraph, three of the lines (1, 2, and 4) rhyme with each other

There are three main **categories of rhyme**, which are partly differentiated by whether they fall on a stressed (strong) or unstressed (weak) syllable.

- **Identical rhyme** is rhyme in which the exact same word is repeated *bones / bones*
- **Perfect rhyme** is rhyme in which one or more syllables are repeated except for the initial sound. Perfect rhyme includes strong syllable rhyme: *bones / loans, bones / atones* and multiple syllable rhyme: *rattle / prattle.*
- **Near rhyme** is rhyme that doesn't meet the criteria for perfect rhyme, but has similar sounds nevertheless. The use of near rhyme can be intentional, chosen because the poet wanted that effect: it doesn't necessarily indicate a failure to find a perfect rhyme. Three widely used types of near rhyme are:

  1. **Assonance**, in which only the vowel sound in the stressed syllable of a word is repeated *over / stones*
  2. **Consonance**, in which only the final consonant sound is repeated *warm / harm*
  3. **Alliteration**, in which only the initial consonant sound is repeated *jogged / jounced / jolted / jarred*

There are three main categories of **rhyme placement:**

- **End rhyme** is rhyme at the end of lines. It is the most often used.
- **Initial rhyme** is rhyme at the beginning of lines.
- **Medial rhyme** is rhyme between a word somewhere in the middle of the line with another word, which may be in three different places:

  1. at the end of the same line (called **internal rhyme**)
  2. somewhere in the middle of the same line (called **close rhyme**)
  3. in the middle of a line before or after the first rhyme word (**interlaced rhyme**)

Here is a chart that shows the placement and category of each type of rhyme that appears in the epigraph. The words that rhyme are bold-faced:

RHYME TYPES	
Placement / Rhyme Type	*Example*
Interlaced assonance (*bones/over*); Internal assonance (*over/stones*) Strong end rhyme (*bones/stones*)	Rattle his **bones** **Over** the s**tones**
Interlaced assonance (*over/only*);	It's **only** a pauper
Interlaced assonance (*only/nobody*); Internal assonance (*nobody/owns*) Strong end rhyme (*bones/stones/owns*)	Who **nobody owns**

A song's content is a useful starting point for analysis. What is the song about? After determining the subject, note the structure, including the use of stanzas (if any) and lines. Try reading the song aloud several times, also noting various types of rhyme and other sound devices and considering the grammar, syntax, and mechanics used in the lyrics. When there is a historical element, as in the epigraph, it's a good idea to look up the original, if it can be found and see what light it sheds. Finally, how do all these devices and information contribute to our understanding of the song's meaning? In writing a poem, a poet works backwards from desired meaning to choices about sound and groupings of lines, grammar, syntax, etc.

In the epigraph, we should note the focus on the long *o* sound, which occurs in all of the rhyme words, whether they use strong rhyme or assonance, and the use of rhyme words within lines, making the structure seem very tight and connected. We might also note the grammatical error (*who* for *whom*), which fits the idea of a nursery rhyme, as does the fairly simple vocabulary. The poem calls up an image of a body being dragged, only to dismiss the cruelty because it's "only" a poor person. I am unable to find a record in nursery rhyme sources, but I did find the same words in a poem by English poet Thomas Noel (1799–1861) called "The Pauper's Drive." Here are the first two verses:

There's a grim one-horse hearse in a jolly round trot;—
To the churchyard a pauper is going, I wot;
The road it is rough, and the hearse has no springs,
And hark to the dirge that the mad driver sings:—
 "Rattle his bones over the stones;
 He's only a pauper whom nobody owns!"

Oh, where are the mourners? Alas! there are none;
He has left not a gap in the world now he's gone,—
Not a tear in the eye of child, woman, or man;
To the grave with his carcass as fast as you can.
 "Rattle his bones over the stones;
 He's only a pauper whom nobody owns!"

In these two verses, the poem more fully develops the dismissive attitude toward the poor that we noticed in the epigraph, depicting the reviled and unmourned pauper. But the material of the epigraph is laid out as a couplet, not a quatrain, and it has the proper *whom*, making it seem more adult, fitting the context. To see how the poem ends, go to http://www.bartleby.com/360/3/117.html

1. Using the information in this lesson as a jumping off point, write an analysis of the song Mrs. Owens sings to Bod. Then explain how the song relates to the plot.

2. Given your analysis, how do the lyrics "hairy bacon" strike you?

3. Write a short hunting song for Jack to sing as he searches for Bod.

Special Vocabulary: a Teacher's Resource

In this feature, you will find vocabulary grouped by topic. Words that Gaiman uses that will be familiar to students are included along with words that are likely to be new and challenging in order to fill out the categories. Categories are arranged in alphabetical order, and include:

- amounts
- art terms
- botanical terms
- categories of being
- clothing
- criminals/crimes
- currency denominations
- environments
- graveyard/architectural terms
- jobs
- locales
- lab equipment
- zoology terms

Remember that the bulk of vocabulary words, along with context-specific definitions—listed alphabetically and with the first chapter of appearance noted—appear in a free download from the garlicpress.com website. That list is grouped by part of speech. In the answers to Strategy 13: Interpreting Dialogue (p. 37), you will find archaic words, Britishisms, civilities, idioms, and similes, along with their chapter of use and definitions. Finally, in the answers to Strategy 15: Interpreting Allusions and References (p. 42), you will find collected vocabulary in the categories: celebrations, historic periods, honorifics, literary references, other aspects of culture, places, proverbs, quotations, and real people, along with definitions and chapter of use. At the end of this feature are suggestions for exercises.

Amounts

accumulation 4 slowly built collection
bellyful 4 an entire meal
clump 3 small, compact lump

multitude 4 large number
powdering 2 sprinkling
smattering 2 small amount

Art Terms

couplet 5 two lines of poetry with similar or identical meter and end rhyme
doggerel 7 badly written poetry
manga 7 style of Japanese comic books/graphic novels
odes 7 elegant lyric poem addressed to a subject (e.g.,"Ode to a Grecian Urn" by Keats)

overture 5 piece for orchestra that begins a voice and orchestra performance (musical, opera, etc.) or an independent, single-movement composition for orchestra
prelude 5 introductory piece of music

Botanical Terms

Acacia 7 thorny tree with clusters of flowers
barley 3 a cereal grain
beetroot 3 red edible root of the beet plant
bluebells 2 European woodland plant with bell-shaped blue flowers that bloom in spring
brambles 4 wild, prickly vines or shrubs
brussels sprouts 3 a vegetable that looks like a small, green cabbage
carnivorous plants 4 plants that derive some nutrients from trapping and digesting animals—usually insects and spiders
daffodil 1 spring bulb with grass-like leaves that produces long-stemmed, bright yellow flowers, with 6 petals and a trumpet (corolla)
duckweed 4 small, aquatic plant that spreads widely over the surface of still water, making it appear green
fungus 3 organisms in the group to which mold, yeast, mushrooms, and toadstools belong
gorse 2 yellow-flowered shrub with spines
hawthorn 4 thorny, flowering shrub in the rose family, used for hedges
hazelnuts 6 small, round, edible nut from the hazel tree
hedges 3 boundaries formed by bushes or shrubs planted close together in a line

holly bushes 7 shrub with glossy, prickly leaves and red berries, closely identified with Christmas
ivy 1 woody, climbing plant with dark green, five-pointed leaves
leaf mold 7 soil mostly composed of decayed leaves
lichens 3 collection of simple, composite plants that combines a fungus w/ an algae partner
monkey puzzle tree 7 scaly evergreen tree with cones, native to Chile
nasturtium 8 trailing plant w/ rounded leaves and bright flowers, ranging from yellow to red, from South America
nettles 4 plant with jagged leaves covered in stinging hairs
primroses 2 short, European, early-blooming, woodland plant with pale yellow flowers
sloe 3 fruit of the blackthorn
stubble cut stalks
thickets 1 dense trees
tulips 2 spring-flowering bulb w/ cup-shaped flowers
undergrowth 1 dense shrubs growing beneath trees
weed 3 plant growing where it isn't wanted, competing with cultivated plants
wildflowers 2 flowers that grow w/out human aid
yew tree 8 poisonous coniferous tree with red berries

Categories of Being

carrion 3 decaying flesh of dead animal
criminals 4 people who have committed one or more crimes
discarnate spirits 1 a spirit that does not have a physical body
ghouls 3 evil spirits who rob graves and eat dead bodies
hellhound 3 demon that has taken the shape of a dog
Hounds of God 3 the background of werewolves as Hounds of God who go into hell and return to Earth comes from the testimony of Thiess of Kaltenbrun of Livonia (now the southern part of Estonia), who admitted in court to being a werewolf
Lycanthropes 3 from the Greek for "wolf man"
parasites 3 organisms that live in or on other organisms and at the host's expense
Providence 7 God as a source of protection

revenants 1 persons who have returned from the dead
scavengers 3 animals that feed on carrion (decaying flesh of dead animals)
solitary types 3 personality type characterized by enjoying solitude, independence, and being calm and unsentimental
souls 3 non-corporeal beings
spinster 4 unmarried adult woman
suicides 4 people who have taken their own lives
werewolves 3 people who change into wolves, often w/ a full moon
wights 1 persons of a specific kind
witch 4 woman who has magic powers, including cursing

Clothing

anorak 2 coat with a fur-lined hood
bonnet 1 hat that ties under the chin for girls and women
cape 1 sleeveless outer garment worn across the shoulders and fastening in front
gown 3 long dress, close-fitting from the bust up, w/ a flowing skirt, usually worn for formal occasions
jeans 4 denim pants
mackintosh 3 full-length, waterproof coat
morning suit I formal daytime dress for men, including striped trousers, a waistcoat, and a morning coat, which has tails
nightshirt 1 long loose shirt worn for sleeping
pantaloons 6 formal name for pants; specifically, close-fitting-men's pants, fastened at the foot or below the calf

Royal Robes 4 official garments of a king
shift 4 long, loose, sometimes sleeveless undergarments
shroud 3 garment in which a dead person is clothed for burial, used figuratively
toga 2 wrapped garment of Ancient Rome, worn over a tunic, worn by male Roman citizens
trousers 6 pants
turban 5 man's headdress
vest 2 sleeveless garment worn as a top
winding sheet 4 sheet in which a corpse is wrapped prior to burial; one type of shroud

Criminals/Crimes

bounder 6 person considered socially unacceptable
coiner 4 archaic term for counterfeiter
crook 4
fibber 2 liar
footpad 4 highwayman who works on foot (rather than mounted on a horse)
gallows-bird 4 thief or pickpocket and their associates

highwayman 4 mounted robber who held up travelers at gun point
nightwalker 4 prostitute
shoplifter 6 person who takes items for sale without paying for them
thug 6 violent criminal
vandalism 1 deliberately damaging or destroying the property of others

Currency Denominations

copper pennies 6 first issued in England in 1788 (previously, pennies had been silver)
guineas 4 British gold coin from 1663 to 1817 with a value of 21 shillings; replaced by sovereign
ha'porth 1 /HAY puth/ abbreviation of half-penny's worth (HAY pnee wurth) - a very small amount
pence 4 plural of penny

pennies 6 plural of *pence*
pounds 4 short for "pounds sterling" - basic unit of UK money, equal to 100 pence
silver groat 4 English coin worth four old pence and created from 1351 to 1662
ten-pound note 7 a pound-sterling banknote
tenner 4 nickname for a ten-pound note

Environments

barren plain 3 flat land with nothing growing on it
cavern 4 large cave
city 3 large town
compost 4 decaying organic matter
desert 1 dry, barren, sand-covered area of land
glacier 8 slow-moving mass of ice
island 2 land surrounded by water
jungle 8 tropical land overgrown with vegetation
marsh 4 low-lying land near the sea, flooded at high tide during wet seasons, and waterlogged all the time
mountain 8 large, natural elevation, higher than surrounding ground

natural amphitheater 1 natural area with a hollow that amplifies sound
nature reserve 1 land set aside by a government to safeguard its plants, animals, and physical features
ocean 8 large expanse of sea
pampas 8 large, treeless plain in South America
pasture 8 land with plants suitable for grazing cattle or sheep
tundra 8 large treeless Arctic region w/ permanently frozen subsoil and no trees
volcano 8 hill or mountain with a vent through which lava and hot gases flow (or flowed)

Graveyard/Architectural Terms

altar stone 7 a stone for celebrating the Mass of the Roman Catholic Church; it contains relics of saints

arch 3 curved shape or structure over an opening

barrows 2 ancient burial mounds

belfry 4 bell tower

casement window 5 window that swings open like a door

catacombs 3 underground cemetery with a large open space surrounded by tombs

cellar 6 storage room below ground in a house; basement

chapel 1 small church for Christian worship

coffin 2

crypt 1 room or vault under a church, used as a burial place

disinterred 7 dug up from a grave

funeral chapel 1 place of religious prayer and worship, dedicated to the celebration of funeral rites

gargoyle 2 grotesque carving of creature mounted at the gutter of a building

goblet 2 metal drinking cup, with a stem and a foot

graverubbing 7 practice of recording an image of the surface of a tombstone by placing a paper over it and rubbing charcoal or wax over the paper

guttering 1 gutters of a building

headstone 4 large slab of stone set at the head of a grave, often inscribed with a name and dates, and sometimes an epitaph

inscription 2 carving on a monument

inter 2 place in a grave

listed building 1 building that has been placed on the Statutory List of Buildings of Special Architectural or Historic Interest in the UK

manor house 1 large country house on a landed estate

masonry 2 stonework

mausoleum 2 large, stately building that houses one or more tombs

memorial plaques 1 ornamental tablets engraved to commemorate a person's life

monument 2 structure built to commemorate a noted person

mortal remains 7 dead body

obelisk 1 stone pillar with a pyramid-shaped top, set up as a monument

parish 4 small section of a worldwide Christian organization, generally consisting of a single church and priest

pavement 6 paved area or surface, which may be lined with asphalt, concrete, bricks, stones, flagstones, etc.

paving stones 5 large flat pieces of stone

pedestrian gate 8 gate for people on foot

pews 1 long bench to seat the congregation in a church

Potter's Field 4 burial place for paupers and strangers

shrine 1 Roman holy place, dedicated to a god or goddess

slab 3 large piece of stone that is thick and flat

spike-topped iron railings 1 fences composed of bars with pointed tops, to dissuade trespassers

spire 1 church tower

steeple 2 church tower and spire

tombs 1 large chambers, especially those underground, for burying the dead

tombstones 2 large flat stones standing at the head of a grave or laid over it, often having an inscription

unconsecrated grounds 4 not set aside as sacred

unhallowed 4 not made holy

unshriven 4 not having been absolved of one's sins in the confession

vault 4 chamber used for burials, located under a church or in a graveyard

Jobs

apprentice 3 novice in training with a master for a fixed period at low wages

archaeologist 4 person who studies human history by excavating sites

architect 6; 7 maker; person who designs buildings

baronet 1 a person with a hereditary title that does not bestow nobility

brewer 1 person whose work is making beer

cabinetmaker 3 an expert in furniture construction

caretaker 1 someone charged with caring for land or property

estate agent 7 real estate agent

guild 1 association of craftsmen

historian 7 person with expertise in happenings of the past, often focused on a time, area, or particular type of event

Lady Mayoress 5 title of the wife of a Lord Mayor, which title is given to mayors in large British cities, including London

police spokesman 7 person who makes statements to the public and the press on behalf of the police

prime ministers 3 principal ministers of a state

proconsul 1 governor of an ancient Roman province

publisher 7 person that prepares materials for publication

undertaker 3 person who prepares dead bodies for burial

Locales

antiques shop 4 seller of old, collectible furniture and art

chip shop 6 take-out restaurant featuring deep-fried, battered fish and thickly cut, deep-fried potato slices (chips)

high street 3 main business street in a British town; downtown

junk shop 4 seller of secondhand goods

pawnbrokers 4 shops that lends money at interest with the security being the article pawned; many also make outright purchases

the Green 4 public grassy area in the center of a town

the Old Town 4 the oldest or historic core of a city

tourist information center 5 visitor center that provides information about local attractions, as well as maps and transportation information

town square 5 open public area in the center of a town

Lab Equipment

Bunsen burner 6 small gas burner with adjustable flame

filter papers 6 porous paper for filtering liquids

gas jets 6 nozzles through which gas is released to be burned

glass beaker 6 cylindrical glass container with a lip, used in laboratories

petri dishes 6 circular, lidded, flat, transparent dish used to culture microorganisms

preservative 6 substance used to keep laboratory specimens

test tubes 6 thin glass tube, open at one end, meant to hold materials for use in laboratories

Zoology Terms

"grey" 1 white horse

arctic viper 4 poisonous snake that lives near the north pole

beast of prey 1 animal that kills other animals for food

beetle 2 insect with a hard wing case

bumblebees 2 insect that pollinates flowers and makes honey

cat 1 small, domestic soft-furred, carnivorous mammal

chimpanzees 3 smaller great ape, capable of tool making (distinguished from monkeys, which have tails)

fox 1 carnivorous bushy-tailed mammal in the dog family

magpie 7 long-tailed crow with white and black plumage

nightbird 1 night owl; person who habitually stays up during the night

parrot 7 brightly-colored bird w/ a hooked bill, able to mimic human voices

porpoises 8 small-toothed whale with a rounded snout

rabbit 1 burrowing, herbivore with long ears and puffy tail

scarlet macaw 7 particular kind of parrot, native to Central and South America

Shire horse 1 heavy, powerful draft horse from the English Midlands

spider 6 eight-legged arachnid that spins webs and eats insects

squirrels 3 (comparison) furry, medium-sized rodents that scamper about on the ground and climb trees

swans 7 water birds considered more majestic than ducks and geese and thought to be silent until immediately before death

vole 1 small rodent of Eurasia and North America, mouselike in appearance

wasp 4 winged insect with narrow waist and venomous sting

weasel 1 small, long-bodied carnivorous mammal, related to minks, skunks, and otters

Words in this resource are grouped by topic because more interesting vocabulary activities are possible using groupings of related words, and more meaningful vocabulary exercises will improve retention.

Fruitful activities include the following.

1. Identify relationships between and among words, creating a web or other graphic that shows these relationships and adding related words.
2. Keep an eye out for multiple meaning words and synonyms and identify context clues to Gaiman's use and other meanings.
3. Use a set of words in a piece of writing, for example a poem, a personal anecdote, a one-act play, or a journal written in the persona of a character.
4. Research the etymology of a set of vocabulary words.
5. Make and exchange puzzles made with vocabulary words.
6. Write and exchange cloze exercises (a blank is left for the vocabulary word, and context provides clues) using the vocabulary words.
7. Identify subcategories of vocabulary, for example, words about nature and hunting, verbs, words naming character attributes, six-syllable words, etc.
8. Identify the role of each word group in the book as a whole: what does it contribute?

Chapter 2

Journal and Discussion Topics

1. Explain how Bod reasons that the Indigo Man is imaginary.

2. Explain how Scarlett's parents reason that Bod is imaginary.

3. Think of another story in which a boy and a girl from different cultures meet get to know each other, and are separated by events beyond their control. Compare Gaiman's handling of the situation with how it is used in the other story. What does it represent or mean in each case?

4. Which aspects of the events in Chapter 2 are realistic (i.e., they could happen in real life)?

5. As you continue to read, char the ups and downs in Scarlett's and Bod's friendship from their meeting to the moment of parting. Label key events.

6. How would you characterize the treasure in the barrow?

7. Scarlett says that someday Bod will have to grow up and go live in the world outside the graveyard. Bod shakes his head. Who do you think is right? Why?

8. What evidence in Chapter 2 supports Silas's assertion in Chapter 1 that the name "Nobody" would help protect Bod?

9. Given your understanding of the developing plot structure, what do you think will happen in Chapter 3?

10. Why were some tombstones better than others for learning letters?

11. What does Bod's being obedient "for the most part" suggest to you?

12. Summarize the chapter from Scarlett's parents' point of view.

Summary

After quickly covering Bod's learning to talk and acquiring the habit of most pre-schoolers of perpetually asking questions, Chapter 2 lightly covers his learning to read and write. He begins with typical alphabet books, but locating letters on tombstones is substituted for finding them on street signs, license plates, and outdoor advertisements. Silas begins Bod's instruction, himself, but by the end of the chapter, he is about to begin learning cursive writing with Miss Borrows.

But the main focus of the chapter is his meeting and becoming friends with Scarlett Amber Perkins. The acquaintance begins with making faces, and within minutes, Scarlett announces that she's not allowed to talk to strangers, but Bod is not a stranger, he's her friend. Bod allows her to join in copying the inscriptions on tombstones, until her mother calls. Based on Scarlett's description, her parents are convinced that Nobody is her imaginary friend, and they are fine with that. As Scarlett continues to visit the nature reserve/graveyard with her Mother, their activities expand to include hide-and-seek, climbing, watching wildlife, and Bod introducing Scarlett to other residents of the graveyard, whom—because she can neither see nor hear them—she assumes are Bod's imaginary friends.

Then one day Scarlett asks who's the oldest person in the graveyard, and Bod guesses Caius Pompeius, but isn't sure. They have an argument because Scarlet wants to go someplace in the graveyard that she physically can't get to, while Bod—having Freedom of the Graveyard can—but Scarlett thinks he's being mean. Scarlett learns from her parents and Bod learns from Silas and Caius Pompeius that there were Celt burials in the graveyard prior to the Roman rule. And Caius tells Bod about the history of the barrow, accessible from the Frobisher vault, and about the two treasure hunters, one of whom never came out, and the other whose hair turned white from ther encounter.

The next time she comes with her Mother, Scarlett ignores Bod for a while, but finally relents and joins him. They compare notes on what they've learned, and she tells Bod that the burial hills were called barrows. He immediately offers to show her one, and has already procured a key. After some discussion of the fact that she won't be able to see and that he shouldn't leave her alone, he guides her down the stairs, acting as tour guide by pointing out the cave painting and the Celtic knot engraved on the wall. At the bottom they find the Indigo man, whom Bod determines is imaginary, locate the corpse of the treasure seeker who never returned, and become acquainted with the Sleer, who are guarding and protecting a cup, a brooch, and a stone knife for their master, whose return they are awaiting. When the leave, they walk into a police investigation, seeking Scarlett, who was believed to have been kidnapped. Scarlett comes once more to say goodbye: her father has gotten a job in Scotland, and the family is moving away.

Strategy 7

Plot—Distinguishing Types of Conflict

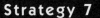

Conflict is at the core of a story's plot. Conflict is both what makes us wonder if the protagonist will attain his or her goal and what adds suspense and excitement to stories. Often there is one overarching conflict that takes up much of the book and stands in the way of the protagonist's progress. But each chapter or scene in a story usually also has conflict on a smaller scale.

The struggles that a protagonist undergoes in a story can be either **internal** or **external** (or both). In an **internal** conflict, the protagonist undergoes an interior struggle. He or she might have:

- conflicting desires,
- values that are at odds with each other,
- clashing personality traits, and/or
- conflicting motives.

An internal conflict takes place in the character's mind and heart. People often have internal conflict as they grow and develop from one stage in their lives to the next, so you will often find internal conflict in novels in which the protagonist is a teenager (although there are often external conflicts as well), and sometimes (though not always) coming to grips with identity is at the root of it. Since we have seen Bod age a number of years between chapters and since he is adopted and his identity has already been the subject of speculation, we can expect that identity will be a growing focus.

In an **external** conflict, the protagonist struggles with something or someone outside of himself or herself. The conflict may be with:

- another individual,
- a challenging or complex task or problem,
- society,
- nature,
- an idea, or
- a force, such as good or evil.

Because Bod begins the novel at about 18 months old, his goals, like those of any toddler, are very immediate, and instead of his struggle, we might consider a struggle taking place *on his behalf.*

The first external conflict reported in this story, though Bod, himself, is not aware of it, is a murderous attempt on Bod's life. Since the first conflict reported in a story can often provide insight about what is to come and since we know Jack is still out there, we may expect more to follow.

1. What are the specific conflicts that are important in Chapters 1 and 2?

2. What appear to be the overarching goals in this story? Cite evidence to support your conclusion.

3. As you continue reading, make notes for each new chapter on the chapter-specific conflict(s) and the overarching conflicts that shape the entire story.

Directions:
First, read the information. Then, answer the question or questions.

Vocabulary

Look at each group of words. Tell why it is important in the story.

1. discarnate spirits, revenants, wights
2. mildewed, Victorian, pews, flush toilet
3. slithering, holy, brooch, treasures
4. Shire horse, masticating, cantering, thunderous
5. tombs, vaults, plaques
6. sober, mop, tousled, mouse-colored, obedient
7. toga, leggings, vest
8. nightshirt, pacifier, tottered
9. crayons, copied, pronounce, tombstones
10. flibbertigibbet, johnny-come-latelies, respectable
11. vole, weasel, rabbit
12. tattooed, yodeling, ululation, gutteral
13. scents, honed in on, tang
14. Freedom of the Graveyard, right of abode
15. grey, shawl, serene, charity
16. distant university, particle physics, grading
17. knot-work, slab, ledge

Essay Topics

1. What evidence in Chapters 1 and 2 supports the age that Bod is said to be in each?

2. In the first two chapters, how do Mr. and Mrs. Owens and Silas carry out their roles with regard to Bod? How does the role of guardian differ from the roles of father and mother?

3. There is no mention of the man Jack in Chapter 2. What do you make of this? What do you think Jack is doing during this time?

4. Why do you think Gaiman chose the book *The Cat in the Hat* as the one story that Silas gave Bod?

5. How would you characterize Scarlett? Her parents? Caius Pompeius? Josiah Worthington?

6. Who has power in the graveyard? Rank the five most powerful characters and explain what gives them power.

7. Give examples of the different types of skills that Silas categorizes. (p. 37)

8. What point do you think Gaiman was trying to make by including Caius Pompeius's characterization of Caledonia?

9. Say aloud the last two words of the Epigraph and the name of the protagonist. Explain what you notice and what you think it means.

10. Bod's age is discussed in Chapter 2, but never directly stated. How old do you think he is? What evidence supports your conclusion?

11. Work out which queen Sebastian Reeder might have seen. Explain your reasoning.

12. Compare and contrast Scarlett's parents relationship with Scarlett and Silas's relationship with Bod.

13. What do you think is the significance of Scarlett to Bod? of Bod to Scarlett?

14. Explain how you adjusted your reading to account for different sections of the text.

15. Identify reversals in Chapters 1 and 2. Explain their effects on subsequent events.

16. If you were the author of this story, what would happen next? How would you develop the plot? How old would Bod be in the next chapter?

Chapter 3

The Hounds of God

Journal and Discussion Questions

1. Do you think the events of Chapter 3 would have happened if Bod hadn't had the experience of Chapter 2? Provide evidence to support your response.

2. Think of another book in which a character feels sorry for himself or herself. Compare how that character overcomes (or doesn't) his or her self pity with what happens to Bod.

3. What did you think about the dog when it first appeared? How and when did your thoughts develop?

4. How does Gaiman create humor in this chapter?

5. What leads to suspense in this chapter?

6. How does the relationship between Miss Lupescu and Bod change through this chapter?

7. What role does food have in this chapter?

8. Characterize the ghouls. What do they all have in common? What traits distinguish the various individuals?

9. Why do you think Miss Lupescu chose the subject matter in which she was originally instructing Bod? Why do you think she chose the subject matter in which she intended to instruct him in the future?

10. What kind of information do you think Silas was seeking? Explain what led to your conclusion.

11. Summarize the chapter from Miss Lupescu's point of view.

Summary

The chapter opens with a description of ghoul-gates and switches abruptly to Silas's imminent departure. Silas says he needs information that he cannot get in the graveyard, and Bod, now 6, has gone from being upset to being angry. He accuses Silas of failing to look after him as promised, and is unimpressed with the replacement whom Silas has found to be Bod's guardian while Silas is away, Miss Lupescu. Miss Lupescu seems equally unimpressed with Bod and tells him that she hopes he will make her long journey to come care for him worthwhile.

The Owenses are relaxed about Silas's departure, but his being away leads Bod to think about what Silas does for him over and above feeding him, and this is immediately contrasted with the food Miss Lupescu provides, which—although she made it herself—is so unpalatable that Bod can hardly keep it down. Adding insult to injury, she also insists on teaching him when he already has plenty of teachers and during high summer, when he should be out playing in the twilight. He endures her lesson about different types of beings, but the food and lessons both get worse: the food is heavy and unappetizing; the lessons focus on calling for help in languages of creatures he doesn't even know, like night-gaunts. Leaving the lesson with a list to learn, Bod puts it under a stone, and —unable to find a playmate—he tries to play with a dog, but when even it won't join him, he throws a clump of mud at it, and finding an old decrepit grave, sits on it and ruminates on all his grievances. He is there when three ghouls, calling themselves after the distinguished persons who supplied their first ghoul meals come into the graveyard, seeking the ghoul gate. When Bod recounts the injustices he's suffered, they beguile him with tales of their home with endless playfellows and loads of delicious food, until he begs to join them, and they carry him off toward their home, Ghûlheim

They swing Bod along, chattering all the while, until it dawns on Bod that he is either going to end up as a ghoul or eaten by ghouls. Spotting a night-gaunt, he calls it, but the ghouls stop him, telling him that they take too long to rot properly for a meal, and Bod's heart falls as it flies away. During the night, while the ghouls sleep, several of their lot disappear, which seems to some to be meaningless, and others to be due to an attack. Hearing a howl behind them and seeing night-gaunts coming, they race up the giant stairs that lead to their city. Bod is stuffed in a sack and thrown over the shoulder of the last ghoul in line, but finds a screw with which he pierces the the sack, planning to get out the hole and run away until spots a monstrous hellhound following. While Bod is debating which is worse, the hellhound tears the sack, Bod falls out, and trying to escape it, he hurts his ankle and then falls off the stairs, only to hear the dog say, "Oh, Bod" in Miss Lupescu's voice and be saved from certain death by a night-gaunt. Miss Lupescu carries him home on her back and offers to teach him constellations next. Reading the list, he learns about werewolves. Silas returns, and Miss Lupescu engages to come back.

Strategy 8 Interpreting Character Names and Development

Character names (and place names) can simply be names, or they can be descriptive or symbolic, carrying an extra layer of meaning. The use of unusual names and the anecdote about how Nobody Owens got his name in Chapter 1 seem designed to draw attention to characters' names, so it seems appropriate to examine them in this book. The key is to find patterns and meanings that augment the meaning of the book, not just collect possibilities. Sometimes this involves looking at etymologies: words' original meanings in their language of origin.

One pattern is that beginning in Chapter 2, residents of the graveyard are introduced by both name and epitaph, the words inscribed on their tombstone. These words serve as epithets, brief descriptions that help to characterize both the characters and the time in which they lived. When you read a book in which names seem meaningful, explore further.

1. Research the names of key characters in the book. Identify the names in the book that seem to you to have meanings beyond their surface and explain what it seems to you is being conveyed by Gaiman's choice of names.

Now, let us turn to **character development**. English anthropologist and linguist Gregory Bateson pointed out in the introduction to his book *Mind and Nature* that things cannot be defined in themselves alone: Understanding the relationships of a thing to its context is an essential part of knowing what something is. In the specific case of understanding character, it is often, if not always, true that the development of character can be marked by the character's changing role in the community.

It often happens that in a book with major and minor characters, some characters will show development and others will not. But there are reasons why a major character might not show development.

2. As you continue reading, gauge Bod's character development from chapter to chapter. What changes besides his age? How do his relationships with those in the community and with locations show this development?

3. Which other major characters besides Bod show character development? Which don't? Explain what the changes in those who do develop add to the story. Explain what the lack of development in the others means in the world of the story.

Directions:
First, read the information. Then, answer the question or questions.

Strategy 9

Relating Setting and Mood

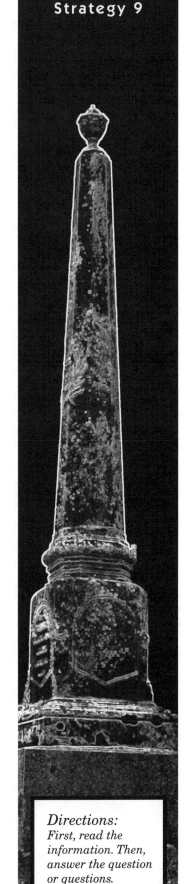

Setting refers to both the world in which the story takes place and the changing scenery that serves as the backdrop for each scene or chapter. Setting includes what the characters can sense in their environment, e.g.,

- time of day
- season of the year
- plants and animals
- natural features

- weather
- landscape
- buildings or other structures
- human-made features

The general setting of this story—the city and country in which it takes place—is never explicitly mentioned, but Gaiman includes many, many clues, some more subtle than others, mainly cultural references. The story begins in Chapter 1 with several specific locales within the unnamed city or town—the home of Bod's family, the hill, the graveyard.

Setting may be a mere backdrop to the story, or it can serve other functions, sometimes even several different functions within one story. Setting often contributes to characterization, when characters are able to choose aspects of their setting. Setting has a particular importance in this story: Bod's choice to change his location saved his life, and the new location has a variety of ways to keep him safe.

Setting may also be symbolic or create conflicts for the characters, hindering the characters in achieving their goal(s), or creating physical hardships or challenges that are difficult to overcome. Setting can also provide materials or resources that help the characters solve problems.

In addition, the settings of a story and how the settings function affect how we and the characters feel about their surroundings. This feeling is called **mood**. The setting can make things seem pleasant or create an air of foreboding that hints that something bad is about to happen, or convey many other moods. The description of the ghoul gate in Chapter 3 is an example of a mood-evoking setting.

Although a novel like *The Graveyard Book* is classified as a narrative—a type of writing that tells a story—sections of a novel that deal with the setting are usually passages of description. You may be aware of the shift back and forth from narrative to description as you read.

As you read descriptions of setting, look at illustrations for the story, or listen to Gaiman read, try to figure out what Gaiman is aiming to convey. Paying attention to the possibilities and problems created by the setting and the mood these functions create will help you reach a deeper understanding.

1. Extend the following chart to create a record of *The Graveyard Book* settings and their functions by skimming the chapters you've already read and continuing to add as you read more.

Chapter	Setting	Function(s) in Story	Mood Created
1			
2			
...			

2. Write a paragraph about the clues that helped you discern the settings.

Directions:
First, read the information. Then, answer the question or questions.

Writer's Forum 2 Writing Description

In descriptive writing, writers share the attributes of something so readers can picture it in their mind's eye. As a writer, you choose the features to mention based on what stands out among the physical properties and internal attributes of whatever you are describing, and these features will be different depending on your subject. If you were describing a person, the features you would focus on would likely be among those discussed in Strategy 5 Interpreting Characterization, p. 22, but in describing objects, places, or ideas, you would choose different features, as appropriate.

There are some general questions you can use to help you formulate your description of an object, place, or idea, as applicable:

- What is its name, species, or type? What is it not?
- What are its attributes and/or parts?
- What is the experience of it like?—how does it look, smell, taste, feel, sound?
- How does it relate to other things in its environment or context?
- What are its possibilities and limitations?
- What is its current state? What is its history?
- How did it come to be?
- What is its value?

The way you organize the information in a description may vary depending on what you are describing. Organization can help convey meaning. You can organize your description in these ways, as appropriate:

- top to bottom
- front to back
- side to side
- around the perimeter
- inside, then outside, or vice versa
- from the beginning to the end of its cycle
- most important trait to least important
- least important trait to most important

Source words that can help you express concepts of similarity and diversity in your description include:

Similarity

- also
- and
- as well as
- similarly
- besides
- furthermore
- likewise
- alike
- in addition
- too
- at the same time
- resemble

Diversity/Dissimilarity

- differ
- whereas
- however
- while
- but
- on the contrary
- conversely
- though
- on the other hand

1. Identify a place in Chapter 3 in which Gaiman writes to appeal to each of the following senses: sight, touch, taste, smell, hearing?

2. Reread the description of Ghûlheim, starting with "Even from the path below Ghûlheim . . ." and ending with ". . . called it home." Then describe some place you have seen in real life, a movie, a photograph, or your imagination, using some of the same techniques, as well as those described above.

Directions:
First, read the information. Then, answer the question or questions.

Strategy 10

Drawing on a Source, Part II
"Kaa's Hunting"

In creating his own version of "Kaa's Hunting" for *The Graveyard Book,* Gaiman makes substitutions, alterations, additions, and deletions. We know to expect parallels of structure (see Strategy 4: Plot—Identifying the Overall Design of a Story), but we should also look for parallels in:

- plot
- characters
- relationships

This does not necessarily mean that there will be one-to-one relationships in every case: there may be a mix of clear substitutions and alterations from the original to better fit the new work.

1. Read "Kaa's Hunting" (pp. 96–105 of this teaching guide). Then re-read the third chapter of *The Graveyard Book.* Explain all the parallels that you see. Consider plot, characters, and relationships. Then, consider and note the differences that strike you.

2. Name and compare the environments that each protagonist came from and went to in Chapter 3.

3. How has Mowgli changed since the beginning of "Mowgli's Brothers"? How does this compare to how Bod has changed since "How Nobody Came to the Graveyard"?

4. Taking each chapter on its own (that is, leaving aside the rest of each book), what themes does its author develop? How do the themes of the two works compare?

5. What do you think a reader gains from reading Chapter 3 of *The Graveyard Book* with *The Jungle Book* in mind? Do you think anything is lost? Explain.

6. Given what's at stake in each story, what do you think a satisfactory ending to each would include?

Directions:
First, read the information. Then, answer the question or questions.

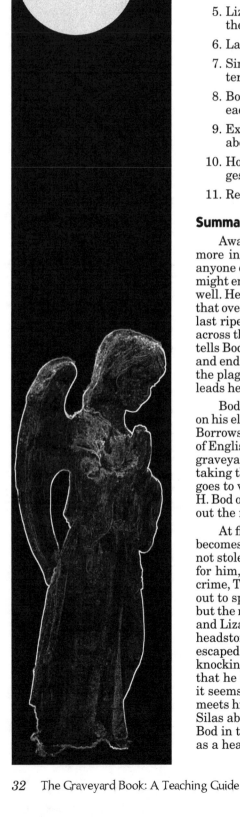

Chapter 4   The Witch's Headstone

Journal and Discussion Questions

1. What differences do you find in how different people answer Bod's questions about the witch buried just outside the corner of the graveyard?

2. What in this chapter sheds more light on the kind of being Silas is?

3. Where do Bod's ideas about what witches might be like come from?

4. What play on words does Mr. Pennyworth make? Do you think it's Mr. Pennyworth's joke or Gaiman's? Explain why you think as you do.

5. Liza's answer to Bod's question about whether she was a witch before she cursed them is a non-answer. Do you think she was? Why or why not?

6. Lack of knowledge of which areas of human life challenge Bod in this chapter?

7. Similes are comparisons using *like* or *as*. Find at least eight similes in this chapter and explain what effect(s) five of them had for you.

8. Bod and Abanazer Bolger each want something the other has. Record the moves each one makes as he seeks to get what he wants, prior to the arrival of others.

9. Explain how two different story strands—Bod's education and his curiosity about the witch—come together in this chapter.

10. How did you feel about the mentions of Jack in this chapter? What do they suggest to you about how the plot will develop?

11. Retell the witch's life story in your own words.

Summary

Aware that there is a witch buried at the outside edge of the graveyard, Bod seeks more information from Silas, the Owenses, and Miss Borrows, but learns little from anyone except Silas, who explains *unconsecrated ground* and details the reasons people might end up there. At this point, Bod's lessons are focused on fading, which are not going well. He is very interested in the witch but also obedient, so he climbs into an apple tree that overlooks the Potter's Field rather than climbing through the fence. Reaching for the last ripe apple, he climbs onto a branch that breaks and drops him onto the grass pile across the fence, where he is greeted by a voice that turns out to belong to the witch. She tells Bod her life story, focusing on the part that begins when she is accused of witchcraft and ends when she has cursed those who drowned and burned her and they have died of the plague, which arrived in a carpet delivered from London. Bod asks her name, which leads her to point out the lack of a grave marker to identify her, an omission she regrets.

Bod begins to plan how to provide Liza Hempstock with a headstone and is focused on his elaborate, complex plans during his lessons, making Mr. Pennyworth despair. Miss Borrows, who is very suggestible, is easily diverted from English grammr to the topics of English money and headstone purchases. Realizing that his fund collected around the graveyard are not sufficient, Bod returns to deep within the barrow and defies the Sleer, taking the brooch despite their claims that the treasure "always comes back." Next, Bod goes to visit Liza to find out what she wants put on her headstone, and she tells him E. H. Bod outfits himself from items left in the gardener's hut, and with trepidation, walked out the main gateway of the cemetery and arrives at Abanazer Bolger's shop.

At first Bolger states that he doesn't buy from kids, but when he sees the brooch, he becomes affable and offers Bod tea in the backroom. He tells Bod he needs to know its not stolen. Bod won't tell where he got the brooch, but gives away that no one is waiting for him, and Bolger locks him in the backroom, closes up shop, and calls a partner in crime, Tom Hustings. Meanwhile, Bod is surprised by the appearance of Liza, who goes out to spy on Bolger, who has recollected a card he's been saving that has nothing on it but the name *Jack*. Bolger and Hustings argue over what to do with both their treasures, and Liza returns to find Bod trying to fade. He finally admits that he's there to get her a headstone, and she decides to help him, enabling him to fade so that the men think he's escaped. Hustings attempts to steal the brooch, Bolger drugs Hustings, and they fight, knocking each other out. Bod pockets a paperweight, a jar of paint, and a paintbrush, that he uses to knock the key out of the lock so he can escape the backroom. Although it seems evil to him, Liza takes the card, which Liza has spotted, to give to Silas. Silas meets him on the way home, and takes him back to the safety of the graveyard. Bod tells Silas about Liza and her assistance, the card, and everything else. Mr. Owens punishes Bod in the manner of his time for breaking the rules, and Bod sets up the paperweight as a headstone for Liza, inscribing it, "E.H. we don't forget."

Strategy 11

Forming Hypotheses

Leading (and misleading) the reader's expectations is something that all good fiction writers do. As readers, we make predictions about causes, results, and intentions. These predictions could be based on various things, such as a gut feeling or what we wish were true. It is only when we base a prediction on evidence that it merits the name of **hypothesis**.

Some people associate the word *hypothesis* strictly with scientific investigation. But that is not the limit of its application. Readers are constantly making and testing hypotheses about characters' reasons for their choices and actions, about what will happen next in the plot, about what is true in the world of the story, and about the author's intentions. Here are some criteria for a good hypothesis.

- **A good hypothesis should be of significance in the world of the story**. If we were reading a journal article on the science of nutrition, the fact that prior to Miss Lupescu's arrival, Bod got most of his food "in packets, purchased from the kind of places that sold food late at night and asked no questions" (Chapter 3) would be of some significance. But in *The Graveyard Book*, it's not important beyond helping to establish that Bod has limited experience of food and—by extension—the outside world. Bod's refusal to simply do as he is told (eat what is set before him) and his success in compromising with adult intentions, however, is likely to be key in how the story unfolds and should hold some interest and focus for the reader. It seems apparent that Gaiman aims to create suspense about whether Bod will be safe, despite being in a community where his safety is a key goal, and often it's Bod's choices that put him in danger.

- **A good hypothesis should be clearly stated and specific so that you can easily tell what it means, but it should reach beyond what you know for certain**. If you formed the hypothesis, *Maybe Bod's lack of unwavering obedience will be important*, it would not do you any good. That Bod not always doing just as he is told is important in this story is something we have already established. A hypothesis is a statement about which you do not yet know the truth.

- **A good hypothesis should clearly state the motivation, result, or intention that you think you have identified**. For example, having seen Bod leave the graveyard without permission and succeed in his quest, learning to fade in the process, suggests that testing the rules is leading to learning and that the adults may be imposing strictures that are too tight. Given the evidence, you might form the following hypothesis: *Maybe the learning that results from Bod's disobedience is critical to his long-term safety*. Once you form a hypothesis, you should look for further information to verify or disprove it as you continue to read

1. Form a hypothesis about Bod, Silas, Miss Lupescu, the man Jack, or some other important part of the story. Collect and record evidence from Chapters 1–4 that supports your hypothesis. Write your hypothesis and explain the evidence that supports it. You may wish to arrange the evidence in order of decreasing importance (most important point first) or increasing importance (most important point last). You'll get a chance to review your hypothesis in Strategy 21: Rereading a Book (p. 53).

Directions:
First, read the information. Then, answer the question or questions.

Strategy 12

Understanding Tropes and Motifs

A **literary trope** is a device that has been widely used—enough so that many readers will recognize it. It may be a recurrent character type, plot development, setting, narrative device, or other literary technique (although tropes are also used in every other story-telling genre, including television shows, movies, and graphic novels). Many tropes have nicknames in order to more easily identify and discuss their use, and Gaiman uses a number of them.

Paper–Key Retrieval Trick

A person locked in a room from which there is no escape, discovers the key inserted in the lock on the outside of the door, places a paper under the door, uses a thin instrument to push out the key, catching and retrieving it with the paper to escape. This technique can also be used to enter a locked room, as Patrick Jane does on an episode of *The Mentalist*.

Sequispedalian Smith

A key character is shown to be key by having a multi-syllable, unusual first name, combined with a very ordinary last name, like Indiana Jones from the movies bearing his name or Coraline Jones from Gaiman's novel *Coraline*.

Free-Range Children

Pre-teen children who roam about freely, due either to parental neglect (Lyra in *The Golden Compass*; Dido Twite in *Wolves Chronicles*) or other factors (Mowgli in *The Jungle Book*).

Happily Adopted

Children for whom adoption is *the* answer, like Anne of Green Gables, Oliver Twist, and Matilda in the books bearing their names.

Motif is the name used for a repeated thematic element of a story that often has a universal meaning. Folklorist Stith Thompson defined it as "the smallest element in a tale having a power to persist in tradition" (*The Folktale*, 1946, p. 415). Thompson defines three classes into which most motifs fall:

- the *actors* in a tale, including heroes, villains, and mentors
- *background elements*, including gifts and task-performing animals
- *single incidents*, including contests of strength and battles of wits

Wicked witches and sets of three tasks are two fairytale motifs.

Motif analysis is most frequently applied to folktales and fairy tales, which are classified by the type, combination, and arrangement of motifs that they include, but *The Graveyard Book* includes elements of fairy tales and folktales, including some key motifs.

1. Explain how each trope listed above applies in *The Graveyard Book*.

2. For each each category named for the three classes of motifs above, tell how it applies in *The Graveyard Book*.

Directions:
First, read the information. Then, answer the question or questions.

Vocabulary

Look at each group of words. Tell why it is important in the story.

1. tendrils, carnivorous, arctic viper, venom, writhed
2. mist-walkers, solitary types, high hunters
3. jogged, jounced, jolted, jarred
4. canine, drooled, fangs, pursuing
5. sanguine, choleric, phlegmatic, melancholic
6. loped, skulked, leapfrogging, scampering
7. Orion, Taurus, rumors
8. bulging, scraggly, rank, fungus, lichens
9. gallows-birds, coiner, highwayman, footpad
10. transformation, tenacity, pursue, duplicated
11. antiques, pawnbroker's, sentimental value
12. unicorn, astride, irrelevancies
13. garden-twine, encrusted, shuffle, dandy
14. Skagh, Thegh, Khavagah, Wegh Khârados

Essay Topics

1. Why do you think Miss Lupescu doesn't teach Bod to say "help" in the ghoul language?

2. What is the ostensible reason that Miss Lupescu suddenly shows up and spends so much time in the graveyard? How much do you know about the real reason? What do you suspect about the real reason? Why does Miss Lupescu develop an alibi for spending time in the graveyard?

3. What does the wolf/hound saying, "Oh, Bod" explain that occurred earlier in Chapter 3?

4. What do the ghouls and the man Jack have in common? How do they differ?

5. How does shifting Chapter 4 between Bod's and Abanazer's perspective enhance the story?

6. What evidence in Chapter 4 would allow you to figure out when Liza was born? In what year was Liza born?

7. How does Chapter 4 depend on things that happened in earlier chapters?

8. Compare the plots of Chapters 3 and 4. How are they parallel?

9. How would you characterize Liza? Abanazer Bolger? Bod at age 8?

10. How did what happens to the brooch in Chapter 4 affect your view of the Sleer.

11. Explain Abanazer's and Tom's discussion. What's at stake? What are the advantages and disadvantages of their various options?

12. Why do you think Liza didn't tell Bod what she'd heard about Jack?

13. Explain the ins and outs of fading.

14. Compare and contrast Abanazer Bolger with Tom Hustings, on the one hand, and Jack, on the other.

15. How do Bod's escapes from danger in Chapters 3 and 4 differ from his escape from danger in Chapter 1?

16. What is the reversal in Chapter 3? In Chapter 4?

17. If you were the author of this story, what would happen next? How would you develop the plot?

Chapter 5

Journal and Discussion Questions

1. What preparations are made for the Macabray?
2. How do the events of Chapter 5 separate Bod from others? How do they join him with others?
3. What changes do Bod's new clothes bring about?
4. Why doesn't the Lady Mayoress know what to do to carry out the tradition? How do the men accompanying her know?
5. If Silas is, as he says, neither alive nor dead, what is he?
6. Who experiences panic or dread in this chapter? What causes it?
7. Why doesn't anyone tell Bod that he can leave the graveyard for the dance?
8. How does the dance change as the evening progresses?
9. Why do you think Silas looks heartbroken?
10. List all the people Bod sees dancing the Macabray. How does this selection match the composite meaning of the couplets that make a motif in the chapter?

Summary

Bod notices signs that something is afoot. Mrs. Owens sends him out of the tomb, although it's winter, commenting on cleaning that needs doing and aspects of her clothing that need attention, singing a couplet that ends with the words *the Macabray,* and then refusing to explain it. He spots Mother Slaughter, who sings another couplet after asking him to check for flowers blossoming, which puzzles him. He is sent away by the Bartleby's who are all excited about "tomorrow night" (thought they won't say why). Bod gives up and goes to wait for Silas, who returns home with clothes for Bod. As he changes from his winding sheet into jeans, a grey sweater, and green sneakers, he asks Silas what they're for and Silas say, "camouflage." After Silas teaches him to tie his shoelaces, he ask him about the Macabray, and learns that it's a dance of the living and the dead, and Silas, not being either, has not danced it. Silas comments that Bod looks like he's lived outside the graveyard all his life, and when Bod asks if he himself and Silas can always stay in the graveyard, Silas answers obscurely.

The next morning, Bod smells an unknown scent in the air and discovers five-petaled white flowers in bloom. He fades when the Lady Mayoress, Mrs. Caraway, and three male advisors arrive. The men guide her to cut the flowers and fill the baskets so that the flowers can be distributed to everyone in the Old Town, as is the tradition, and, the smallest of the men dredges up a couplet from a far away memory, but she remains skeptical.

The scene switches to late afternoon: it is dusk, and Bod can find no one in the graveyard. Bod panics as Silas, too, fails to return. Walking to the main gate, he hears music unlike anything he has heard before, and slipping out the locked gate, follows it into the Old Town. He sees confused people accepting flowers without fully understanding why, as he follows the music, and claims a flower, himself, from one of the men he'd seen earlier, but has to assure the man that he lives in the Old Town. Forgetting that he is forbidden to leave the graveyard, Bod wanders the Old Town, and at the stroke of midnight, the dead come marching down the hill, terrifying at least some of the living in the square. Josiah Worthington walks up to the Lady Mayoress and—in another couplet—invites her to dance the Macabray with him. She hesitates, but with her husband's blessing, agrees. Liza takes his hand as the dance begins and the living and the dead dance toegether. Bod asks Liza questions, but only learns that it always happens and the dead remember it, though the living "may not remember." Then the Lady on the Grey arrives and joins the dance, and just as Bod thinks to himself, "everyone is dancing," he spots Silas standing in the shadows, not dancing. He calls Silas, but Silas disappears.

Bod dances with the lady, and she promises him that he will one day ride her horse, just as everyone does. The clock strikes twelve again, and Bod wonders if they'e danced 12 hours or 24 or no time. The dead disappear, and the living, who no longer seem awake, seek their homes. The next day, upon trying to discuss the dance with the residents of the graveyard, Josiah telllls him that the dead and the living don't mix; that the dead may have danced with the living, but they would not speak of it to the living. Bod protests he is one of them, and Josiah tells him, "not yet . . . not for a lifetime." Bod then accosts Silas and insists he not deny he saw the Macabray, then tells him about dancing with the Lady. Silas is not forthcoming, so Bod asks why nobody will talk about it, and Silas gives him three reasons. Bod sees that Silas looks heartbroken, and as he is trying to think what he can say, it begins to snow for only the third time in Bod's life.

Strategy 13   Reading Dialogue

Dialogue is the name for conversation that takes place in narrative. Even one person speaking is characteristically referred to as *dialogue*, even though normally *dialogue* refers to a conversation involving two or more people. Dialogue is distinguished from narration and description.

Sometimes dialogue is attributed with dialogue tags like "said Bod." Sometimes writers omit dialogue tags when other clues indicate who is speaking. Look for the following signs:

- **Alternating dialogue**. Dialogue between two people goes back and forth, by nature. It is an exchange of ideas, views, thoughts, and the like. So every *other* line (1, 3, 5, 7, 9 or 2, 4, 6, 8, 10, if they were numbered) is spoken by the same character. An example occurs between Mrs. Owens and Silas after Bod finishes the banana in Chapter 1.

- **Vocatives**. A *vocative* is a word that shows who is being addressed in a sentence. When—during the discussion about Bod's being allowed to leave the graveyard in Chapter 1—Silas says, "I am infinitely older than you, lad," he leaves no doubt about whom he is addressing. Almost always, the next person to speak after a sentence with a vocative is the person addressed.

- **Content**. There are certain things that only one person could say in response. For example, in the debate about adopting the baby, the person who says, "Then yes. If you'll be its Mother, I'll be its father," can only be the husband of the person who spoke immediately before—Mrs. Owens.

- **Speech characteristics**. Just as people have certain habits of movement, they have certain habits of speech—characteristic expressions that can help you to recognize them, even when you have very little else to help you recognize who is talking or word choices that characterize their speech. This is called *idiolect*, which simply means "an individual's speech." For example, Silas's speech is more formal and uses more sophisticated vocabulary than anyone else's.

There are many different speech characteristics that can go into making up an idiolect. Here are some of the ones Gaiman uses prominently in *The Graveyard Book*.

PRONUNCIATION

The word *colloquial* refers to the informal elements that are added to spokin language, as opposed to written language. While we might write "Bod is not awake"; we might say "Bod *isn't* awake," using a contraction. While we might spell phrases correctly, in speaking we may run words together saying "gonna" for "going to" or "Whaduhya want?' for "What do you want?" When writers record dialogue, they may choose to give language a colloquial feel by spelling actual pronunciation.

ARCHAIC WORDS AND PHRASES

As time goes on, new words and invented and others go out of fashion. Words that are no longer in use are called *archaic*. Because *The Graveyard Book* takes place in a cemetery used for burials across hundreds of years, characters' speech reveals the words of their times. Archaic words are identified in dictionary definitions.

Directions: First, read the information. Then, answer the question or questions.

DIALECT

A *dialect* is a form of a language that is usually regional: people in a certain area share a dialect that distinguishes it from the speech in other regions where the same language is spoken. Characters in *The Graveyard Book* come primarily from different parts of England, although Caius Pompeius is Roman, and Scarlett has spent most of her life in Scotland. Even people who live at the same time and both speak English, may speak different dialects of English, for example, calling *potatoes* either *taters* or *spuds*. Gaiman chooses to record dialectical differences, which can include vocabulary, including both words and *idioms* (phrases with a figurative meaning that cannot be derived from the meanings of the individual words, like "It's raining cats and dogs"), and pronunciation. Note that idioms can also be shared across dialects.

CIVILITIES and OATHS

The words we use to carry out many basic social interactions—bestowing and accepting things; showing gratitude and accepting gratitude; asking after another's health and responding about one's current state of health—are called *civilities*. They are somewhat standardized (e.g., *please, thank you, you're welcome*), but have also changed over time. *Oaths* are expressions of frustration or fury. Gaiman records the civilities and oaths appropriate to his characters' ages, station, and circumstances.

PROVERBS

Proverbs are brief sayings expressing in a standard way something that is considered—at least by some—to be a truth. Examples include:

- What's sauce for the goose is sauce for the gander; and
- To each his own.

Notice from the above examples that proverbs may contradict each other. In the past, proverbs were more often used than today, and some of the characters in *The Graveyard Book* quote them more often than others.

1. Which characters use archaic language? How else is archaic speech used? Find ten examples of archaic language, using a dictionary to confirm its status, and also tell what each one means.

2. Which characters characteristically use civilities? Which character speaks with oaths? Find ten examples of civilities and two oaths and tell what each one means.

3. Who says each of these proverbs? What is its significance?

   - It will take a graveyard.
   - Everything in its time.
   - Everything in its season.

4. Find five idioms that are spoken by charactes speaking British English but that you recognize to also be used in American English.

5 Now that you've studied some of the elements in Gaiman's dialogue, write a paragraph describing in general the dialogue in *The Graveyard Book*. What elements mark the characters' speech as British English, as opposed to American English?

6. Write an analysis of Bod's speech and how it changes through the book.

7. What special features do you find in Miss Lupescu's speech?

Writer's Forum 3   Writing Dialogue

Dialogue is a particularly powerful way to reveal a character's thoughts, personality, tastes, and culture. The language that each character uses can reflect such important characteristics as age, education, and background. The level of formality the character uses can reflect his or her personality and approach to life as well as the social situation in which the speech takes place. Dialogue can also reveal relationships. How two (or more) people speak to each other shows a lot about their feelings for each other. Do they give each other a turn to speak? What tones of voice do they use? Do they use polite phrases or insults? Do they make each other laugh?

In terms of text organization, dialogue can help to break up narrative passages and can be more interesting than paraphrased speech.

Rules for Writing Dialogue

A. Start a new paragraph each time you switch speakers, or if a speaker speaking for a long time switches topics.

B. Punctuate dialogue to clearly show which words are the exact words that each speaker says. Follow these rules:

• For tags before the speaker's words:
1. Begin the tag with a capital letter.
2. Follow the tag with a comma, a space, and an opening quotation mark.
3. Begin the quotation of the sentence with a capital letter.
4. End the quotation of the sentence with the proper punctuation (./?/!)
5. Close the quotation marks.

• For tags in between the speaker's words:
1. Begin with opening quotation marks, followed by a capital letter.
2. Follow the first part of the quotation with a comma if it is in the middle of a sentence or if it is the end of a sentence that would normally end with a period (or ?/! if it is the end of an interrogative or exclamatory sentence), end quotation marks, and a space.
3. Write the tag and follow it with a comma, a space, and opening quotation marks.
4. Finish a sentence by beginning with a lowercase letter (unless it's a proper noun); start a new sentence with a capital letter. End either with the proper punctuation (./?/!)
5. Close the quotation marks.

• For tag after the speaker's words:
1. Begin with opening quotation marks and start the quotation with a capital letter.
2. If the quotation would normally end with a period, substitute a comma. If it would normally end with a ? or !, use the ? or !
3. Follow the end punctuation with closing quotation marks and a space.
4. Add the tag.
5. End the sentence with the appropriate punctuation, usually a period.

1. Pick two characters in the story with strong speech traits. Say, Mr. Dandy and Silas. Imagine them meeting. Write a dialogue for them.

Directions:
First, read the information. Then, answer the question or questions.

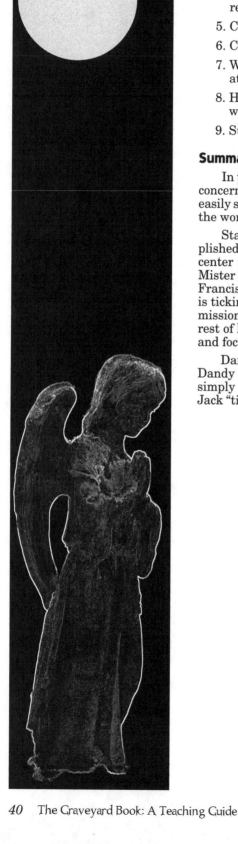

Interlude

The Convocation

Journal and Discussion Questions

1. How is this part of the book different from the rest?

2. Where else in the book has the narrative shifted from Bod's experience?

3. How has San Francisco been referenced before? What do you make of this?

4. In what context was the Convocation mentioned before? How does this chapter relate to that reference?

5. Characterize Mr. Dandy.

6. Characterize Mr. Dandy's manner of speaking.

7. What did you learn in this Interlude about the murder of Bod's family and the attempt to murder Bod that you did not know before?

8. How would you describe the man Jack's current situation? What do you think will happen if he fails? What do you think will happen to *him* if he fails?

9. Summarize the chapter from Mr. Dandy's point of view.

Summary

In the Washington Room of a hotel, a private function is being held. No information concerning it is available, but if one had a chance to glance around the room, one could easily see that it is an international gathering of men only. Though they come from across the world, all wear similar black suits and speak English.

Standing on the dais, a man in a morning suit is announcing the good deeds accomplished under the auspices of the organization gathered in the room, while at the front center table, the man Jack is in conversation with a silver-white haired man named Mister Dandy. Although Jack is bringing up excuses—the relevance of an event in San Francisco; the fact that time is not out for accomplishing what he was sent to do—Dandy is ticking him off, trying to impress upon him that time is running out for fulfilling his mission of finishing what he started, i.e., killing Bod, in addition to having killed the rest of his family. A waiter and other men at the table politely ignore the conversation and focus on the speaker.

Dandy tells Jack he's now on deadline. Jack claims to have leads, but admits when Dandy quesitons him, that the secretary (the man at the podium) dismissed them and simply wants the matter handled and done. Dandy has the last word, telling the man Jack "time's a-ticking."

Strategy 14

Analyzing Narration and Point of View

A story is always told by someone called the narrator. Usually the narrator of a work of fiction is a **persona** created by the author for the purpose of conveying the story. The narrator may be someone who participates in the action of the story, or someone outside the action of the story. The narrator may have limited knowledge, or may know everything there is to know about the story. The narrator may also be reliable or unreliable. All of these factors go into forming the characteristics of the narrator. The term **point of view** is used to identify one of the important characteristics of a narrator. There are three main viewpoints.

Stories can be told in the **first-person point of view**. In this case, the narrator is usually someone who was present or involved in the action of the story, and this person tells the story using the pronoun *I* to indicate personal involvement. A first-person narrator's perspective is limited by what he or she knows, sees, hears, and is told, as well as any mistakes or misconceptions he or she has. First-person point of view creates a certain intimacy because the narrator is speaking of his or her own experience.

Stories can also be told in the **second-person point of view**, which is distinguished by the fact that the narrator speaks to the reader as *you*, and addresses the reader directly, as if they were speaking together. If the reader understands him- or herself as "you," this creates another type of intimacy: that of a story shaped and styled for this very reader and no other.

The **third-person point of view** is the point of view of a narrator who is separate from the action and tells it from a greater distance than a first-person narrator would. This is the least intimate way of telling a story.

A second- or third-person narrator can be **omniscient**, knowing all the action of the story—even including what is going on in all the characters' minds and knowing what will happen before it happens—or **limited** to only the perspective of one character.

1. How much of *The Graveyard Book* did you need to read before you could identify the point of view? From what point of view is it told?

2. Identify two passages that show that the narrator is telling events from the perspective of the future, looking back on past events, not unfolding events as they happen.

3. In third-person point of view, the main character—the one from whose perspective the story is told—is often named and described to some degree in a paragraph or several close to the beginning of the book. Explain how the narrator reveals the basic facts about the main character. How is this approach unusual?

   - name
   - family members
   - appearance
   - age
   - location
   - key characteristics

4. What is the narrator's tone or attitude towards the reader? Cite the passages that support your conclusions.

5. How would you describe the personal attributes of the narrator?

Directions:
First, read the information. Then, answer the question or questions.

Strategy 15

We're going to make a distinction. We'll define a **reference** as an explicit mention of something outside the work you are currently reading. It could be a reference to something real or imaginary, but it's plain and out in the open. Here are some items that might be referenced.

- celebrations   • events   • places   • people   •books
- historic periods   • literary characters   • other aspects of culture

An **allusion**, then, we'll define as an indirect reference—one that you need to recognize as a reference without the author telling you that it is one. After you recognize the allusion, you need to figure out what it means in context. There are different types of allusions. Sometimes an author will include clues like quotation marks or introductory words ("as the great philosopher once said...") or use a name. But sometimes—especially if recognizing and understanding it are not essential to the author's point, the author assumes that virtually every reader will recognize the allusion, or the search for allusions forms an important (if puzzling) part of the reading experience—the author may not signal the allusion. Instead, the author may rely on readers sharing a common knowledge of literature, history, biography, science, and art that in most cases will help readers figure out meanings or treat the allusions like private jokes, inserted for those who can get them. When they are understood, allusions can help the reader see the work as part of a greater tradition.

Many allusions are to things that support or reinforce the meaning in the text.

1. Make a list of four references in *The Graveyard Book* to each of the following and tell what role they have in the book:

   - celebrations

   - real people

   - real places

   - civilizations and eras

2. Research each of the following allusions. Tell where the words come from and what they mean in the context of *The Graveyard Book*. Then tell whether you recognized the allusion yourself or not, and tell what, if anything, it added to your experience of the book:

   - "… but like the flowers that bloom in the spring, tra-la, absolutely nothing to do with the case." Mister Dandy, Interlude

   - "the Man in the Moon who came down too soon."

   - a lad who "put in his thumb and pulled out a plum"

   - a young country gentleman whose girlfriend had, for no particular reason, poisoned him with a dish of spotted eels

   - "Here comes a candle to light you to bed
     and here comes a chopper to chop off your head."

Directions:
First, read the information. Then, answer the question or questions.

Chapter 6

Nobody Owens' School Days

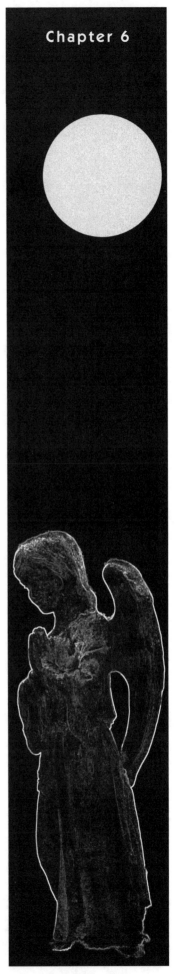

Journal and Discussion Questions

1. How are Nick and Thackeray alike?

2. Both Silas and Liza talk to Bod about the differences between the living and the dead. What does each of them say? Compare and contrast their analyses.

3. The narrator often uses simile, but in this chapter he uses a metaphor, a comparison that says that one thing is another (rather than using like or as). He says of Silas, "At the best of times his face was unreadable. Now his face was a book written in a language long forgotten, in an alphabet unimagined." What does this mean? Explain why and how it is effective.

4. The trope **Chameleon Camouflage** refers to the ability to avoid notice, not by being invisible, but by being difficult to recognize as present. Explain how this trope plays a role throughout the book so far.

5. Explain step-by-step how Bod outsmarts Nick and Mo.

6. Summarize the chapter from Mo's point of view.

Summary

On a rainy day, Bod is in hiding, reading a copy of *Robinson Crusoe*, that he'd sneaked away from Thackeray Porringer. He has just reached the part at which Crusoe spies a footprint in the sand and knows he is not alone on the island when Thackeray—who died in a rage and is still furious—comes after him. Bod returns the book after offering to read it to Thackeray and gets punched. As he leaves, Tom Sands and Euphemia Horsfall let him know that Silas is looking for him, which surprises Bod because it's still day.

Silas tells Bod that it's time for Bod to know where he came from. Bod politely says it doesn't have to be now, but Silas continues, first reminding Bod of what he already knows—that he's different from everyone else in the graveyard in being alive; that the Owenses took him in; and that Silas agreed to be his guardian. He continues by telling Bod that he had parents and a sister; that they were killed; and that the man who killed them is still out there and intends to kill Bod. Bod responds that being dead isn't so bad. Silas explains the key difference between the living and the dead: that the living have potential and are able to act in ways that change the world. Bod surprises Silas by concluding from this that it is important for him to go to school to be able to survive "out there" and—one day—confront the killer. Silas agrees to find him a school.

At first, hardly anybody notices Bod, and when they do, the attention is somewhat misdirected, as when two teachers discuss whether his family is religious—and they cannot remember him when he is gone. This comfortable anonymity starts to crumble after he begins to get involved with his fellow students—a move prompted by Bod's awareness that Nick Farthing and Maureen (Mo) Quilling are blackmailing Bod's classmates out of their pocket money and Bod taking the initiative to stop them by telling his classmates how to get out of their power. Mo and Nick come after him and Bod leads them into a cemetery, where they think they've cornered him. He fades as Nick punches him, resulting in Nick hurting his hand, Mo getting a fright, and the Persson family being extremely impressed and recommending that Dreamwalking and Visitation might be good follow-up techniques. The Perssons send their regards to Silas, and obliquely refer to him as a member of the Honour Guard, a fact that Bod files away.

That night, Bod follows up on their suggestions with Mr. Pennyworth, but the next day, Nick stabs the back of Bod's hand with a pencil when the teacher isn't looking, and Bod—realizing that he has become a presence rather than an absence—confesses to Silas, leading to their first serious argument and Bod walking out of the graveyard. He creates a scary Dreamwalk for Nick, and is heading out into the wide world when Liza catches up with him and reminds him of all the reasons he has to go home, which he decides to do when suddenly Liza tells him to run or fade, and he doesn't have time before a police car with two officers and Mo in the back seat stops him. Mo (falsely) accuses him of vandalism, and because he won't identify himself or his family, the officers, one of whom is Mo's uncle, are taking him to the station, when suddenly something black appears before them, and they hit it.. They stop the car, and Bod pounds on the window till they let him out and he positively IDs the "dead" victim as his dad and predicts that the officers wil lose their jobs. As they begin to argue, Silas, whom Liza had alerted, takes Bod home. Bod gives Mo a visitation and threatens to haunt her. Silas and Bod talk and make up. Silas appreciates that Bod needs to be among his own kind, though it is more challenging to protect him when he is out in the world. They make plans for Bod to learn in other ways, using libraries, theaters and cinema, and sporting events.

Strategy 16 Interpreting Irony

Irony comes from a Greek word meaning "someone who hides under a false appearance." When irony is used, things appear different from, or even the opposite of, what they really are: unexpected events happen; what people say is not what they mean. Authors use irony to create interest, surprise, or an understanding with their readers that the characters do not share. There are three main types of irony used in this story.

Verbal irony is irony in the use of language. Verbal irony means that what is said is different from or the opposite of what is meant. It is often indicated by a conflict between the content and the tone of voice in which it is said. When Silas says he is "delighted to have made [the man Jack's] acquaintance," we may not know everything Silas is thinking, but we can be quite sure he isn't delighted with a new acquaintance with whom he intends to fraternize frequently.

Situational irony can occur either from the point of view of a character or the reader. It refers to either a) a situation when something that is expected with a great deal of certainty doesn't happen as expected (this can be from either point of view) or b) a situation when something that is intended fails to materialize (this is only possible from a character's point of view, except in Choose-Your-Own Adventures or other books in which the reader participates by making a choice). For example, Bod is certain that the choice between the ghouls and the wolf is a choice between two horrible evils, whereas it is really a choice between death and protection, for the wolf is Miss Lupescu.

In **dramatic irony**, there is knowledge that the narrator makes available to the reader, but the the main character is unaware of it. This technique forms an important part of this book, as the older audience is enabled to see beyond Bod's toddler and child views of the world and knows things about his past that he was too young to remember.

The inkling that the characters do not understand as much as you do or the suspicion that a character's words can be interpreted in multiple ways are signals that should encourage you to examine whether irony is taking place.

1. Keep a record of other examples of each of the three types of irony in this story as you review chapters already read and continue to read.

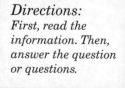

Directions:
First, read the information. Then, answer the question or questions.

Strategy 17   Tracing the Hero's Journey

Mythology expert Joseph Campbell characterizes the hero's journey as having a set pattern that can be varied in infinite ways. The hero leaves his ordinary life on a journey into a region where he confronts the supernatural. He wins a victory and returns to the world he left a changed person.

1. Read each summary of a stage in the hero's journey to determine to what extent it characterizes Bod's experience in *The Graveyard Book*. Expand on your answer as you finish reading, explaining how each stage fits or doesn't and identifying any stages that aren't present.

Departure

I. The Call to Adventure

The hero can enter into the adventure by mistake, or by being called by a herald who summons the hero. The call comes at a time when the hero is ready for inner growth. The hero's focus shifts from home to a distant place.

II. The Refusal of the Call

The hero is not always eager to assume the adventure offered. The hero has the opportunity to reject the call. If the hero refuses, his or her life may enter a state of paralysis until something happens to release him or her.

III. Supernatural Aid

The hero encounters a helper as the journey begins, a guide and protector (often an old woman or an old man) who provides special powers to keep the hero safe in his or her encounters with evil. This protector usually appears to one who has already accepted the call, but not always. In fairy tales, the helper is often a wizard, hermit, smith, or shepherd.

IV. The Crossing of the First Threshold

The hero, accompanied by the guide, goes beyond the boundaries of his or her everyday life, enters the wilderness, and has a first encounter with the dangerous forces of the unknown.

V. The Belly of the Whale

The hero is swallowed up by the unknown.

Initiation

VI. The Road of Trials

The hero undergoes a series of trials often on a perilous journey. The guide or other helpers support him. Each trial may bring new insight. Victories may be repeated, but are not lasting.

Return

VII. The Magic Flight

The hero's return to the world from which he or she came accompanied by his or her guardian.

VIII. The Crossing of the Return Threshold

The hero leaves the realm of the unknown and returns from the dark to the light. The transition is not easy.

IX. Master of the Two Worlds

The hero, through the journey, has won the ability to pass back and forth from one world to the other.

X. Freedom to Live

The hero can now live with new freedom as a result of the journey, having matured and grown.

Directions:
First, read the information. Then, answer the question or questions.

Test: Chapters 5–6 and Interlude

Vocabulary

Look at each group of words. Tell why it is important in the story.

1. shoplifter, thug, intimidate, pocket money
2. municipal gardens, Old Town, information center
3. wicker basket, tarnished, clumps, blossoms
4. abreast, Lord have mercy, it's a judgment on us
5. apoplexy, apprentice, initiation, slushy
6. underfoot, couplet, cobwebs, hemming
7. winding sheet, camouflage, shoelaces
8. bud, bloom, blossom, fade
9. secretive, brutish, sensitive, diverse
10. fiddle, swells, prelude, overture
11. crewed, cutlass, captor, reform
12. exotic, excursions, kidney machines
13. Visitation, Dreamwalking, Honour Guard
14. tread, curtseyed, bowed
15. Bunsen burners, petri dishes, preservative
16. tracks and traces, football match, cinema

Essay Topics

1. How does Bod's experience of the the Macabray differ from the experience of the dead? From the living? From Silas's experience? What are the reasons behind these differences?

2. Discuss Bod's garb through the book and the significance of each outfit he's worn.

3. How does Bod understand what the Lady in Grey says to him at the Macabray? How do you understand it?

4. How is Bod's departure from the graveyard in Chapter 5 different from his departures in Chapters 3 and 4?

5. How do you think Silas disposed of Jack's card?

6. How is the plot of Chapter 5 different from the plot of Chapters 1, 3 and 4?

7. Compare and contrast Silas and the Lady in Grey.

8. What do you think is the significance of Silas watching the Macabray, rather than staying in the graveyard and ignoring it?

9. Describe the music of the Macabray.

10. Why do you think Gaiman chooses to include the woman's reminiscence about Aunt Clara?

11. Discuss reversals in Chapters 5 and 6.

12. Explain the relationship between the word *Macabray* and the chapter title *Danse Macabre*.

13. What are the three reasons that people don't talk about the Macabray after it's been danced, according to Silas. Explain to whom each reason applies and why.

14. If you were the author of this story, what would happen next? How would you develop the plot?

Chapter 7

Every Man Jack

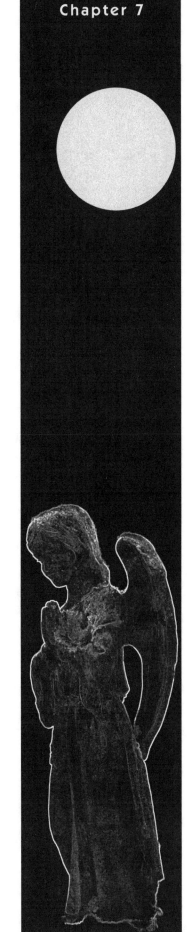

Journal and Discussion Questions

1. What clues hint at who Mr. Frost really is?

2. Compare and contrast the events of Chapter 1 and the end of Chapter 7.

3. Does Bod follow the Sleer's advice? Does he follow Nehemiah Trot's? Explain.

4. Describe Scarlett's relationship with her Mother.

5. What explanation can you offer for Scarlett's abilities that are similar to those Bod receives with the Freedom of the Graveyard?

6. List all Bod's previous experiences that go into his being able to deal with the Jacks and explain the role each played.

7. Write a news story, giving an objective report of Bod's struggle with the Jacks.

8. How does Gaiman use the following tropes in Chapter 7?

   • **Missed the Bus/Took the Wrong Bus**: Counting on transportation goes wrong, with dire consequences.

   • **Wolf in Sheep's Clothing**: Someone who appears to be nice turns out to have affected this personality only to accomplish his or her evil ends.

9. What is left to wrap up before this book can reach a satisfactory end?

10. Summarize the chapter from Mrs. Owens's point of view.

Summary

After months of intermittent absences, Silas mysteriously disappears. Bod learns the man Jack's name from Mrs. Owens. Meanwhile, Scarlett, now 15 and her parents having split up, has moved back with her Mother, Noona Perkins. Scarlett, who is angry with the world, has gotten on the wrong bus, and ends up near the graveyard. Feeling that she's been there before, she walks through the gates and accurately predicts to herself the presence of a church with a bench before it. She is called over by a friendly-looking man to assist with a grave-rubbing. When it starts to rain, he offers her a ride home. He introduces himself to her Mother as *Jay Frost* and is invited in for tea and then for Saturday dinner. As they talk, Mrs. Perkins recalls Scarlett's "imaginary friend," Nobody, whom Scarlett doesn't remember until later that evening, when she Dreamwalks with him, leading her to recall the Indigo Man and the Sleer.

Bod—who has food stashes and is not leaving without Silas or Miss Lupescu present—is outgrowing his childhood graveyard friends, who do not age and is being not-spoken-to by Liza. He misses the world of the living and is upset that he did not recognize Scarlett on her return. Wandering in the northwest portion of the graveyard, he recalls falling into Carstairs' very deep grave when he was 9. He consults poet Nehemiah Trot, who convinces him to Unfade for Scarlett, though Bod is concerned that this will lead to others seeing him. But when Scarlett next comes, she can see him even when he's faded and can also read in the dark. She hugs him, proving to herself that he's real, and they agree to meet on the weekend.

As Silas and Miss Lupescu, joined by a mummy and Ifrit, are fighting an unnamed foe in Krakow, Scarlett and Bod are together again, discussing the murder of his family. Bod explains that Silas is concerned that if he tells Bod too much, Bod will seek vengeance, but he won't say more about his guardian, and Scarlett leaves in a snit to rejoin Mr. Frost doing grave rubbings. She asks him how she would find out about a local murder, and—saying he's a wimp about such things—he suggests the library, where Scarlett founds a suspiciously incomplete record that omits any mention of Bod. Scarlett calls Mr. Frost prior to their dinner to inform him that the murder took place in his house. Meanshile, Miss Lupescu, who is critically wounded, finds the strength for one last battle to save Bod. Bod asks the Sleer for advice and is told to find his name.

On Sunday, Mr. Frost calls Scarlett and suggests she bring her friend over to see something he's found. She does, and Mr. Frost attempts to kill Bod, who escapes with Scarlett to the graveyard, despite four Jacks on the doorstep. With Scarlett hiding in the barrow, Bod drops three Jacks down the ghoul gate and one into Carstairs' tomb with the help of the graveyard. Confronting the man Jack in the barrow, Bod saves Scarlett, convincing Jack to declare himself the master the Sleer has been awaiting, and they subsume him. Scarlett is able to see Jack and hear his pleading as the Sleer take him, and she calls Bod a monster. Silas appears and takes her home, convincing her Mother to return to Glasgow, and wiping her memories. Silas tells Bod of Miss Lupescu's death. They go out for pizza, and Silas promises to stay with Bod until he's grown.

Strategy 18

Engaging with a Text Through Imaging and Mapping

IMAGERY

When there are few or no illustrations, during the act of reading, the words of a book are translated into experience by the reader, experience that for many readers can include **imaging** (seeing, hearing, taste, etc.) and feelings. There is an important distinction to be made between **induced images**—those aroused by text in the mind of the reader—and **imposed images**—those provided by an illustrator. The role of imaging in your reading process will be limited in cases where images are provided for you, whether occasionally, as in the print editions of *The Graveyard Book*, or throughout, as in the graphic novel version.

In either case, the meaning of a work of literature is felt by readers as they enter into the story in their imaginations. Writing instructor Janet Burroway explains that "Fiction tries to reproduce the emotional impact of experience. And this is a more difficult task, because written words are symbols representing sounds, and the sounds themselves are symbols representing things, actions, qualities, spatial relationships, and so on. Written words are thus at two removes from experience. Unlike the images of film and drama, which directly strike the eye and ear, they are transmitted first to the mind, where they must be translated into images [by the reader]" (*Writing Fiction: A Guide to Narrative Craft*, sixth edition, New York: Longman, 2002, p. 54).

Different texts foster different amounts and different kinds of imaging and feelings (also called "affect"). In part, these differences can result from the author's use of more or less description and more or less sensory language, the author's degree of focus on abstractions as opposed to concrete things, the relative complexity of the writing style, how plain or academic the diction is, and so on. As a result, your imaging won't always be exactly the same, and different senses may be emphasized at different times. Even when your imaging is at its most vivid, it is likely that it will not be as specific as a photograph or movie is. The visual images we create in our minds are characteristically not sharp and finely focused, a quality that literary critic Wolfgang Iser calls "optical poverty." This is an important point because you shouldn't expect these images to be something they're not or force them into a mold. Just let them come into your head, watch them, and take note.

Sensory language, often used in description, engages the senses of sight, hearing, smell, taste, and touch, by fostering images that appeal to the senses. Sight is the sense most often invoked, and taste, usually the least. Sensory language helps readers imagine the scene in the "movie" in their minds. It helps bring the black and white of the printed book or eBook or the sound of an audio recording to life. Keep an eye (or ear) out for such words as you read.

Musical Imagery

One way of using your imagination when you read that is not often discussed is imagining the music that the writer describes (for instance, the music for the Macabray) or imagining music for songs for which the writer supplies the lyrics. A simple melody can help you make such parts of a book more rich, meaningful, and memorable.

Directions: First, read the information. Then, answer the question or questions.

MAPPING

Another way in which writers encourage reader engagement is by providing sufficient location information that readers understand the spatial relationships between portions of the setting and become able to navigate in the world of the book as if they had a **map** in their mind and were able to use the mental equivalent of Google street view to walk through the world of the story.

Writers use direction words and location words to assist readers in gaining the lay of the land. Here are some words you can look for as you are working to figure out where each location is in relation to the others:

- north
- south
- east
- west (& combinations thereof)
- beyond
- beside
- past
- near
- behind (etc.)

The action of Chapter 7, for example, is challenging to understand without a thorough understanding of the layout of the graveyard. In books such as *The Graveyard Book* in which geography is important and no map is provided, it is often a good idea to make one. It is useful to begin this exercise with a compass rose—the indicator that identifies north, south, east, and west—so that you can be sure of marking things on the map with a consistent reference.

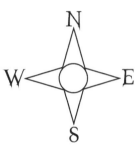

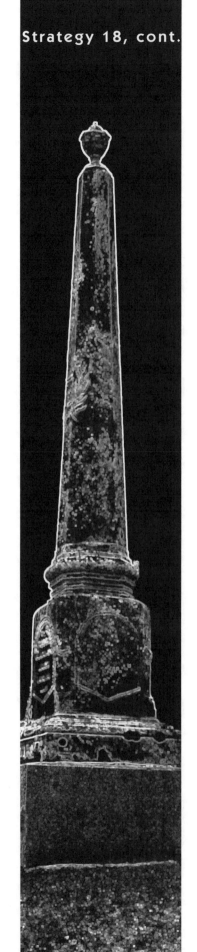

1. Make up a melody for the lullaby that Mrs. Owens sings to her son, guessing what might work for the ending. Record your tune with a mic and an app like GarageBand or—if you know how—by writing the notes on a music staff. Note that Mr. Gaiman owns the rights to the words, and while you can privately sing your musical version to yourself, you should check with your teacher before using it in any other way.

2. Using examples, explain to what effect Gaiman uses sensory language in Chapter 7. Tell which senses his words appeal to and how this use affected your experience of the events of the chapter.

3. To keep track of your imaging, it is useful to write about or draw what you've seen in your mind's eye. Record the most striking image(s) that you recollect from each chapter. Don't worry about your drawing ability; just do the best you can in whatever medium is most comfortable for you or best conveys what you want to communicate or recollect about your experience. Create a record for Chapters 1 through 7 now, and add a final one after you read Chapter 8

4. Make a map of the graveyard, putting in all key locations in the story as best you can, showing both the where in the graveyard prominent features appear and their relative position with regard to each other.

Writer's Forum 4

Writing a Short Research Report

A short research report is a 3–5 page paper that reports the results of a well-organized investigation of a suitably narrow topic, casting light on it through the use of multiple, appropriate sources. Your task is to explore the various Jacks in Chapter 7 to determine what they have in common and why Gaiman chose them. You will need to use *The Graveyard Book*, as well as authoritative sources that speak to the origins of their names. Use your research as a basis from which to assess the role of these characters individually and as a group in the story.

1. a. Reread Chapter 7. Write a preliminary thesis statement stating what you think the main idea of your paper will be. Your research may alter your main idea. That's fine: it's part of the process.

   b. List the Jacks. Write a short point-by-point outline, discussing each Jack before moving on to the next).

   c. Locate sources of information. You may access **primary sources**— ones with the first use of the names of the various Jacks—and **secondary sources**—interpretations, evaluations, or critiques of one or more primary sources. You can choose either **print sources**—those that have a physical existence on paper—or **digital sources**—computer files, in this case, eBooks—to conduct your research.

   d. In order to select which sources of information to use, you should evaluate them for appropriateness. These questions may help:

   • Is the source reliable and authoritative?

   • Is the source on-topic?

   • Is the source at a level that I can understand?

   You must choose a minimum of two sources besides *The Graveyard Book*, but not Wikipedia, because it is neither reliable nor authoritative. You may not use analysis of *The Graveyard Book* that answers the question for you by having undertaken the same research. You may need to locate more than two sources in order to find two that meet the criteria. JSTOR and other databases, Google Books, and a reference librarian may be of value in locating sources.

   e. Take notes on your source, using your outline to organize your notes. Use **paraphrasing** (expressing the same thing in different words) and—as needed—short **quotations** and avoid **plagiarism** (unacknowledged use or overuse of someone else's words) by citing properly, following whichever guide your teacher suggests.

   f. Following your outline, use your notes to draft your paper, which should have an introduction that states your topic, a body, in which you provide the similar or contrasting information, and a conclusion, in which you review your points and derive what meaning you can. Be careful to use quotation marks to show others' words. Consider your teacher as your audience. Give your piece a title, when done.

   g. Create a bibliography in the style that your teacher suggests.

Directions:
First, read the information. Then, answer the question or questions.

Strategy 19

Drawing on a Source, Part III
"Tiger! Tiger!"

You will remember that Gaiman has acknowledged using *The Jungle Book* as a framework for developing *The Graveyard Book*. We have determined that we should look for parallels in

- plot
- characters
- relationships

without necessarily expecting one-to-one relationships in every case: there may be a mix of clear substitutions and alterations from the original to better fit the new work.

1. Read "Mowgli's Brothers" (pp. 88–95 of this teaching guide). Then reread the first chapter of *The Graveyard Book*. Explain all the parallels that you see. Consider plot, characters, and relationships. Then, consider and note the differences that strike you.

2. How has Mowgli changed since "Kaa's Hunting"? How does this compare to how Bod has changed since "The Hounds of God"?

3. Taking each chapter on its own (that is, leaving aside the rest of each book), what themes does its author develop? How do the themes of the two works compare?

4. What do you think a reader gains from reading Chapter 7 of *The Graveyard Book* with *The Jungle Book* in mind? Do you think anything is lost? Explain.

5. In Strategy 10, you predicted what would be involved in a satisfying ending for each story, given what was at stake in the story. Did the two chapters, "Tiger! Tiger!" and "Every Man Jack" supply what you expected? Explain, telling how your expectations were fulfilled, or—if they weren't—offering some rationale for what each author chose to do instead.

Directions:
First, read the information. Then, answer the question or questions.

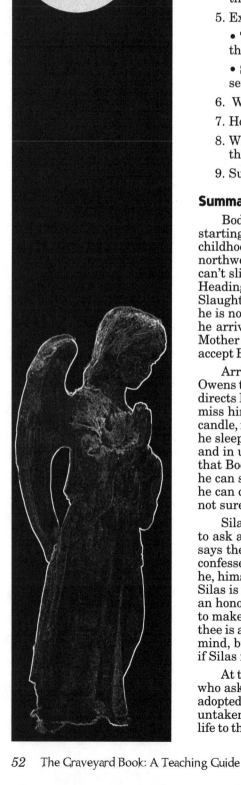

Chapter 8   Leavings and Partings

Journal and Discussion Questions

1. Compare Mother Slaughter's account of Bod's acceptance into the graveyard with what actually happened? How do you account for the differences?

2. How does what happens in Chapter 8 relate to Bod's coming of age?

3. When the narrator says, "there was kindness in Silas's voice, and something more," what is the "more"?

4. Gaiman creates a motif by repeating near the end of Chapter 8 words that were used in Chapter 1. Identify the words, and explain what the Chapter 8 version of them means and how they relate to the meaning and themes of the entire story.

5. Explain how Gaiman uses the following tropes in Chapter 8:

   • **The Magic Goes Away**: After evil is defeated, temporary power granted to those who fought them are lost.

   • **Sugar and Ice Personality**: A character who is primarily distant and reserved has moments of warmth, emotion, and tenderness.

6. What is the significance of Bod deciding he didn't want to know his birth name?

7. How did Mrs. Owens's completion of the poem effect you?

8. What is your response to the last sentence of the chapter? Explain why you think as you do.

9. Summarize the chapter from Mrs Owens's point of view.

Summary

Bod begins to lose the powers bestowed on him with Freedom of the Graveyard, starting with lapses in his ability to see the dead. Animals that he had known since childhood begin to avoid him, and he has difficulty slipping through the ivy to reach the northwestern part of the graveyard. He goes to see Alonso Jones, hoping for a story, but can't slip his head into the grave to call Jones, getting a painful bump on his forehead. Heading towards the southwestern slope, he sees no one until he comes upon Mother Slaughter, for whom he picks nasturtiums. She cleans his forehead, pointing out that he is no longer a boy, but a young man. She gives him an incorrect account of the night he arrived at the graveyard in which the Lady on the Grey tells the dead to listen to Mother Slaughter, leading everyone to agree with Mother Slaughter to be charitable and accept Bod. Saying she doesn't know when she'll see him again, she tells him to stay safe.

Arriving at the Owenses' tomb, he finds his parent standing formally outside. Mr. Owens tells Bod how proud they are of him, but Mrs. Owens has slipped away. Mr. Owens directs Bod to Silas, but on the way he meets Liza, who kisses him and tells him she will miss him always. Arriving at the chapel, he finds he can't see anything, so Silas lights candle, revealing Silas's leather bag and a steamer trunk, which Silas explains is where he sleeps when he is away from home, where he will now return, but which is far away and in uncertain condition. Bod protests that Silas is his guardian, and Silas responds that Bod is old enough to guard himself and he has other things to protect. Bod asks if he can stay in the graveyard, but Silas tells him he needs to leave and live. Bod asks if he can come with Silas, and when Silas says no, asks if he will see Silas again. Silas is not sure if Bod will see him, though he is certain of seeing Bod.

Silas points out a case packed for Bod, a miniature version of his own. Bod interrupts to ask about the Honour Guard, and Silas explains that they protect the borders. Bod says they did the right thing stopping people like the Jacks, who were monsters. Silas confesses that when he was younger he did worse things than any of the Jacks—that he, himself, was a monster, and worse than a monster. When Bod seeks to confirm that Silas is not a monster any longer, Silas says "People can change." Then he adds, "It was an honor to be your guardian, young man." He hands Bod a wallet with enough money to make a start in the world, and when Bod asks if he can see the world, Silas tells him thee is a passport in his suitcase. Bod begins to ask if he can come back if he changes his mind, but realizes the graveyard will never again be his home. He offers to help Silas if Silas is ever in need, and after first saying he never is, Silas more graciously accepts.

At the pedestrian gate—which is, for once, unlocked and open—he meets his Mother, who asks about his plans. She sings him the full lullaby that she had started when she adopted him, punctuated by his commentary. Confirming that he will try to "leave no path untaken," he tries to hug her, but she has become like mist. He leaves, meaning to live life to the full, before he returns to the graveyard, riding with the Lady on her giant Grey.

Strategy 20

Rereading a Book

As we discussed in Strategy 2: Understanding the Reading Process and Strategy 19: Engaging with a Text Through Imaging and Mapping, reading fiction is meant to be an experience. Novelist Joseph Conrad wrote, "My task, which I am trying to achieve, is, by the power of the written word, to make you hear, to make you feel—it is before all, to make you see. That, and no more, but it is everything."* In other words, we don't read literature just for the words that make up the story or to get at the facts; we read it in order to pass through (in our imaginations) the sequence of events the author proposes, allowing our minds and hearts to respond to these events.

But all of this doesn't happen without the extended and complex act that we call reading. And in our first reading of a text, we cannot give ourselves fully to experiencing the story because we have to perform all of the tasks that make up the reading process, from recognizing the symbols as letters and words, to figuring out the meaning of unfamiliar words, to recollecting the sequence of events, etc.

It is worth recalling what Vladimir Nabokov said:

> ". . . one cannot read a book: one can only reread it. . . . When we read a book for the first time the very process of laboriously moving our eyes from left to right, line after line, page after page, this complicated physical work upon the book, the very process of learning in terms of space and time what the book is about, this stands between us and artistic appreciation. . . . In reading a book, we must have time to acquaint ourselves with it. We have no physical organ (as we have the eye in regard to a painting) that takes in the whole picture and then can enjoy its details. But at a second, or third, or fourth reading we do, in a sense, behave towards a book as we do towards a painting" (*Lectures on Literature*, New York: Harcourt Brace, 1982, p. 3).

Rereading is also important when we want to clarify, re-experience, or check on our understanding of links between different parts of a book. Furthermore, rereading gives us an opportunity to review our hypotheses and their accuracy. It is possible, even likely, that we will see things we missed on the first reading.

1. Reread *The Graveyard Book*. Keep track of things that you notice in your second reading that you bypassed without paying attention the first time. Write a brief compare and contrast essay, to show the similarities and differences in the two readings.

2. Track each of the following tropes through your second reading:

- **Ancient Conspiracy**: A powerful group has skulked through history gaining power, but now they face extinction unless the fulfill a task.

- **Don't Fear the Reaper**: Death is not something to be feared: its personification is compassionate rather than menacing.

3. Identify all the characteristics that mark Silas as a typical vampire.

4. Review the hypothesis you formed in Strategy 11 (p. 33). Write a paragraph about it from the perspective of having finished and reread the book.

Directions:
First, read the information. Then, answer the question or questions.

*(Preface to *The Nigger of the "Narcissus,"* Oxford: Oxford University Press, 1984, p. xlii)

Writer's Forum 5

In a **book review**, you identify the work you are considering by its title, author, and genre; briefly summarize the plot; and then state your evaluation of the work.

When you write the **summary**, it is standard practice to identify the main characters, including the protagonist and antagonist, if the story has them. You should also include basic plot information, including a brief description of the main conflict, the setting, and the background of the situation, while avoiding spoilers that could ruin the reading experience for your audience.

Evaluation involves holding the book you're reviewing up to a set of preestablished criteria and then judging it based on those criteria. It requires much more than "I like it" or "I don't like it," although that kind of personal, gut-level reaction can form a part of an evaluation. But after that (or, perhaps, before that), it's time to become analytical and describe why and how the book in question succeeded in meeting or failed to meet your criteria. So your statements of judgment should include your general evaluation of the work as a whole (usually, book reviews are only written when a reader has finished a book) and show how your analysis of and reaction to elements of the work led you to that response.

For example, you might respond positively based on the following:

- The plot is suspenseful and interesting.
- The themes resonate with you.
- You like or admire one or more of the characters.
- The vivid description catches your imagination.
- The book is amusing and enjoyable.
- You learn something valuable.
- You are so absorbed that you can't wait to read more.
- You find insights or understandings that enrich your life.

Your evaluation need not only include favorable responses, however. You may judge the work unfavorably, if you think, for example, that the

- dialogue is unbelievable,
- characterization is weak,
- characters' motivations are not convincing,
- plot is convoluted or unbelievable,
- attitudes expressed seem inappropriate to you, and/or
- the genre doesn't appeal to you.

If your criteria don't match those stated above, you should clarify for yourself what you expect from the plot, themes, characters, language, dialogue, etc. and include your criteria in your review.

Sometimes readers change their minds about a work as they read, and it is also possible to write a review in which you explain how you began with one judgment and detail how and why your judgment changed.

1. Write a review of *The Graveyard Book*. Identify the book, summarize the plot, and provide a criteria-based evaluation, supported with evidence from the book.

Directions:
First, read the information. Then, answer the question or questions.

Writer's Forum 6

Comparing Two Treatments

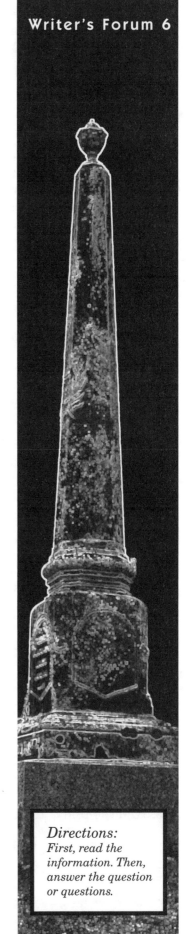

In a compare and contrast essay, you show the similarities and differences between two people, things, ideas, approaches, etc., and draw some conclusion(s) based on this examination. You choose the categories to compare and contrast based on your purpose and your topic.

Sometimes you will want to compare and contrast multiple treatments of the same subject in different genres or media. You might want to do this if a work has been adapted or translated to create a new work, if a work has inspired or influenced another work, or if they have the same subject and enough in common or such wide differences that you think it would be fruitful to assess how the two treatments, with their similarities and differences, each make meaning and achieve their effects.

In this particular case, you are going to contrast the illustrated text edition of *The Graveyard Book* with the audio recording (available at http://mousecircus.com/videotour2.aspx?VideoID=1). Usually it is easier to do this if you both read the book at least twice and listened to the audio attentively, while taking notes for your paper. Alternatively, you could compare the print edition with the graphic novel version, which has more adaptation of the text. Here are some questions that could be useful to examine, citing evidence as appropriate:

- What does the other form have that the text edition doesn't? How is the experience of the story different as a result?
- The two-volume graphic novel adapts the text of the book. What, if anything, is omitted or compressed? How did this affect the story?
- Images in a graphic novel may have additional material not included in the book, or may make changes in the book. What additions and/or changes do you notice? Did they add value? Did they make sense in the context?
- How did Gaiman's voice and gestures contribute to your understanding?
- How did your imaginings of the characters, settings, and actions of the book differ from the way they were presented in the audio or graphic novel? Compare the characterizations carefully. Did the audio or graphic novel provide you with new insights?
- Did the audio or graphic novel work as an experience in itself? Did it hold your interest? Was it worthwhile?
- Did the theme(s) you identified in the book come out in the audio/graphic novel? If not, what message(s) did it give?
- Which version do you like better? Why?

Source words that can help you express concepts of similarity and difference include the following:

• as well as	• likewise	• at the same time	• similarly
• alike	• resemble	• on the contrary	• while
• conversely	• whereas	• on the other hand	• but
• though	• however	• differ	

Directions:
First, read the information. Then, answer the question or questions.

1. Write an essay comparing and contrasting two versions of *The Graveyard Book*.

Test: Chapters 7–8

Vocabulary

Look at each group of words. Tell why it is important in the story.

1. islands, porpoises, glaciers, mountains
2. Glasgow, Scotland, splitting up
3. publisher, architect, Dorian, foul play
4. borderlands, weary, monster
5. fawn-colored, biscuit tin, portfolio, Mini
6. uncharacteristic gesture, transpires, regret
7. crikey, bit of a wimp, gives me the shivers
8. rustle, steamer trunk, immutable
9. engulfed, spread-eagled, flailing
10. The Old Country, *Nimini*, pet name
11. Assyrian mummy, Ifrit, hackles
12. too stupid, perplexed, wrong-footed, lumpkin

Essay Topics

1. In Chapter 6, Silas said there were many reasons why it was important to keep Bod safe. What do you now understand to be the reasons?

2. Explain how Bod goes from being just "boy" to something more in multiple relationships in this book.

3. In arguing that he should be able to go to school, Bod implies that experience in the outside world will help prepare him to deal with the murderer of his family. Is he right? Explain.

4. Sometimes authors invoke motifs and tropes only to play with them. It might be said that Gaiman does this with the "Finding True Love" motif that runs through fairy tales. Explain how Gaiman's plot development might expect readers to expect a romance that doesn't materialize.

5. What does Bod secure in Chapter 7? What does he lose?

6. The word *bait* is used twice in Chapter 7. Explain the significance of each statement and how they relate to each other.

7. The word *monster* is used twice in Chapter 7. Explain the significance of each statement and how they relate to each other and to the discussion of the word *monster* in Chapter 8.

8. How do the past and present intersect in *The Graveyard Book*?

9. Tell where the words "when the battle's lost and won" come from and what they mean in the context of *The Graveyard Book*. Then tell whether you recognized the allusion yourself or not, and tell what, if anything, it added to your experience of the book.

10. How do you feel about Miss Lupescu's death?

11. Read this trope definition: **Bittersweet Ending**: An ending that has positive aspects that come at a cost. Explain how Gaiman used this trope in ending *The Graveyard Book*.

12. Explain the significance of Robinson Crusoe in *The Graveyard Book*.

13. Tell the tale of the Honour Guard vs. the Jacks of All Trades in chronological order.

14. How does Gaiman make jokes with the words *grave* and *frost*? What do they add to the story?

15. Now that you know how the lullaby ends, revise your melody from Strategy 19.

16. If you were the author of this story and were writing an epilogue, what would it contain?

Theme Page

Maturity and Adulthood

1. How does Gaiman's plot for this story emphasize maturity as a theme?

2. Why is talking about maturity in relation to the population of a graveyard ironic?

3. That the prophecy about Bod is fulfilled suggests that Bod is an adult, although a 14-year-old isn't generally considered grown up. What characteristics and/or actions that Bod takes confirm his maturity? What more does he need?

4. Soviet psychologist Lev Vygotsky studied how children learn to become adults. He defined "the distance between actual developmental level as determined by independent problem solving and the level of potential development as determined through problem solving under adult guidance, or in collaboration with more capable peers" as the **Zone of Proximal Development**. Give an example from *The Graveyard Book* of Bod working in the zone of proximal development. Provide evidence to support your answers.

Identity

1. Adolescence is a time of internal change and development during which teens build and discover their identities. In our world, this is played out through engaging in activities and making choices, and discovering one's gifts, talents, inclinations, and disinclinations. Bod's ability to do this is limited. Do you think this interferes with his ability to develop his identity? Explain.

Appearance vs. Reality

1. Appearance can be different from reality for many reasons. List as many reasons as you can for a gap between how someone seems and who he or she really is.

2. Backstory is further details about characters, including how and why they became the way they are. Backstory can help provide depth to a character that seems to be a stereotype. For which characters in *The Graveyard Book* did additional information from their backstory change and deepen your impression of them? Explain what happened in each case.

3. Does Silas deceive Bod about who he is? Does Miss Lupescu deceive Bod about who she is? Does Gaiman deceive his readers about who Silas and Miss Lupescu are? Explain your answers.

4. How does the behavior of the man Jack make appearance vs. reality a critical theme in this story?

Education and Reading

1. What is education? What is its purpose? How does education relate to adulthood and maturity? Consider this quotation: "I have never let my schooling interfere with my education." —Mark Twain

2. Evaluate Bod's educators in light of this quotation: "Educators should be chosen not merely for their special qualifications, but more for their personality and their character, because we teach more by what we are than by what we teach." —Will Durant

3. What are the goals of education in *The Graveyard Book* as delivered by (a) the schools, (b) Miss Lupescu, (c) Mr. Pennyworth, (d) Silas?

4. What is the importance of reading in *The Graveyard Book*?

5. How has the experience of reading and thinking about *The Graveyard Book* contributed to your education? To your becoming a mature individual? To your becoming an adult? Explain.

Civility and Manners

1. What behaviors are indicative of good manners in the Graveyard? in the town?

2. How does Bod demonstrate good manners in the way he behaves to others?

Answer Pages

Strategy 1: Beginning a Book, pages 9–10

1. Answers will vary depending on how students characteristically read.
2. Answer will vary depending on students' prior experience.
3. Answers will vary. Students may predict a book about ghosts, murder, or a mystery being solved.
4. Answers will vary depending on version. The audio recording and the US text version both have a broken angel monument with a deep blue background and gold lettering, as well as the Newbery Medal. The UK version shows a vampire and a boy both looking at the reader in a graveyard. The graphic novel is in two versions. Volume one shows a Vampire protecting a boy in a graveyard in which the dead are also visible. Volume 2 shows a man being engulfed by a serpentine creature in the midst of a graveyard. A knife flying out of his hand is heading toward a teenage boy. Those with the audio or US version may have similar answers to 3 above. Readers with the UK version may think it's a story about a boy who befriends a vampire or vice versa. Readers of the graphic novel may be puzzled by the quite different covers and not know how to encapsulate the story from such different representations.
5. 2008; number of years since 2008.
6. Possible response: People who are poor may be considered useless by those who have more.
7. Those with the audio or US version may think that the chapters make it seem as if the book will be episodic, and may think that there's someone named Nobody Owens and somebody named Jack. Neither the UK version nor the graphic novel has a table of contents. Students are unlikely to be able to assign a chapter to the cover illustrations.
8. Possible observations: The writing is leisurely, evoking suspense through detail rather than dramatic statements or exclamations. It is also conversational—it sounds like the kind of work that was written with reading aloud in mind.
9. Possible response: The narrator seems objective about his report of the murders, but he also begins by presenting Jack's hand and knife as disembodied—separate from the man, which could be a subtle commentary on the man Jack's inhumanity. The detail and apparent care the narrator takes to describe things accurately suggests trustworthiness. The audience is not yet clear.
10. There are only two characters we know of who are still alive: perhaps Jack and the escaped child he was meant to kill are the key characters.
11. Beyond the fact that it is in a place with houses with several stories and the terrain isn't flat, it's hard to say much about the setting, including—based solely on the text (not the images or chapter titles), whether it is real or not.
12. Possible response: whether the child gets away from the man Jack; who else is important in the story.
13. Answers will vary. The title, chapter names, and illustrations suggest fantasy.
14. Possible response: staying alive.
15. Possible response: We'll be introduced to the child.

Chapter 1 How Nobody Came to the Graveyard, page 11

1. Possible response: The graveyard's efforts to protect Nobody Owens and Jack's efforts to find and kill him.
2. The first break shifts the focus from Jack's efforts to kill the child to exposition about the child and his actions this particular night. After the second break, the narrative shifts to address the reader as *you*, and the focus shifts to the graveyard at the top of the hill, and specifically, the Owenses and the interactions within the graveyard with a) the baby and b) the man Jack. The third break shifts from the communal discussion to follow Mrs. Owens and Silas and then report the visit of the Lady on the Grey and the resulting decision. The fourth break is a time break to just before sunrise, and the following section describes the baby's situation, Silas's pre-sunrise actions, and ends with focus returned to the man Jack. Aside from the exposition, sections 1 and 2 are more or less simultaneous; the following three sections are sequential. Breaks are more subtle in the audio version (rendered with pauses and changes in tone) and are rendered with a change of place/characters shown rather than space in the graphic novel.
3. Combining the fact that Chapter 1 begins and ends with Jack and chapter titles (if their edition has them), students may conclude that even though Jack may be out of the picture for awhile, there will be a confrontation with him in Chapter 7.
4. The narrator points out Silas's superiority in the areas of height, darkness of clothing, and scariness. Students may also note that Silas is ironic, persuasive, sophisticated, and clever, while Jack is literal, easily persuaded, crude, and nowhere near as clever as Silas, and Silas acts in multiple ways to protect the child

that Jack is bent on murdering. With regard to other members of the graveyard, Silas appears to be better educated, better traveled, more sophisticated, and have particular persuasive powers that are in the realm of magic. Unlike the dead, he can leave the graveyard and he eats (although he consumes only one food), and he is there not because his bones are buried there but because he has been given Freedom of the Graveyard. Students using the UK or graphic novel version may immediately detect that he is a vampire, whereas everyone else in the graveyard is either a ghost or the living baby.

5. First, naming a child is the right and duty of parents, so it represents Mrs. Owens' truly becoming the child's Mother (although, the fact that she can hold him has already suggested a bond between them that is outside the norm). Second, as Silas implies, those who mean to kill him have only his previous name to go on, so a new name will help keep him safe. Third, there is a literary tradition in this regard, notably Odysseus claiming the name "No One" (Οὖτις) to avoid being identified by the Cyclops Polyphemus and his father, Poseidon in the *Odyssey*.

6. Possible responses: The way Gaiman speaks about the knife makes it seem almost magical, creating an expectation that Jack will succeed. That Gaiman leaves the youngest, most vulnerable, and most innocent member of the family to last for Jack to kill creates the fear that he will be the easiest prey. The debate about whether the graveyard will or won't accept the baby makes his fate uncertain. When Jack gets into the graveyard, the reader doesn't know of Silas's experience, and there is no reason to expect that the Owenses could fend off the man Jack from harming the baby.

7. Bod's name, home, family, guardian, community, and his chances to live to adulthood all change in Chapter 1. Astute students may add that his frame of reference shifts from the current time of the story to the past, because that is the frame of all of the graveyard residents except Silas.

8. The reader learns that the hit was on behalf of "the Convocation" and that—for some reason—it did not need to be done immediately: Jack still has time to successfully complete his mission. Readers with a table of contents may note that between Chapters 5 and 6 is an "Interlude" titled *Convocation*.

9. Students may identify her as Death or as a kinder, gentler counterpart to the Grim Reaper or the Boatman on the River Styx—the one who guides people in their transition from life to death.

10. Mrs. Owens holds the baby, rocks him to sleep, sings to him, makes sure he's fed, cleans him up, and protects him.

11. Answers will depend on the edition the student is using. Gaiman's British accent and his differentiated accents for the characters are likely to make it clear to students that the book is set in England. This may not be clear to readers. The graphic novel is likely to make it clear that Silas is a vampire and the imposed images may help students clearly recall the narrative development, since they have an image for each key point. Students with the US version may be extremely puzzled. The man Jack looks clownish, his face appears to be falling off on p. 4, and the house on pp. 4–8 seems to be either designed by an architect intent on avoiding 90° angles or ramshackle and about to collapse. All of this is misleading as far as the facts of the story go, and potentially distracting. Teachers whose students have the US edition may wish to suggest they ignore the art for these reasons (or students may choose to do so on their own). Students watching the video of Gaiman's reading will also see the US images.

12. In the first sentence after the first section break, the masculine pronoun and the word *boy* indicate that the toddler is a boy. It is likely that it is revealed here, in the context of a description about the child's place in his family because it was important to them. The only thing important to the man Jack, who dominates the first section, is that the child be dead.

13. In chapter order: Mr. Owens argues based on the division between the living and the dead and the fact that the babe belongs with its (living) family. Mrs. Owens argues based on the child's Mother asking her to protect him. Jack argues that "anyone" would follow the sound of a baby crying. Mr. Owens argues that Mrs. Owens sees caring for the child as doing her duty. Josiah Worthington argues that graveyard residents have a duty to the graveyard and that the child belongs in its "natural home." Caius Pompeius argues that Mrs. Owens is not in a position to either feed or care for the child. Mrs. Owens argues that she is able to touch and hold the child (suggesting that this is evidence that she is meant to have him because in general, it seems that the living cannot touch the dead and vice versa). Mother Slaughter asks where he would live (implying that there is no suitable place). Mrs. Owens argues that they could give the child Freedom of the Graveyard based on the precedent of having given it to Silas. Caius argues that that was different because Silas is not alive. Silas argues that the rest of the graveyard should honor Mr. and Mrs. Owens's decision to take the child under their protection. He adds that he will provide food. Mother Slaughter argues that if Silas left for any length of time, the child could die. Silas responds to this argument by undertaking to be

the child's guardian and to ensure a substitute to care for the child should he be away. Josiah Worthington argues based on tradition that a graveyard is not a nursery. Silas concludes that part of the argument by agreeing with Josiah and changing the subject to the child's name. After the child is named, Josiah implies that Nobody could bring trouble to the graveyard. After Caius Pompeius sends Mrs. Owens away and the debate continues, the narrator tells us that the Owenses' respectability and Silas's agreement to be guardian both weigh in favor of keeping the child. At this point the Lady on the Grey arrives and says, "The dead should have charity," which decides the matter.

Strategy 2: Understanding the Reading Process, pages 12–13

1. Answers will vary. Particularly students reading the graphic novel, but also any student reading an illustrated edition, may slow down to examine illustrations, as well as words, in more detail. Students may slow down over the excerpt from Chapter 2 on the first page of the US version (which you might wish to encourage them to skip), the epitaph (which refers to the same person with both masculine and neuter pronouns and is somewhat cryptic in any case), or the table of contents. They may also slow down just after the breaks to reorient themselves, and speed up in spots of suspense to find out what happens.

Strategy 3: Marking a Text, page 14

1. Students' approaches to marking their text will vary. If you are distinguishing an aesthetic reading from an analytic reading, this should be saved for the analytic reading.

Strategy 4: Plot—Identifying the Overall Design of a Story, page 15

1. Overall, the structure is three parts: 1) from the beginning to "Danse Macabre"; 2) from the Interlude to the death of Jack in Chapter 7; 3) from Jack's death to the end. In each act, a significant action by Jack has dramatic repercussions in Bod's life, until—at the end—he is free of Jack's influence for the future. In the first two acts, we begin with the man Jack's point of view, and thereafter, the plot is played out from Bod's perspective. In the third act, Jack's view no longer intrudes in Bod's life. Further observations: Gaiman explains part of his approach in his Newbery Medal Acceptance Speech: "I wanted the book to be composed of short stories, because The Jungle Book was short stories. And I wanted it to be a novel, because it was a novel in my head. The tension between those two things was both a delight and a heartache as a writer." (US edition, p. 321). In following this design, the story of Jack's attempts to kill Bod on behalf of the Convocation is background for large parts of the book, which—when all is said and done—deemphasizes the murder plot in favor of the coming-of-age story. Because the reason for murdering Bod is presented as a mystery, exposition takes place throughout the book, up to the very last conversation between Bod and Silas, in which we finally understand the role of the Honour Guard.

Strategy 5: Interpreting Characterization, page 16

These questions build on the initial questions about the narrator in Strategy 1.

1. (Readers of the graphic novel may grasp a great deal that isn't explicitly stated in text about appearance and attitude.) Bod is characterized by his new name and by the actions he takes that puts him in the hands of people who will care for him and that endear him to them (e.g., smiling) and what others say about him, as well as exposition telling how they feel about him. He is not illustrated in any of the text versions, and the only word he says is, "Narna," naming the banana he has just eaten, which Mrs. Owens thinks is clever. Mrs. Owens is characterized largely by interactions: her quick understanding of Bod's situation and what his dead Mother is trying to communicate to her; and her attitudes: her willingness to undertake Bod's care, her protectiveness, warmth, and tenderness toward Bod, her tenacity in convincing her community, her willingness to learn new things (bananas). Bod's Mother is primarily characterized by her actions to try to protect her son. The man Jack is characterized by the physical description of him, in the beginning of the chapter, by his ruthless action, and by his almost magical capacity to discern smells in the first section. When he meets Silas, he is characterized by his interactions, and astute students might characterize Silas and Jack as character foils—characters whose traits are implicitly or explicitly contrasted. At the end of the chapter, Jack is characterized mainly by his thoughts. The Lady in Grey is characterized by her presence, by the graveyard's response to her, and by her words.

2. Students using different editions are likely to have quite different responses. Those reading the graphic novel may be unable to separate the influence of the illustrations from that of the text, taking it all in as a whole (which is, quite frankly, the intention). Those with the UK edition have an image of Jack, but may

not recognize Silas from the cover, and have only their imaginations create images for the rest. Those with the US edition may, as noted above, find the illustrations more problematic than helpful.

3. Silas is ironic; persuasive with the dead and able to change the thought of the living; sophisticated; and clever, generous, and protective. Neither living nor dead, and going out only at night (and/or the cover illustrations of the UK or graphic novel version may let readers know he is a vampire (more clues are dropped throughout the book, though the word *vampire* appears nowhere in the novel).

4. Possible response: It seems like Jack is the antagonist, but a) since Bod is a baby, having no particular goals, and b) since his safety is now the concern of the entire graveyard community (including Silas and the Lady in Grey), it seems as if there is a larger protagonist than just Bod. Some students may go on to characterize the book as depicting a battle between good and evil.

Strategy 6: Drawing on a Source, Part I "Mowgli's Brothers," page 17

1. To avoid spoilers, have students stop reading at "And that is how Mowgli ws entered into the Seeonee Wolf Pack for the price of a bull and on Baloo's good word." (p. 91)
   Parallels: *Plot*—Male toddler being chased by "inhuman" killer takes refuge in an environment not his own, with different rules, customs, and culture from the world he comes from and finds a home with a family, with the mother of that family making the initial decision to keep him. The child is presented to the larger community, who accept him after the intercession of two characters who are semi-outsiders but who have standing in the community. The child is fed, made comfortable, and given a name by the Mother who adopted him. *Characters*—Jack/Shere Khan; Bod/Mowgli; Mr. and Mrs. Owens/Mother and Father Wolf; Silas/Bagheera; The Lady on the Grey/Akela—as the one with ultimate authority in the community; the graveyard community/the wolf community. *Relationships*—Both boys are hunted by a crude and defiant killer who violates an area in which he does not belong to get what he wants. Both lose and acquire a mother and father; both gain a guardian (though Bagheera is not named as such), who is wise, persuasive, and has special knowledge and special interest in his safety. Both are accepted by the wider community.
   Key Differences: The characters of Tabaqui and Baloo have no discernible parallel in Chapter 1; Akela and the Lady on the Grey do not have the same role in the decision to keep the child; Bod's plays with other community children rather than step-brothers and sisters; Jack is sent off and has no voice or influence at the council; Chapter 1 covers only a single night, therefore, none of the events when the child is older.

2. Bod comes from a family home at the bottom of a hill and wanders into a graveyard; Mowgli is apparently at a woodcutter's campfire near a village and wanders into the jungle. In both cases, one would usually think the original environment was safer (but in both cases, it was made unsafe by the killer). For Mowgli because he is adopted by the wolves (and ultimately the tribe and Bagheera) who know, have insight into, and hate Shere Khan, and for Bod because he has lost his family where he came from and has a substitute family and a guardian who seems to have some ways of dealing with and some insight into Jack, the environment which would initially seem unsuitable is actually a haven.

3. Possible response: *The Graveyard Book* seems to be primarily focused on the role of the community and treats Jack's mission to kill as a mystery, which will presumably be unraveled as the book progresses. *The Jungle Book* seems to be exploring the role of humans in relation to animals and how external influence can fragment a community, while Shere Khan's intent to kill Mowgli is simply a personal vendetta against "the one who got away."

4. Possible response: The similarities and differences may both help cast Gaiman's choices into relief, leading to a greater understanding of the unity that Gaiman is creating. If any of the material that Kipling includes when Mowgli is older is going to appear later in *The Graveyard Book*, it may diminish/ruin the suspense.

Writer's Forum 1: Analyzing and Composing Lyrics, pages 18–19

1. Possible response: The song is about the possibilities that a baby has as it grows up, including some of the things that are most desired: love (kiss a lover), happiness (dance a measure), creating a sense of identity (find your name), and finding something completely worthwhile (and buried treasure). It has two verses with four line stanzas (this can be judged by the change of rhyme, with perfect end rhyme on lines 2 and 4. By adopting Bod and saving his life, Mrs. Owens has (along with her community) made it possible for Bod to grow up and (potentially) fulfill all the wishes expressed for him in this song; had they not acted, all his possibilities would have been at an end. [The graphic novel does not even include one entire stanza and treats "babby-oh" as "babby./Oh"].

2. "Hairy bacon" does not seem in keeping with the serious and uplifting nature of this lullaby. Gaiman likely used it for comic relief.

3. Answers will vary. Possible response (couplets with four stresses in the first line and two in the second):

Three of four are dispatched,
My next plan hatched.
For this most important crime
I still have time.
Polished bone knife in the dark:
Find your mark.

Chapter 2 The New Friend, page 24

1. Because Scarlett can see the Indigo Man, although she can't see dead people, and maybe also because the Indigo Man does not react to Bod's assertion that he has the Freedom of the Graveyard.

2. According to Scarlett, her friend has a completely unlikely name and lives in a place where no living people reside, and her father's understanding that imaginary friends are age appropriate seems to confirm it—i.e., if it wasn't age appropriate, they might have followed up more.

3. Answers will vary depending on the story chosen. Possibilities include Lyra and Roger (or Will) in *The Golden Compass* trilogy; Katniss and Peeta in The Hunger Games trilogy (although both are from District 12, they are from opposite sides of the tracks); Romeo and Juliet from the Shakespeare play that bears their names; Tony and Maria in *West Side Story*; and Jesse and Leslie in *Bridge to Terabithia*. In many (if not most) cases, the connection is between older children, and it is often a romantic relationship.

4. It is realistic that children: use ambient material to learn the alphabet (e.g., billboards and streetsigns); have prior knowledge about different things, depending on their backgrounds; ask the adults they know for more information about topics of interest; play in the environment they find themselves in; have mis-understandings and disagreements; sulk; explore in places that are not entirely safe; are affected by their parents' emotions; sometimes lose friends because their families relocate.

5. The key events are: the argument about what Scarlett can do in the graveyard; the visit to the barrow; their farewell before Scarlett moves to Scotland; the Dreamwalk; Scarlett feeling insulted over Bod's re-fusal to talk about Silas; the visit to Jack Frost's house; the attack of the Jacks in the cemetery, leading to Scarlett seeing Bod in a much different light.

6. Possible response: It's not very extensive and doesn't seem very valuable—maybe its value is more symbol-ic than monetary.

7. Possible response: Scarlett is correct in that almost every one leaves home when they've grown up in order to earn a living and live their life. Also, Bod is being kept safe in the cemetery primarily because Jack is trying to kill him: presumably this conflict will be resolved and Bod will either be safe—so able to leave the cemetery. However, eventually, Bod will die—as everyone does—and so become a permanent resident of a cemetery, so Bod is correct in this regard, although this is not what he means: the fact is that he cannot, at this point, imagine a life outside of the community that is all he knows..

8. The name *Nobody* is one of the things that convinces Scarlett's parents that her friend is imaginary, help-ing to ensure that nobody in town is talking about a boy living in the cemetery.

9. Possible response: I think Bod will be several years older and have some apt experiences for that age that are complete in themselves, while advancing the larger plot at least a bit.

10. Some are new and clear, whereas others are aged and no longer readable.

11. Possible response: It suggests that his not being obedient will play a role in the story, sooner or later.

12. Summaries should include: taking Scarlett to the nature reserve because their flat has no garden, and allowing her to roam on her own for only 30 minutes at a time, with strict instructions "not to get into trouble or talk to strangers"; Scarlett reporting on an imaginary friend; Scarlett asking about the history of England prior to the Roman occupation and learning about the Celts; Scarlett reading with her Mother on the bench and then going for a walk; being unable to find Scarlett and calling the police; Scarlett being found by a policewoman; Scarlett's parents fighting with each other and drawing conclusions about how dangerous the world is; the argument between Scarlett's father and the policewoman; Mr. Perkins's new job in Scotland; Scarlett's insistence on a last visit to the graveyard.

Strategy 7: Plot—Types of Conflict, page 25

1. The conflicts in the first two chapters are exclusively external, as characters come up against impediments

to their individual goals. Bod in Chapter 1 and Scarlett and Bod in Chapter 2 are too young to have the kinds of internal conflicts that usually show up in fiction. Chapter 1: Jack's attempt to fulfill his murderous mission despite the disappearance of his final quarry; Mrs. Owens' attempt to gain community support for saving Bod. Astute students may suggest that Silas is somehow involved in a larger conflict—he seems to be attempting to discover more about and thwart the plans of the organization behind Jack (this explains his conversation with Jack, his support of Bod's adoption, his taking on the role of guardian, and his visit to the scene of the crime). Chapter 2: Scarlett has a minor conflict of not being allowed to talk to strangers, but wanting to be friends with Bod; Bod and Scarlett have conflicts as one might expect children of their ages to have (students may note that they have to do with trust). There is an apparent conflict with the Indigo Man, but he turns out to be imaginary. Their goal of friendship is interfered with by the move of Scarlett's family to Glasgow.

2. The overarching goal is to keep Bod alive so he can get the chance to grow up, make his choices, and live his life. Students who have particularly noted Silas's actions may suggest another overarching goal of defeating the Convocation. (The evidence for this is limited, but solid, and keeping Bod alive seems to form part of this greater program.)

3.

3	Hound of God, Night-Gaunt, and Bod vs. Ghouls—for Bod's life and safety	4	Bod, Liza, and Silas vs. Abanazer Bolger, Tom Hustings, and Jack—for Bod's life and safety	5	There isn't a conflict of the standard type in this chapter. Bod is trying to figure out what's going on.
I	Jack vs. Jack Dandy and the Convocation—for Bod's life and safety.	6	Bod, the graveyard, the Perrsons, and Silas vs. Mo and Nick—for Bod's anonymity, therefore his life and safety	7	Bod, Scarlett, the graveyard, and Silas vs. the Jacks—for Bod's and Scarlett's life and safety and the defeat of the Jacks of All Trades
8	Bod vs. his destiny—Bod is conflicted over leaving the graveyard, but by the end has accepted that his future lies ahead of him and among the living.				

Test: Chapters 1–2, page 26

Vocabulary

1. Names of the types of beings to whom—according to Josiah Worthington—Mrs. Owens has a duty (i.e., not the living).
2. These are furnishings of the crypt.
3. These words have to do with the barrow and the Sleer.
4. These words are related to the Grey that the Lady rides.
5. These are items that are visible in the graveyard in the moonlight.
6. A description of Bod's appearance as a young boy.
7. These form a portion of Caius Pompeius's attire
8. These words describe Bod upon his first appearance as he heads towards the graveyard.
9. These are key elements in Bod's process of learning to read.
10. The first two are what the Owenses are not, the third what they are—and this factors into the debate about keeping Bod.
11. Animals that confirm that dual nature—graveyard and nature reserve—of Bod's new home.
12. These words have to do with the Indigo Man.
13. These words have to do with Jack's extraordinary sense of smell.
14. These words have to do with the way that Silas, who is not dead, is allowed to reside in the graveyard.
15. These words are related to the Lady on the Grey's appearance in the graveyard.
16. These words have to do with the work of Scarlett's Mother and father.
17. These words have to do with the appearance of the tomb in the barrow.

Essay Topics

1. Possible responses: Chapter 1—Bod's disposable diaper, pacifier, sleeping in a crib, climbing out, pronunciation of *banana*, messy eating, reaching to be picked up, etc. Chapter 2—Interest in learning, initially not wanting to share, being mostly-but-not-entirely obedient, getting into an argument with a playmate because he can't explain why things are different for him and for her, making up games with what's at hand, exploring. Some students may feel that Bod's reasoning skills as demonstrated in the Barrow are a bit above his age level.

2. Possible response: In Chapter 1, the Owenses adopt him and take care of holding and cleaning the baby and giving him a place to sleep. In Chapter 2, the only mention of the Owenses is in regard to their lack of interest in reading—we assume that Bod still sleeps in their "fine little tomb," and that they oversee his bedtime, etc. In Chapter 1, Silas provides everything from the outside world (the world of the living) that Bod needs (he offers to let Bod sleep in the crypt, but is turned down by Mrs. Owens), and goes to Bod's original home, presumably to try to figure out what Jack's motivations and plans are. In Chapter 2, Silas answers Bod's questions on a wide range of topics, procures materials for him to learn to read, listens to his tales of his exploits, finds a new teacher when Bod wants to learn something new, and tries to help Bod understand—without mentioning Jack—why Bod is safe in the graveyard but not in the world beyond.

3. Answers will vary. Students may see the role of Jack as providing the inciting incident for Bod's early life and development, to which he is not party, due to the protection the graveyard has provided for Bod. They may imagine that Jack is searching hopelessly for Bod out in the world beyond the graveyard.

4. Possible responses: It is the first book that many children read on their own, one that a bookstore owner would be likely to recommend as a first reader. It is a book about an outsider, of whom (like Silas) the children's Mother would not approve, so it might be meaningful to Silas.

5. Scarlett is confident, self-possessed, and matter of fact. She can hold a grudge, but can also let it go. She is enthusiastic in her praise, as she is in her criticism. Scarlett's parents are both thwarted in their careers—she by teaching at a distance; he by being unable to find a permanent position—and "modern" in their child rearing, using external norms to judge whether Scarlett's experience of an imaginary friend is normal. They are also both volatile after Scarlett's temporary disappearance, showing no self-restraint in their treatment of each other or the policewoman, and in controlling their emotions. They are concerned enough about Scarlett's development that they heed her plea to visit the graveyard one last time, though her Mother doesn't control her voicing of her own opinions. Caius Pompeius is a bit stiff and pompous, as fits his name, and holds outdated opinions that we are likely meant to think were typical in the age in which he lived (e.g., about the furry orange Caledonians). He has a good memory, is truthful, and is fond of Bod. Josiah Worthington, Bart., is also pompous, as well as formal, condescending, self-important, and aggrieved by others' lack of gratitude for his gift of the graveyard.

6. List from most powerful first: The Lady in Grey—akin to a deity; Silas—who has standing that caused him to be given Freedom of the Graveyard (we will later learn, as a member of the Honour Guard); Josiah Worthington—due to social standing, Caius Pompeius—due to being the oldest member of the graveyard, after the barrow resident; Mrs. Owens—who, despite having none of what empowers the others, is able to use logic and argument to help bring about Bod's rescue and adoption.

7. Answers will vary. Possible responses: Skills attained by education: Multiplication; using a microscope; analyzing a work of literature; learning a language. Skills attained by practice: throwing a football; climbing a tree; sewing a straight seam. Skills attained by time: [It is debatable whether there are such skills in the real world that are functions of time and not education or practice. Students who believe in an afterlife may suggest an ability to exist as pure spirit, without a body; students who don't may be at a loss.]

8. Possible response: That people have always had a fear of and held misconceptions about those different from themselves.

9. *Nobody Owens* and *nobody owns*, sound nearly identical. Possible response: The name is ironic because whereas in the poem, the words literally bespeak a human being who is completely alone with no connections, in the novel, the name is the sign and symbol of Bod's adoption and the commitment of the community to care for him, changing his state from "a pauper whom nobody owns" to a beloved child in the care of many.

10. His aptitude for reading suggests that he is somewhere between four and six. His being shorter than Scarlett could be due to a variety of reasons, including genetics. His reasoning abilities as demonstrated in the barrow make him seem a bit older, and for this reason, students may have trouble drawing conlusions about his age.

11. Sebastian Ryder died in 1583. Of the queens he might have been alive to see, there are Catherine of Aragon, Anne Boleyn, Jane Seymour, Anne of Cleves, Catherine Howard, Catherine Parr, Jane (if she's counted), Mary I, and Elizabeth I. Of these, only Anne of Cleves spoke no English.

12. The relationships are similar in that: the adults are a bit hand's-off, allowing the child a certain amount of freedom; they do not show excessive interest in the child's play—they listen to their stories and move on. Silas, however, seems more self-possessed and urbane, is certainly in better control of his emotions, is more sophisticated and has a wider knowledge of affairs and the bigger picture for his charge than the Perkinses

do. Also, they are living,

13. Scarlett is likely even more important to Bod than Bod—as her real or imaginary friend—is to Scarlett because Scarlett is the one living person whom Bod has any interaction with, and likely, any conscious memory of: she may anticipate making new friends in Scotland, whereas for Bod, her departure is more on the lines of a devastating loss with no immediate hope of replacement.

14. Answers will vary. Students may have slowed down for the discussion between Bod and Caius Pompeius, which has a number of references to places the students may not recognize (Caledonia, Camulodonum, Gaul) and customs that they are unlikely to recognize.

15. The reversal in Chapter 1 is the graveyard residents, Silas, and the Lady interceding on Bod's behalf and making him off limits to Jack—who one would otherwise expect to succeed without problem in killing an 18-month-old. The reversal in Chapter 2 is Scarlett's family moving, which effectively prevents Bod's and Scarlett's friendship from developing further.

16. Answers will vary. Students may suggest that since Bod aged about 4 years between Chapters 1 and 2, there may be the same length of time between 2 and 3. They may suggest that the plot will be self-contained, like that of Chapter 2. Since the most important thing for Bod's safety is that he stay in the graveyard and since he is only mostly obedient, they may suggest that Bod will leave the graveyard or attempt to do so.

Chapter 3 The Hounds of God, page 27

1. Answers will vary. Some students may think that in addition to Silas being away, Bod's loss of his friend Scarlett contributed significantly to the self-pity that put him at the mercy of the ghouls. Others may think that Silas's absence in itself was enough to disturb the order of Bod's life because of all the things Silas meant to Bod. In either case, they should cite textual evidence to support their opinions.

2. Answers will vary depending on the character chosen for comparison. Possible choices include: Denethor in *The Lord of the Rings,* in response to the visions he saw in the palantír, which he took to be true; Robinson Crusoe and his pitying parrot; Brian Robeson in *Hatchet* by Gary Paulsen; Collodi's Pinocchio; Silas Marner in the book that bears his name; the Mayor of Casterbridge in the book that bears his name; Moaning Myrtle in the Harry Potter series.

3. Answers will vary. Students who have read other books with werewolves and/or who know the species name *Canis lupus* and connect this to Miss Lupescu's name are apt to figure out the connection more quickly. Very astute students may make the connection early because they notice that Miss Lupsecu walking around Bod and sniffing him is canine-like behavior.

4. Students' responses should include: the disconnect between the names of the ghouls and their speech and behavior; Miss Lupescu's attitudes, speech, and terrible cooking.

5. Students' responses should include: the description of the ghoul-gates with which the chapter begins (implying that they will be important); Silas's departure, which may concern the reader as it concerns Bod; Miss Lupescu's apparent incompetence to protect Bod (as evidenced by her cooking and her seeminly irrelevant lessons); the apparent hopelessness of Bod's situation when it seems that he must become a ghoul or a ghoul's meal; the apparently terrible choice between allowing the ghouls to take him to Ghûlheim and being eaten by the wolf.

6. They come to understand one another, to trust one another after each finding that s/he has underestimated the other, and to find common interests.

7. Food provides comic relief (through Miss Lupescu's terrible cooking); a temptation (through the ghoul's description of the delicious food that awaits Bod if he were to be allowed to accompany them); a threat (when it seems that Bod's choice is to either eat corpses or become a corpse and be eaten; a sign of both truce and friendship when Miss Lupescu brings Bod a meat pie and chips (as we imagine Silas might have done) and (unlike Silas) shares the chips with him.

8. Possible response: Ghouls are disgusting and gruesome creatures, as well as silly, self-important chatterers, who name themselves after their first meal and act as if they deserved the honors associated with those names. Tenacious and single-minded as far as eating, anti-everything that isn't ghoul, and afraid of both night-gaunts and werewolves, they are distinguished by their attempts to impersonate the people after whom they name themselves, attempting to speak with their diction and dialect.

9. The original subject matter was chosen to help keep Bod safe (although Miss Lupescu failed to communicate this to Bod, leaving him with the feeling that he was having to memorize a lot of useless stuff). She intends to teach him to name the stars and constellations because it is a subject of mutual interest.

10. Silas holding his right arm stiffly suggests that he has been in battle; his gift to Bod suggests that he's been in San Francisco.

11. Possible response: Miss Lupescu comes to the graveyard from the Old Country to care for Bod in Silas's absence with serious reservations, unclear that Bod is worthy of her attention. Her impressions are not enhanced by his responses to her home-cooked meals or his sometimes flippant, sometimes inattentive attitude towards the important lessons she is trying to teach him. She is likely further put-off when he throws a clump of mud at her when she is protecting him in wolf form. She learns of Bod's ghoul-napping from the night-gaunt that Bod calls to for help, and rushes in wolf form to save him, assisting to tear a large enough hole in the sack that he has already damaged so that he can escape, only to have him push past her and hurt his ankle falling down the next stair. In wolf form she carries him back to the graveyard on her back after the night-gaunt catches him when he falls off the stairs to Ghûlheim. On the way back, when Bod admires the night sky, she offers to teach him the names of stars and constellations, and delivers him safely to the Owenses. The next day, in her human form, Miss Lupescu goes to the chemist (drugstore) for an ankle bandage. Later she brings him a meat pie and chips—the kind of food he is used to—and shares the chips with him. When Silas returns, Miss Lupescu admits to having learned things while he was away, and undertakes to return to teach Bod the next year, which Bod says he would like.

Strategy 8: Interpreting Character Names and Development, page 28

1. Silas—this name may be an oblique allusion to the novel *Silas Marner*, in which the life of Silas is transformed by the adoption of an orphan who wanders to Silas's house after her Mother dies.

Sleer—an obsolete variant of the word *slayer*

Nick Farthing—*Nick* means "steal"; *farthing* is money

Scarlett Amber—The bright colors of her name and attire contrast the world of the living with the world of the dead (and Bod's grey winding sheet)

Lupescu—related to *Canis Lupus*, the species name of the gray wolf

2. Bod continues to form warm attachments to those who enter his sphere (Liza), and (following the model of the graveyard, although this is never stated explicitly), becomes involved in the life of the school community to ensure the safety of its members, even though this puts him at risk. He forms alliances to get out of the scrapes he gets into, always contributing in some way to his own rescue, until—when he faces the Jacks—he has grown to be able to direct a winning battle, working with his allies.

3. Most of the characters do not change because they are dead, and that is one of the key characteristics of being dead: there is no more change. Mr. and Mrs. Owens change in adopting Bod, but since we meet them just as they meet Bod, we don't see much change other than we know that they have never before cared for someone the way they care for Bod. Scarlett changes, growing up and becoming a disaffected teenager, but still maintaining her fondness for Bod until she sees what happens to the man Jack, whom she cannot entirely detach from the kind Jay Frost who she knew, at which point she sees Bod as a monster. What would have happened next is unknown, because (for the safety of all) Silas wipes her memories. Miss Lupescu changes, learning from Bod, as he learns from her. She becomes more flexible, less standoffish, warmer, and more invested in Bod's future. Silas, though his change is more subtle, also show signs of increased tenderness towards Bod in Chapter 8—at one point he seems to wipe away a tear, and he changes his response to Bod's offer of help, should Silas ever be in need. It should be noted that the dramatic change in the man Jack (as Jay Frost) is not character development but disguise.

Strategy 9: Relating Setting and Mood, page 29

1. Students may interpret moods differently. Samples are provided for the first three chapters. You may wish to have students distinguish different areas in and around the graveyard.

	Setting Description	Function(s) in Story	Moods Created
1	Bod's family home; hill; graveyard	reveals Bod's homelife; shows his escape from Jack; introduces his new community/home	terror, heartbreak; hope, love
2	graveyard	provides opportunities for learning and fun; scary, but when understood, less scary; confining place of separation from life outside	nurture; interest and invitation; fear; comprehension; loneliness
3	graveyard; desert through the ghoul gate; Ghûlheim; back to the graveyard	interpreted as unwelcoming/uncaring; dangerous/alien; welcoming, desirable	rejection; abuse; hope, love

		Setting Description	Function(s) in Story	Moods Created
4		graveyard, Abanazer Bolger's shop in the Old Town		
5		graveyard, the Old Town		
I		The Washington Room at a hotel		
6		graveyard, school, other places in town, including small graveyard, outside Nick's house, outside Mo's house, police car		
7		graveyard, Mr. Frost's car, Scarlett's apartment, Mr. Frost's house, the hill		
8		graveyard; the world		

2. Answers will vary depending on which version students are using. Those listening to the audio version may assume from the start that the setting is England. Those using the US version may pick up clues from common British English vocabulary, such as *flat* for *apartment*, *chemist* for *drugstore*, *Honour Guard* for *Honor Guard*, and *grey* for *gray*. Those using the graphic novel may notice the double decker buses, the car with the steering wheel on the right-hand side, etc.

Writer's Forum 2: Writing Description, page 30

1. Answers will vary. Possible response: *Sight:* "bluish-green color of the veins of mold in a cheese"; *Touch:* "He felt the tip of it, sharp to the touch."; *Taste:* "vinegary tomato"; *Smell:* "smelled of nothing worse than dusty wood"; *Hearing:* "a guttural cry, like an eagle's call."

2. Answers will vary depending on what students choose to describe, but in any case, they should evaluate it using objective criteria, use metaphor and simile to describe it, and describe the emotional response of those whose it is.

Strategy 10: Drawing on a Source, Part II "Kaa's Hunting," page 31

1. <u>Parallels:</u> Because his teacher (Baloo/Miss Lupescu) is a bit harsh and makes him memorize long lists of items (master word/ways of saying help), Mowgli/Bod is feeling sorry for himself and takes up with the Bandar-log/ghouls, who carry him off, out of the area where he is safe, swinging him between them as they travel toward the abandoned city (Cold Lairs/Ghûlheim) that they have taken over, promising that they will appreciate him, and bragging about their wonderful lives. Both boys use what they were taught to signal to a flying creature (Kite/Night-Gaunt) for help, and the message is carried back to their teacher, who comes to their aid. Both boys are carried home on the back of a four-footed animal.
<u>Differences:</u> In *The Graveyard Book*, Bod only has two allies available to help him against the ghouls (Miss Lupescu and the Night Gaunt), and he is aware of only one, initially. Silas (unlike Bagheera) is away and only learns of the episode at a distance. There is no battle between the ghouls and those who have come to rescue Bod. Besides calling for help, Bod also assists in his own rescue by getting out of the bag. Bod does not initially recognize Miss Lupescu. bod has been warned obliquely against the ghouls; Mowgli has not been told about the Bandar-log. Unlike the ghouls, the Bandar-Log are desperate to be noticed by the folk of the jungle, and to this end, tease and taunt them whenever possible, while the ghouls avoid what they perceive as danger. There is more of a transition in Bod's and Miss Lupescu's relationship as she agrees to teach him a subject of common interest, rather than one that is simply needful for his safety, and they have grown fond of each other.

2. Mowgli goes from the part of the jungle inhabited by the people under the law to the abandoned and falling down city built by men, which all the other animals avoid. Bod goes from the graveyard through the ghoul-gate and across a desert to the stairs leading to Ghûlheim ("Home of the Ghouls" in German without the circumflex), a repulsive (*unheimlich*), abandoned building that the ghouls took over.

3. Both boys now have teachers dedicated to their safety. Mowgli cannot kill yet, but he can drive goats so that predators can kill them, thus he is more involved in the business of his own upkeep than Bod is in his. He is beloved of Bagheera, and though Baloo dotes on him, Mowgli doesn't love Baloo as well, and this echoes Bod's relationships with Silas and Miss Lupescu. Mowgli is clever, knows the Law of the Jungle, and doesn't like learning, like Bod. He gets into trouble because he is irritated with Baloo, but he is just in assessing his liability for bringing his friends into harm's way, and this is similar to Bod. By the end of the adventure, he is on a friendly footing with Kaa, and this, combined with his ability to avoid Kaa's magic, which Baloo and Bagheera cannot, makes him appear more mature in Jungle dealings than Bod is current-

ly in graveyard dealings.

4. Kipling focuses more on the dangerous alliance that is formed with Kaa for the sake of saving Mowgli and how much risk his friends are put to on account of his foolishness and the stark differences between those who do and do not follow the Law of the Jungle. Miss Lupescu and the Night-Gaunt do not experience as much danger or as much damage, and Gaiman's emphasis is more on the trouble resulting from a lack of trust on both sides (Miss Lupescu does not tell Bod she is a werewolf or why she's teaching him so many ways to say help) and a deepening of the teacher–student relationship.

5. Possible response: The similarities may allowed me to pick up the ill intent of the ghouls earlier than I might have otherwise, and so actually increased the suspense, as I recognized danger before Bod did. There are enough differences in the key plot points that the Kipling chapter did not spoil the Gaiman chapter development for me.

6. Possible response: The young boy growing to manhood and being able to take on the killer of his own accord, with help from those allied with him.

Chapter 4 The Witch's Headstone, page 32

1. Mrs. Owens tells him it's not healthy for the living; Mr. Owens says it's "not a good place"; Silas explains about unconsecrated ground and the beliefs that led to people being buried there, correcting Bod's assumption that they were all "bad people"; Miss Borrows responds with social snobbery, saying that those buried there are not "our sort of people."

2. Although the word "fly" is not used, Silas takes Bod back to the graveyard through the air.

3. The description of an old, iron-toothed woman who travels in a house on chicken legs describes Baba Yaga; the thin, sharp-nosed witch who rides a broomstick could be the Wicked Witch of the West from *The Wizard of Oz* or many other fictional witches.

4. Mr. Pennyworth says, "Where you are is nothing and nobody," a pun because where Nobody Owens stands is always "nobody." Because the narrator has made puns about Bod being "grave" previously, students may suspect that this line is boilerplate to Mr. Pennyworth, while a pun to Gaiman. In addition, Mr. Pennyworth does not go in for humor of any kind, as far as can be told, let alone puns, which are considered "low."

5. Answers will vary. Some students may suggest that her power to curse arose on account of the abuse she suffered and if it's true that magic wasn't necessary to lure Solomon Porritt, it supports the idea that she wasn't a witch. Other students may say that she was being evasive (which she certainly is) and that her continuing powers shown throughout the chapter suggest that being a witch is somehow intrinsic to her, and therefore was probably always part of her. Also, in Abanazer Bolger's back room, she says, "I may be dead, but I'm a dead witch, remember," and that seems to settle it.

6. Bod lacks knowledge about money and the price of things; how living people dress; the kinds of dealings that go on in pawn shops; the ways in which a child seller can be taken advantage of by an (unscrupulous) adult buyer; the import of the question about his folks (until it was too late).

7. Students answers about the effects of the similes and metaphors will vary. Similes they may include: "noise in the spire like a fluttering of heavy velvet"; "felt something like warm fur beneath him"; "dropping like a thunderstone"; "like so many pigwiggins scrubbed clean for market day"; "like a goblin"; "like dancing it was"; "like a rotten tooth"; "like the tendrils of some carnivorous plant"; "smelled like motor oil"; "like a man stroking a kitten"; "like a whirligig"; "like a wet silk scarf against his skin"; "sounded like a distant wind"; "lit his face like the flash of a lightbulb"; "rain on the boy's face, running down like tears"; "like a fluttering of heavy velvet"; "as if he'd been bitten in the heart by some arctic viper and it was starting to pump its icy venom through his body"; "dark as a tin mine." Metaphors they may include: "His business was an iceberg. Only the dusty little shop was visible on the surface. The rest of it was underneath."

8. Bod says he has something for sale. Bolger says he doesn't make purchases from kids; Bod puts the brooch on the counter. Bolger offers him tea and biscuits in the backroom. Bod explains his mission. Bolger, ignoring what Bod says, leads him into the storeroom and—offering him a cookie—determines for himself that the brooch is priceless, but tells Bod it probably isn't worth much and he needs to know it isn't stolen. Bod indicates that he didn't steal it. Bolger asks where he got it. Bod doesn't answer. Bolger pushes the brooch over to Bod and tells him he can't do business without trust. Bod volunteers that the brooch came from an old grave but he can't say where. Bolger asks if there's more like it. Bod responds that if Bolger doesn't want it, he'll take it elsewhere. Bolger asks if his parents are waiting and Bod says no before realizing the implications of doing so. Bolger, satisfied that there will be no immediate search for the boy, again demands the exact location of the find. Bod claims he doesn't remember. Bolger tells him its too late for that and

tells him to think about it, exiting the storeroom and locking Bod in, taking the brooch with him.

9. Fading, which Mr. Pennyworth is trying to teach Bod, becomes an essential part of his escape. And if Bod had recognized more about Bolger's temperament/humor/personality, he might not have gotten locked in. Thus, again, Bod's education is—although he does not see it at the time—key to his safety.

10. Because Gaiman doesn't completely connect the dots—Bolger mentions to Hustings that Bod is the "right sort of age," dressed oddly, and found the brooch; he does not mention that Bod indicated there are no parents waiting for him—and this may lead some students to find the introduction of Jack, and his apparent mind-reading, far-fetched. Astute readers will remember that at the end of Chapter 1 Jack thought of "the calls he would need to pay on certain of the townsfolk, people who would be his eyes and ears in the town" and reason that Bolger is one of these people. Also, the degree to which Silas and the Owenses are upset with Bod is justified only by the fact that he has revealed his whereabouts to Jack. Students may expect Jack to come after Bod, now that he knows where he is.

11. Liza lived in a village, where she was a laundress. One morning, members of her community came to her house, dragged her out of bed, and put her on trial for witchcraft. Based on the supposed evidence of soured milk, lame horses, and Mistress Jemima's claim that Liza stole her boyfriend by magic, she is tested by drowning: according to the test, the woman who drowns is innocent and the the one who doesn't is guilty, and Mistress Jemima's father bribed the duckers to hold the stool down extra long. Liza reports that the water "done for me" (killed her), but then she says she was "nine-parts" dead when taken from the water. At that point, Liza cursed those who had watched her drown with her last breath and died. Then they burned her body and put her in a hole in the Potter's Field with no headstone. But on account of the curse, a carpet delivered to town the following Saturday carried the plague and killed those she'd cursed. All the bodies were thrown in a plague pit dug outside the town borders.

Strategy 11: Forming Hypotheses, page 33

1. Answers will vary depending on the subject of the hypothesis, but should be grounded in the story.

Strategy 12: Understanding Tropes and Motifs, page 34

1. **Paper-Key Retrieval Trick:** This trick, which Bod has never seen, but gets the idea for from the available materials, is his contribution (as well as maintaining the Fade that Liza helps him achieve) to escaping from Abanazer Bolger's backroom.
   Sequispedalian Smith: Ironically, Bod's name, which serves to hide and protect him, also falls into this category because his surname is common, while his first name is highly unusual.
   Free-Range Children: Scarlett and Bod can be considered Free-Range children in their visit to the barrow.
   Happily Adopted: By the end of the book, it is clear that Bod's adoption does just what his parents and guardian hoped—keeps him alive long enough to grow up and live his life.

2. **Actors:** Miss Lupescu is both mentor and hero, dying in the fight with the Jacks to save Bod; Silas is also both mentor and hero, allowing himself to be hit by a car, and fighting with the Jacks along with Lupescu and in San Francisco, etc., also to save Bod; the Jacks of All Trades are villains; Bod is also a hero in his own story, freeing Scarlett from Jack Frost and overcoming the last of the Jacks. Liza is also somewhat in this category. **Background elements:** Bod receives the gift of a safe haven; the Night-Gaunt fits the category of a task-performing animal. **Single Incidents:** *The Graveyard Book* runs more to battles of wits than contests of strength: cleverness is involved in 1) recognizing the Indigo Man for the imaginary being he is; 2) escaping the ghouls by calling the night-gaunt and making a hole in the bag; 3) escaping from Abanazer Bolger's back room with Fading and the paper-key retrieval trick; 4) assembling the items to make Liza a headstone; 5) stopping Mo's and Nick's abuse of their classmates; 6) helping distract the police so Silas could get them away; 7) orchestrating the escape from Jack Frost's house, the dropping of one Jack into Carstairs' deep grave and three down the ghoul-gate; and 8) tricking Jack Frost into volunteering to be master of the Sleer.

Test: Chapters 3–4, page 35

Vocabulary

1. These words have to do with Bod's visit to the barrow to remove the brooch.
2. These words refer to three of the categories of being that Miss Lupescu is teaching Bod.
3. These words characterize Bod's experience riding in the sack on the way to Ghûlheim.

4. These words describe the creature pursuing Bod to Ghûlheim.
5. These are the four temperaments that Mr. Pennyworth is teaching Bod, but he incorrectly lists them as the four humours.
6. These words describe the movement of the ghouls.
7. These words come from the conversation with Silas when he returns from San Francisco.
8. These words describe the ghoul-gate.
9. These words list some of the criminals buried in the Potter's Field with Liza.
10. These words come from the definition of the Hound of God on Miss Lupescu's purple mimeographed sheet.
11. These words have to do with Abanazer Bolger's shop.
12. These words come from Mr. Pennyworth's hyperbolic comparison that aims to show just how dismal Bod's attempt at Fading is.
13. These words have to do with Bod's attempts to dress himself for the outside world before going among the living to purchase a headstone for Liza.
14. These are words in the Ghoulish language.

Essay Topics
1. Possible responses: Bod and the Ghouls both speak English; Ghouls would not help Bod—their characters mean that they could only do him harm.
2. The ostensible reason is that she is a historian who researches old graves. We only know that she is temporarily (and a bit unwillingly) replacing Silas as Bod's guardian, while he goes away on an undisclosed mission. Given what we know of Silas, students are likely to suspect that Miss Lupescu has some powers that will help to keep Bod safe.
3. It explains the presence of a dog in the graveyard and the dog/wolf following the ghouls who were taking Bod to Ghûlheim.
4. Jack and the ghouls are all unheimlich beings that have designs on Bod, but Jack is under orders, while the ghouls happened upon Bod by chance; Jack wants to kill Bod, while the ghouls will be happy either to eat him or to have him become one of them.
5. Possible response: Knowing what is going on in the front room while Bod is locked in the backroom is enlightening; knowing what Abanazer Bolger thinks when it is different from what he says is also useful in understanding the situation.
6. Liza was born the year that Elizabeth I died—1603.
7. Bod's learning of the alphabet in Chapter 2 allows him to create Liza's headstone; his visit to the barrow and getting over fear of the Sleer in Chaper 2 provides him with the knowledge of where to find an item to trade; his escape from Jack and taking refuge in the graveyard in Chapter 1, of course, underlie all that follows.
8. In both chapters, Bod leaves the graveyard and is only able to return with assistance from another member of his community.
9. Liza is pretty, sassy, witch who feels sorry for herself because she was drowned, burned, and buried without a headstone. Grateful to Bod, who—she says—is the first one in 500 years to show her any kindness—she enhances his ability to fade, reports to him what is going on in the outer office in a way that assists him, but shields him from the discussion about Jack. Abanazer Bolger is a sly, greedy, conniving cheat, out to make a buck any way he can, and perfectly happy to lie his way there, no matter who gets hurt. Bod at eight is warm-hearted, generous, sympathetic, clever, and not entirely obedient.
10. Despite his firm intention to sell it, Bod brings the brooch back to the Sleer, apparently showing the truth of their claim, "It always comes back." It lends credibility to their other claims.
11. Abanazer suggests that there's more like the brooch in the barrow it came from. Tom suggests they consider having it declared a treasure trove—the legitimate, aboveboard way to claim treasure—which he names with his surname before Abanazer's. Abanazer reverses the names, putting his first, and says he knows people who would pay more than market value. Then Abanazer shows Tom the card and suggests that Bod is the party that Jack is looking for. Tom argues that there's no reason to think it's him. Abanazer provides some evidence, but is not convincing. Tom asks what happens if Bod is the person Jack is looking for. Abanazer implies by quoting a nursery rhyme that Bod will be killed, and Tom completes the rhyme, showing his understanding. Tom points out that if they lose the boy, they lose access to the rest of the treasure. The argument is suspended while they go to speak to Bod—who has faded and cannot be seen—and picks up again when they return to the outer office, with Abanazer concluding that the boy got away, and Tom responding that Jack won't like that. Abanazer asks who's going to tell him, and then realizes that

Tom has pocketed the brooch, calling the brooch *his*. Tom corrects him that its *ours*, and Abanazer objects that Tom wasn't there when he (Abanazer) got it from the boy. Tom points out that Abanazer has lost the boy and predicts Jack will be in a state when he finds Abanazer has found the boy and let him go. Abanazer now argues that this boy probably is not the boy Jack is seeking. Abanazer gets some whisky and spikes the bottle, but doesn't drink himself. He realizes that Tom has pocketed the brooch again, and accuses Tom of taking "my" brooch at the same time that Tom realizes the drink is spiked. They fight and knock each other unconscious.

12. Answers will vary. Possible responses: Given the power of Bod simply holding the card near his heart, it's possible that Bod knowing more about its meaning would communicate with Jack even more powerfully. If Bod knew that there was a man nearby who had killed his family, it's possible that he would want to bring him to justice, and he is not ready.

13. Fading is different for the living and the dead: the dead are difficult to see and have to work hard to be noticed, so fading is easy; for the living it isn't easy. Bod is only able to Fade with the assistance of a spell Liza casts on him.

14. Abanazer, Tom, and Jack are all lowlifes who don't appear to have any morals. Tom Hustings is bigger than Abanazer, which is useful for scaring people into doing what is wanted. Abanazer is aware of being lower down the ladder in the big scheme of things than the man Jack, whom he can "invite" but not "summon." Also, Jack is affiliated with "The Convocation" (whatever that is), and Abanazer and Tom seems to be independent operators. Unlike Abanazer and Tom, Jack has some supernatural powers—a preternaturally developed sense of smell and an eerie connection to the card he gave Abanazer, so that he is aware when Bod touches it. It's not clear exactly what Jack is (i.e., into which of Miss Lupescu's categories he'd fit), but he's not a regular person, living or dead.

15. In Chapter 1, the first part of his escape is all him—he walks out of the house and up the hill—while the second part—the graveyard community's acceptance of him—is entirely out of his hands. In Chapters 3 and 4, his escapes are the product of joint effort: Bod contributes, as do others, and working together, his safety is assured.

16. One could argue several points for the reversal in Chapter 3, the first being Bod's call for help to the Night-Gaunt, which starts the chain of all else that follows that works to save him from the ghouls. In Chapter 4, Liza's magic, which allows Bod to successfully fade is the beginning of the turning tide in Bod's chances of surviving the encounter without falling into Jack's hands.

17. Answers will vary. Students may predict that Bod will be 10 (like Mowgli, if they've read *The Jungle Book*) or 12 (aging another 4 or so years, as between Chapters 3 and 4) in the next chapter, that he will have increased interaction with the living or that he will be more fiercely protected after having aroused Jack's awareness of his presence in this chapter (if, indeed, Silas is aware of this).

Chapter 5 Danse Macabre, page 36

1. Graveyard residents: Cleaning, tidying, repairing clothes. Silas: purchasing clothes for Bod that will camouflage him when he is among the living. Lady Mayoress and party: filling four baskets with white flowers found to be blooming in the graveyard in winter.

2. Bod is sent away by all the graveyard residents (except Silas) as they prepare for the dance, and then (apparently) abandoned as they disappear and he is left alone in the graveyard. He is joined with various of the dead as he dances the Macabray, and in the dance he participates as a living individual along with the other living of Old Town.

3. Bod's new clothes allow him to walk among the living as one of them, and he learns to tie his shoes.

4. The Lady Mayoress doesn't know about the tradition because the previous Lord Mayor didn't experience it, so wasn't able to pass it on—the flowers had not blossomed for 80 years. It is not explained how the chubby man and the small man with the Lady Mayoress obtained their knowledge, and it is puzzling since—as far as we know—the dead don't talk about it and thevast majority of the living don't remember it.

5. A vampire.

6. Bod experiences panic when he can find nobody in the graveyard and thinks he has been abandoned by the dead. People in the Old Town feel dread when they see the dead coming to join them.

7. Answers will vary. There is no explanation in the book—Silas giving him the clothes makes it possible for him to do so, however, without being noticeable.

8. The one-on-one dances became line dances, danced with ancient steps.

9. Answers will vary. Possible response: In general, the dead are separate from the living, and being among

the dead, Silas is similar to them. But during the Macabray, in which everyone else can join, Silas is separate from everybody and everything and he feels the separation deeply then.

10. Josiah Worthington, the Lady Mayoress, Mother Slaughter, the Lady Mayoress's male associates, the businessman, Louisa Bartleby, the old newspaper seller, Mr. and Mrs. Owens, a small girl; Liza Hempstock, Fortinbras Bartleby, Abanazer Bolger, Miss Borrows, the Lady on the Grey. It includes "rich man, poor man" and "one and all"—people of all ages and stations and occupations and levels of morality and across the range of living–dead joined together.

Strategy 13: Reading Dialogue, pages 37–38

1. The residents of the graveyard who died sometime in the past use archaic language, and Bod sometimes does in imitation of them because that is the language he hears. Archaic language is also used in the epitaphs. Possible responses: *betwixt* - between; *compleat* - complete; *derring-do* - heroic bravery; *en't* - isn't; *like unto a* - similar to a; *lykewise* - likewise; *medical gentleman* - doctor; *why do you not?* - why don't you; *amn't* - aren't.; *a-tatter* - old and torn adj; *dun't* - doesn't; *cos* - because; *ennit* - isn't it?; *thou dost have a face like unto a squishèd plum* - you have a face like a squashed plum.

2. All the graveyard residents are polite except for Thackeray, who uses oaths. The ghouls use civilities in their fake homages to each other that are actually due to their namesakes, and oaths when they, for example, are irritated by the night-gaunts. See below for lists of possible responses.

3. Silas/Mother Slaughter/Silas. The first is a parody of "It takes a village to raise a child." With this phrase, Silas acknowledges that raising the baby is not just a matter for his adoptive parents and tries to enlist the commitment of the wider graveyard population. Mother Slaughter is referring to the cycle of life, ostensibly in reference to the timing of the blooms that signal that it's time to dance the Macabray. Silas says his version in answer to Bod's questions about his future and his desire to believe in his ongoing safety and the support of the graveyard community, and especially Silas.

4. See list below.

5. While some authors make very little differentiation between their characters' speech other than content, Gaiman thoroughly and consistently embues dialogue with characterization based on era, social status, region, level of formality, and age. He conveys British English by showing pronunciation (e.g., with the ghouls), and through word choice, as well as content.

6. In Chapter 1, Bod says only one word and uses a typical toddler pronunciation of *banana* (Narna). In Chapter 2, Silas corrects Bod's use of *amn't* (doubtless picked up from one of the older members of the graveyard), when the current usage among the living is *aren't*, and Bod uses the typical childhood pronunciations *Nuffing* for *nothing* and identifies pig and cow by reference to an alphabet book ("like *P* is for Pig?"). He makes a grammatical mistake in response to Scarlett's ungrammatical question about his birthday ("I didn't," said Bod. "I never was."), and abbreviates *of course not* to *course not*. From Chapter 3 on, his speech is mainly unexceptional—which would be the ideal for staying camouflaged. In Chapter 3, Bod's ordinary speech contrasts with the speech of the ghouls and that of Miss Lupescu, in Chapter 4 with that of Liza, in Chapter 7 with Scarlett's Scottish-inflected language, etc.

7. Miss Lupescu uses some Romanian words (*Da* - yes; *Nimini* - nobody, which some Romanians report is a misspelling of *Nimeni http://roen.dict.cc/?s=nimeni*), and some speech patterns characteristic of speakers of Eastern European languages speaking English ("You understand, boy?"; "Is good for you"), as well as some non-standard words ("stew-soup").

Britishisms - sometimes written to show British pronunciations

7	a wee bit	a small amount
1	airing cupboard	heated linen cupboard
3	'ave a 'eart	be merciful; have pity on
7	awful cheek	not showing proper respect
5	baby buggy	four-wheeled vehicle for pushing a baby, baby carriage
4	bag-of-lard	a fat person; a worthless person (insult)
7	biscuit tin	metal container for cookies or crackers
7	bit of a wimp	something of a coward
6	bollocking	crude expression for a scolding or spanking (*bollock* means "testicle")

7	cheek	sass
3	chemist	drugstore
4	common	used disdainfully before an occupation that the speaker considers to be a crude or criminal
3	coot	fool
7	cuppa	short for *cup of tea*
7	dealt with them	euphemism for killed them
4	done for me	killed me
1	dunderheads	fools
3	dustbin	garbage can
2	flat	apartment
6	football	soccer
7	frightful	terrible (as in "frightful imposition")
3	get on	become friends
4	go sour	become rotten and unsuitable for eating
7	go spare	go wild with anxiety
7	got a good nose on him	has an exceptional ability to distinguish smells
3	high summer	hottest part of the summer
7	hop it	get a move on
4	I'll be bound	I feel fairly certain; I'd bet
4	lummox	someone who moves clumsily; a fool
8	lumpkin	clumsy, foolish person—from Tony Lumpkin in *She Stoops to Conquer* (1773) by British playwright Oliver Goldsmith
3	makes me mouf water	makes me drool
3	makes me tum rumble	makes me hungry
7	mam's	mom's
6	match	game
3	meant to	supposed to
7	Mum	Mom
6	newsagent	shop or person that sells newspapers and magazines
4	nicked	stole
3	not so as you'd notice	either means "not much" or "a lot, but you're no longer in a condition to register it"
3	nuffink	nothing
3	offal-hole	modeled on *cakehole* and *piehole*. *Offal* means "decomposing animal flesh"
4	on the turn	about to go bad
4	packet	package
4	plague-pits	informal British term for mass graves used to bury victims of the plague
6	pocket money	allowance
4	popped	moved something quickly
3	porkies	lies
4	prattle	foolish talk or talk about trivial things
3;4	proper	real; really
6	properly	as in "can I look properly?"; thoroughly or completely
2	quite	to a fairly large extent
6	so that's ... , then	cutting way of stating results of a stupid action
7	stroke of luck, really	due to happy coincidence, rather than careful thought or knowledge
5	stuff and nonsense	said of an idea that is perceived as foolish or worthless
4	t'aint	it isn't

4	t'other	the other
7	that's a bit much	polite complaint that something is unreasonable (mitigators and intensifiers)
7	tickety-boo	fine—from the armed forces, possibly from Hindu tikai babu ("it's all right, sir")
7	toddling off	leaving
8	too stupid	missing what is right in front of your face
4	treasure trove	English procedure for claiming ownerless property; from Anglo-Norman French *tresor trové*, literally "found treasure"
3	ware (the dog)	short for "beware"
6	worked a treat	functions very well
5	wossit	What is it?
8	wrong-footed	surprised, embarrassed, and uncertain how to respond
3	yar	I agree; yes
6	year seven	grade seven

British Oaths

6	blast your eyes	swear word - expression of anger and annoyance
3	bleeders	swear word used to abuse other beings
5	blimmin 'eck	mild swear word (dialect pronunciation of *blooming heck*); *blooming* is a substitution for the stronger word, *bloody*; *heck* is a substitution for the stronger word hell
3	blinking	mild swear word; *blinking* is a substitution for the stronger word, *bloody*
3;6	bloody	strong swear word; Adj ("Bloody stealers") - terrible; awful. Adv. used as intensifier ("You've got to be bloody kidding me"), adds negative impact to whatever it modifies.
3	blooming	mild swear word, substitute for *bloody*. Used as intensifier,
3	blow me down	mild swear word used to express surprise, shock, or confoundedness
5	confounded	mild swear word; substitute for the stronger damned
7	crikey	mild swear word (substitution for *Christ*!
6	damm'ee	mild swear word (substitute for *damn*!)
3	lumme	mild swear word - exclamation of surprise (shortened form of *Lord love me*)

Civilities - examples

3	'ave the honor to be	have the privilege of being
3	charmed, I'm sure	delighted to meet you
6	fare-thee-well	goodbye and stay healthy
5	Gracious Lady	polite expression, used to address women of high social status or royalty
3	hat your service	ready to assist you in any way (*at your service*)
4	how-de-do	short form of *how do you do*? (how are you?)
8	I trust you are keeping well	I hope you are enjoying good health
8	it was an honor	I am pleased to have (done whatever it was)
5	This I pray	I ask this of you
3	Your Grace	style of address and honorific for bishops
3	Your Worship	style of address and honorific for mayors

Longer Phrases

1	There never was such a boy for . . .	of all the boys that ever were, he was the most engaged in . . .
1	what would that be when it was at home?	what does that mean in ordinary, everyday language?
3	what's this when it's at home?	what does that mean in ordinary, everyday language?
7	you're all as bad as each other	none of you get the point (contextual definition)

Idioms

7	all his tomorrows	the rest of his life
3	arm themselves	locate and take possession of weapons
6	as good as ever	recovered from illness or injury (adj)
7	at our lowest ebb	at the most dire moment in our history
7	at the zenith	at our highest point
7	bad Juju	bad luck; dangerous magical powers
4	behind the counter	in illegal trade
3	between the devil and the deep blue sea	caught in a difficult choice
8	bidding him goodbye	saying goodbye
7	blurting it out	saying something suddenly without accounting for situation or feelings
7	came into focus	became clear
4	catch your death	get so sick you'll die
6	close on his heels	following closely
5	cocked his head	tilted his head to the side, often done while listening intently
3	committed to memory	memorizing
4	common (knowledge)	widely held
4	corner of the world	region
6	creeping her out	scaring her
1	cut the final thread	from Greek mythology, according to which the Moirai were three sisters who spun the thread of life, allotted the length, and ended life by snipping the thread.
I	cut you any slack	be forgiving about behavior or performance that is not up to standard
3	decline to elaborate	refuse to say anything more
4	Devil's own luck	such phenomenal luck that it can only be attributed to having made a deal with the Devil
7	don't be like that	a warning or request to change attitude
7	don't make me—	Don't make me laugh.
7	downright	intensifier - see proper and common etc.
1	drank like a fish	was an alcoholic
4	empty your mind	try not to think about anything
5	every man Jack	From two traditions about "Jack": 1) Jack is used generically to refer to every man; 2) Jack is used interchangeably with "knave" (as it is in cards) to refer to a dishonest man or a man of questionable character.
6	filed it away for later	made a mental note of it, w/ intent to think about it again soon
7	find it in your heart to	allow yourself to; decide to, even if at first not inclined to
4	for the sake of all that is holy	mild swearing, indicative of irritation (substitution for "For God's sake!")
7	gave me a lift	drove me in a car
7	give balm	help to ease
7	gives me the shivers	makes me nervous
6	go and boil your fat head	mild swear (substitution for Go to hell!) meaning "Go Away!"
7	go wild	have a riotous time (ironic)
4	gone lame	become unable to walk normally due to an injury or illness
3	grub	food
3	have to get up pretty late at night to put anything past	ghoul version of "have to get up pretty early in the morning to put something past . . . "—it takes a lot of work and planning to have a shot at tricking this person
8	high adventure	adventures worthy of a hero
7	high and mighty	acting as if one is more important than others
1	honed in on	focused in on
1	in a manner of speaking	in some sense
4	in the back room	where secret, illegal transactions take place

7	indecision	inability to decide quickly
5	it's a judgment on us	it's a sign that we have offended God and are being punished
7	it's no skin off your nose	it won't cost you anything
7	jack of all trades	Jack of all trades and master of none
1	johnny-come-latelies	recent arrivals; upstarts
6	keep a low profile	avoid attention
7	little pitchers have big ears	young children understand more than one would think
6	look properly	get a good look
5	Lord have mercy	prayer to God for removal of current bad circumstances
8	lull … to sleep	sooth to the point of sleep
3	made a … circuit	walked all the way around something
3	making a break for it	trying to run away
7	master of his own small world	in charge (or seemingly in charge) of a very limited area, à la Yertle the Turtle
5	month of Sundays	long time
1	naked (emotion)	undisguised; exposed and vulnerable
I	nearly only counts in horseshoes and hand grenades	"close only counts in horseshoes" is a proverb from Indiana (Wolfgang Mieder: *A Dictionary of American Proverbs*); first printed record of "horseshoes and grenades" is in Iowa in 1970 (Fred Shapiro, ed. *The Yale Book of Quotations*)
3	no love lost between	said of people who hate each other
4	none of your beeswax	beeswax is a corruption of business
7	not an option	not an available choice
4	not be advisable	be a poor choice
4	not our sort of people	we think we're better than they are
4	not the end of the world	not as important or dire as it seems
4	off the subject	away from the topic
6	olden times	long ago
4	on the not entirely unreasonable basis that	suspecting that
5	once in a blue moon	not very often
7	Once is a mistake . . . Twice is a disaster	expresses the limit to forgiveness
4	over the counter	in an ordinary retail purchase (vs. under the counter or behind the counter, which refer to illicit or illegal sales)
7	penny for your thoughts	I wonder what you're thinking about.
5	perception	Bod's ability to hear
7	pet name	nickname given because of fondness
5	pick up the habit	get used to doing something
6	pitched and rolled	rotated on the axes side to side and front to back
4	plane of existence	dimension; specifically, death
I	private function	event to which entrance is permitted by invitation only
7	put her out of her way	inconvenience her
7	put in an appearance	show up
6	put things at risk	make it dangerous
7	pyramid days	in the time of the pharaohs
3	rap his knuckles	punish by hitting on the knuckles, often w/ a ruler
7	revenge is a dish best served cold	Proverb of unknown origin: Vengeance is most successful and enjoyed when not exacted in the heat of the moment, but saved for when one's head is cool.
6	right enough	certainly
6	rue the day you were born	in so much pain that you'll wish you were dead

4	send … flying	cause something or someone to be thrown without aim
4	sentimental value	worth only because of the tender feelings associated with it
4	shifting	selling
7	squashed it	kept it quiet
7	swept under the carpet	concealed
1	take …'s point	agree
7	the Deuce take you	swear in anger (substitute for the Devil take you)
7	there's always room at the top	this may mean either that ambitious people always succeed or that the number who rise to the top is always small (so there's always room) or that when you're at the top, there is nothing above you, so there's always room
7	to oblige you	to make you happy; to serve your purposes
5	to someone's satisfaction	to the point at which someone was pleased
8	tolerably well	pretty well
7	took the liberty	acted without asking first
6	tracks and traces	term from zoology, paleontology, and archaeology - the signs of animal or human life that help to build an idea of features and activity
8	trust you are keeping well	intensifier
6	turn over a new leaf	start behaving in a markedly different (and better) way
I	we're none of us getting any younger	our opportunities and capabilities are always diminishing
7	welling up inside her	starting and becoming more intense
7	what do you reckon?	what do you think?
6	without a warrant	without the legal document that permits a search or arrest
6	wouldn't want to be in her shoes	wouldn't want to be her
7	wound down	rolled down
7	wreak vengeance	inflict revenge

Writer's Forum 3: Writing Dialogue, page 39

1. Students' dialogues will differ depending on the characters they choose, but should have proper formatting and exhibit the characteristics that Gaiman gives their speech.

INTERLUDE The Convocation, page 40

1. Prior to the Interlude, there have been very few shifts from narration behind Bod's shoulder, as it were, and no section of the book prior has been entirely without any material from Bod's perspective. The name of the room in which the group meets might tend to make us think that the hotel is in the United States, which—if true—would also make it the first scene not set in England.
2. In Chapter 1—the book begins with Jack and Jack's perspective ends the chapter—and Chapter 4—with shifts to Abanazer Bolger's, as well as Jack's, perspectives.
3. When Silas returns at the end of Chapter 3, he brings Bod a model of the Golden Gate Bridge in San Francisco. Silas (and friends?) were the cause of the trouble the Convocation experienced in San Francisco.
4. At the end of Chapter 1, Jack thought to himself that he did not need to tell the Convocation that he'd failed.
5. Mr. Dandy is well-dressed and neat, with silver-grey hair, and a cool customer. He ranks higher than Jack in the Convocation, and is in a position to tell him off, which he does in a colorful way. He likes his comforts (he sugars his coffee excessively), but a little sloppy in his eating (he slurps). He treats Jack with condescension and suspicion: he doesn't trust him.
6. Mister Dandy's speech is highly individual, characterized by alliteration ("time's a-ticking"), aphorism ("we're none of us getting any younger"), quotation ("the flowers that bloom in the spring, tra-la … [have] nothing to do with the case"—from Gilbert and Sullivan's comic operetta *The Mikado*), and proverbs ("*Nearly* only counts in horseshoes and hand-grenades"; "time and tide wait for no man"). When he is not using these, he is curt, speaking in single syllables.
7. We learn that the murder of the baby in the family was somehow the most important part of the mission and that something will change for the worse for the Convocation if that baby reaches adulthood. Jack's

suggestion that the "business in San Francisco," the timing of which seems like it might match Silas's extended absence from the graveyard, supports the idea that Silas, Miss Lupescu, and others (?), are engaged in a war with the Convocation, which astute readers might have suspected ever since Chapter 1, when Silas altered Jack's memory and visited the scene of the crime.

8. The Convocation is not happy with Jack, but they are not offering him any additional resources to meet his obligation, and he has a strict deadline to meet. It seems like something bad will happen to the whole Convocation if he fails, but it's not clear what this bad thing is. Students might suspect that Silas and company will gain the upper hand in this case. Since it is not clear what kind of being Jack is, it is not clear if he can die, but he'll certainly be in big trouble, and likely be severely punished or killed.

9. Mr. Dandy comes to the meeting in the Washington Room with a double purpose—to attend the assembly of the Convocation and to tell off Jack, who has an obligation that he has not yet fulfilled, having killed three of four members of a family, but not the all-important one, the baby, whose coming of age would mean very bad things for the Convocation. While sitting with other guests and enjoying a cup of coffee, he tries to impress upon Jack that the Convocation's patience with Jack is running out, and there will be consequences if Jack doesn't perform.

Strategy 14: Analyzing Narration and Point of View, page 41

These questions build on the initial questions about the narrator in Strategy 1.

1. Possible response: As soon as the reader starts the second section s/he can see that the narrator is omniscient (because the narrator can see both Jack's thoughts in the first section and the baby's in the second) and in the third person.

2. Answers will vary. Passages students choose should not be in the present time of the story.

3. Name—Bod is not named until the end of Chapter 1 (in fact, we never learn the name he was given at birth). Family members—We learn of Bod's parent and sister in the narrator's record of their deaths in the fourth paragraph. Appearance—Bod's appearance is not described until the opening of Chapter 2. Age—Bod's approximate age is given in the description of the toys he falls on when he escapes for his crib, which were presents for "his first birthday, not six months gone." Location—aside from house, hill, graveyard, and Old Town, the location is never directly mentioned. This is all highly unusual: introducing the protagonist with all of these elements is usually done within the first few pages of a novel.

4. Possible response: The narrator uses *you* quite a bit in Chapter 1 to address the reader, as if he were telling the story directly to the reader—which he is when he reads it aloud: perhaps he had reading aloud in mind when he wrote the book.

5. Possible response: The narrator notices small, tender details in interpersonal relationships, such as Miss Lupescu's growing fondness for Bod, and thus seems kind, thoughtful, and warm. The narrator does not tell everything about the world of the story—we never learn why Scarlett can dreamwalk or see in the dark when she comes back to the graveyard or how the men accompanying the Lady Mayoress know about the Macabray traditions or all of the details about the Jacks of All Trades and their goals, but this does not seem to be a problem for him.

Strategy 15: Interpreting Allusions and References, page 42

1. *Celebrations*: Christmas, Guy Fawkes Night, Hallowe'en, New Year's Day
Real People: 33rd President of the United States, Bishop of Bath and Wells, Duke of Westminster, Emperor of China, Lord Mayor, Victor Hugo
Real Places: Alaskan gold mine, American Colonies, Bangladesh, Caledonia, Camulodunum, City Center, Dragon's Den, Gaul, Glasgow, Golden Gate Bridge, Inverness, Krakow, Melbourne, Moscow, New Amsterdam, New York, Pampas, San Francisco, Scotland, Vancouver, Wawel Hill
Civilizations and Eras: Celtics, Druids, Pagan, Romans, Gothic, Victorian

2. Students may or may not recognize the allusions and their impressions may be quite different. Those who recognize "Oranges and Lemons" from its use in Orwell's *1984* may find it particularly chilling. Those who know that Ko-Ko is the Lord High Executioner, may find the *Mikado* quotation (from Ko-Ko's verse of "The Flowers That Bloom in the Spring" in Gilbert and Sullivan's comic opera) particularly apt. The nursery rhymes seem very appropriate for Bod, but the ballad may draw different opinions (though he was not of an age at which he would likely understand the storyline).

Man in the Moon from a nursery rhyme: The man in the moon came down too soon, and asked his way to Norwich; He went by the south, and burnt his mouth with eating cold plum porridge.	*Put in his thumb* from a nursery rhyme: Little Jack Horner Sat in the corner, Eating a Christmas pie; He put in his thumb, And pulled out a plum, And said, "What a good boy am I!"	
Poisoned with ... spotted eels from the ballad "Lord Randall"		
Where have you been all the day, Lord Randall, my son? Where have you been all the day, my pretty one? I've been to my sweetheart, Mother x 2 Chorus: Make my bed soon For I'm sick to my heart And I fain would lie down. What have you been eating, Lord Randall, my son? What have you been eating, my pretty one? O eels and eel broth Mother, x 2 Chorus Where did she get them from, Lord Randall, my son? Where did she get them from, my pretty one? From hedges and ditches, Mother x 2	Chorus What was the colour on their skin, Lord Randall, my son? What was the colour on their skin, my pretty one? O spickit and sparkit, Mother x 2 Chorus What will you leave your father, Lord Randall my son? What will you leave your father, my pretty one? My land and houses, Mother x 2 Chorus What will you leave your mother, Lord Randall my son? What will you leave your mother, my pretty one? My gold and silver Mother x 2 Chorus	What will you leave your brother, Lord Randall my son? What will you leave your brother, my pretty one? My cows and horses, Mother x 2 Chorus What will you leave your lover, Lord Randall my son? What will you leave your lover, my pretty one? A rope to hang her, Mother x 2 Make my bed soon For I'm sick to my heart And I fain would lie down.
Here comes a candle - the last couplet of the nursery rhyme "Oranges and Lemons"		
"Oranges and lemons," say the Bells of St. Clement's. "You owe me five farthings," say the Bells of St. Martin's "When will you pay me?" say the Bells of Old Bailey.	"When I grow rich," say the Bells of Shoreditch. "When will that be?" say the Bells of Stepney.	"I do not know," say the Great Bells of Bow Here comes a Candle to light you to Bed Here comes a Chopper to Chop off your Head

Chapter 6 Nobody Owens' School Days, page 43

1. Possible response: Nick and Thackeray are both angry bullies, who would as soon use their fists as words. They think they are entitled to special treatment and that everyone else should make them feel good. Neither can take a joke.

2. Silas talks to Bod about his potential to "do anything, make anything, dream anything" - while for the dead, potential is finished. Liza talks to Bod about the dead being always just what they are, never disappointing you because you get just what you expect, while the living , who still have choices, can change, can disappoint the expectations of those who care about them. The statements contrast in that Silas's is overly optimistic while Liza's is overly pessimistic. This is the one thing that Silas says to Bod that is inflated and therefore misleading—we all have limitations: none of us can "do anything" - because there are things to be done for which any one of us may lack the means, the experience, the talent, the skill, the location, etc. On the other hand, disappointing others, while it is a potential difference between the living and the dead, is not as widespread and unmitigated as Liza makes it seem. Many people know each other for years without feeling that the other has disappointed them. The truth seems to lie somewhere in between.

3. The metaphor means that Silas and his experience are totally alien to everyone else: he cannot even begin to be interpreted because the starting materials are unavailable or non-existent. Answers about how this works and is effective will vary. Possible response: It demonstrates how much Silas cares about Bod by showing his retreat to the furthest reaches of his being, where he cannot be touched or hurt. It is effective because it shows how much Silas cares about Bod without having him break character and do something emotional, like cry or yell or beg or plead.

4. Bod's Chameleon Camouflage starts with his name and includes his ability to Slip and Fade, his appearance (mousy hair and the grey clothes that Silas got for him), his staying within the graveyard, and his avoiding notice by only speaking when spoken to at the beginning of school.

5. First, Bod helps Mo's and Nick's victims understand how they can get out from under their thumbs. Then

he leads Mo and Nick to a nearby graveyard and Fades just as Nick is going to hit him, scaring Mo, which scares Nick, and also leading Nick to hurt his hand, as he punches a gravestone where Bod was but no longer is. The following day, Nick stabs the back of Bod's hand with a pencil when no one is looking. In the evening, Nick creates a scary Dreamwalk for Nick, but as he walks home, he is stopped by two police officers, one of whom is Mo's uncle, based on Mo's (false) complaint that Bod's been vandalizing homes. Silas flies in front of the policecar and then plays dead, and Bod follows his lead, accusing the police officers of killing his father on purpose and suggesting their careers are over. As they step aside to talk, Silas flies Bod back to the graveyard. Later, Bod uses a Visitation on Mo and threatens to haunt her.

6. Maureen Quilling, called *Mo*, has formed a team with Nick Farthing to blackmail their classmates (based on first convincing them to steal something). Using the time-honored division of labor—brains (Mo) and brawn (Nick)—she identifies kids who are likely to be intimidated and Nick intimidates them. This goes well for awhile, and Mo is pleased about being part of a team, as well as enjoying the proceeds and talking like a hard case. But one day, just as she is comparing herself and Nick (inaptly) to Batman and Robin, she hears someone say, "More like Doctor Jekyll and Mister Hyde." Afterwards, Paul Singh won't give them his pocket money, and then five more of year sevens not only refuse, but demand their money back, and threaten police action. Mo identifies "Bob Owens" as the one who started the rebellion, and they go after him, following Bod after school. Mo threatens "Bob," who corrects her pronunciation of his name, and Nick threatens Bod with death. Mo starts to get nervous when "Bob" says he has friends in the graveyard. Bod tells the pair to stop blackmailing their fellow students, and Mo tells Nick to hit Bod. But when Bod swings at Bod, Bod is gone, and Nick connects painfully with a gravestone. Mo asks where Bod went, and Nick's answers don't satisfy her. She gets scared, and her fear affects Nick, who turns and runs. Reaching Nick's house, Mo calls her Mom and demands to be picked up as she is afraid to walk even the short distance because it is night. Back in school, Mo meets Bod in the hallway, and even though she looks scared, she takes the offensive, telling Bod he's weird and has no friends. When he doesn't react, she tells him she's not scared of him. That night, Mo sees Bod walking down the street. Soon, she is in a police car with her uncle and another officer. They stop Bod, and he won't answer their questions, so they put him in the back of the car with Mo, who tells him that she saw him out her window, so she called the police. Her Uncle Tam drops her off at home. Things look excellent, but that quickly caves. Nick stops speaking to her; her Uncle shouts at her and tells her never to mention the evening again or else; her parents are furious; and the year sevens are no longer scared of her. She concocts elaborate revenge schemes against Bod, but they don't really help. Then comes a day when Mo is supposed to clean up the science lab—with Bod, but he hasn't been to school in a week. Her science teacher is there at first, and praises her work, which comforts Mo, who doesn't like the preserved animals and is generally creeped out by the science lab. She discovers that Mrs. Hawkins doesn't remember Bod, as none of the other teachers do, and then the teacher leaves, and Mo starts to feel cold. And then she feels as if she's being watched, which she puts down to the dead animals in jars. But when she says aloud to comfort herself, "I'm not frightened," a voice answers her. Mo throws a beaker at Bod but misses. He parries every verbal move she makes: she tells him nobody remembers him, he reminds her that she remembers him; she tells him the police were looking for him, he askes after her Uncle Tam. Bod tells her that she's won in one respect because he's leaving school. And then he asks her if she's every been haunted. She draws the obvious conclusion, and her voice trembles. Bod stares at her while making her schoolbag fall to the floor across the room. Then she can no longer see him.

Strategy 16: Interpreting Irony, page 44

1. Possible responses:
   Verbal Irony: Silas in Chapter 1: "I applaud your public-spiritedness." Interlude: Mister Dandy calling the man Jack "Sunshine."
   Situational Irony: The book begins with situational irony experienced by Jack—now that he's killed the older members of the family, he expects killing the baby to be a piece of cake. Except that it's not, and ten years later, he's no farther along. Abanazer Bolger experiences situational irony in Chapter 4 when his reason tells him that a boy locked in his storeroom will still be there when he opens the door, and yet, when he opens the door, it seems that the boy is gone.
   Dramatic Irony: In Chapter 3, Mrs. Owens tells Bod, speaking of Silas: "Back when you were born he promised us that if he had to leave, he would find someone else to bring you food and keep an eye on you, and he has. He's so reliable." The reader knows, and Bod does not, that this promise was actually made when he was just under 18 months old on the day his family was murdered. In fact, Bod does not seem

to yet know anything about how he ended up in the graveyard. Also in Chapter 3, a reader who has had access to the table of contents may feel certain that Bod will survive to participate in the chapter called "Nobody' Owens' School Days," something that Bod cannot know as he is being carried off by the ghouls and chased by the wolf.

Strategy 17: Tracing the Hero's Journey, page 45

1. Answers will vary. Some students may suggest that just as interpreting the story with Bod as protagonist when he is only about 18 months old at the start is challenging, so is tracing the hero's journey with such a young "hero" to start with. Some may say that Bod is called when Jack attacks his family, but through the intercession of the graveyard community, the call is refused and supernatural aid provided. They may identify the Crossing of the First Threshold with his entry into the graveyard and the Belly of the Whale with his trip through the ghoul-gate. The trials can then be seen as the encounter with Abanazer Bolger and Tom Hustings, his challenges with Mo Quilling and Nick Farthing and the police, and his run-in with the Jacks of All Trades. In this case, the Return does not involve his guardian's accompaniment, but Bod does, indeed, return to the world from which he came—the world of the living—crossing the threshold with his passage through the pedestrian gate, and his freedom to live founded in his education and the tools that Silas has provided for him. But since man cannot be master of the two worlds—the living and the dead—at any one time, Bod lose his mastery of the world of the graveyard in order to return completely to the tasks that face him in the land of the living.

Test: Chapters 5–6, and Interlude, page 46

Vocabulary

1. These words refer to Nick Farthing's activities.
2. These words name places Bod passed as he wandered the town before dancing the Macabray.
3. These words have to do with the gathering of the winter blossoms to be handed out to the living prior to dancing the Macabray.
4. These words have to do with the arrival of the dead in town to dance the Macabray and the crowds' reaction to them.
5. These words relate to the circumstances under which Thackeray died.
6. These words relate to Mrs. Owens's sending Bod away so she can prepare for the unnamed coming event, which we later learn is the Macabray.
7. These words are from the change of clothes that Bod undergoes in Chapter 5.
8. These are the stages of the life cycle of the flower, as explained by Mother Slaughter.
9. These words describe the diversity of faces of the men in the Washington Room.
10. These words characterize the music that precedes and makes up the Macabray.
11. These words relate to Nick's dream of captaining a pirate ship.
12. These words have to do with the generosity of the Convocation, as described by the secretary.
13. These words are mentioned by the Persson family as they congratulate Bod on his treatment of Nick and Mo in their graveyard.
14. These words name moves in the Macabray.
15. These are some of the items in the science lab that Mo has to clean.
16. These words come from Silas's ruminations about how Bod can interact with the living more surreptitiously than by going to school and still be able to learn the things he wants/needs to learn.

Essay Topics

1. Bod's experience is different than the experience of the dead in that he gets to wander the town prior to the dance; he dances only with the dead and Death (the Lady on the Grey), while they dance only with the living; he notices and feels bad for Silas, who is unable to participate, while they do not show awareness of him (as far as we know); he is under no compulsion not to speak of it afterwards. Bods' experience is different from the experience of the living because he sees and hears about the preparations of the dead and the preparations of the Lady Mayoress; he is in a less dreamlike state leading up to the dance; and he remembers the experience afterwards. Bod's experience is different from Silas's because Silas, being neither alive nor dead, cannot dance the Macabray and does not wish to speak of it, possibly because it makes him more deeply regret what he has lost, while Bod can dance it and wants to discuss it.
2. Bod begins the story in a disposable diaper and nightshirt, typical sleepwear for a living boy his age, but

loses the diaper in his progress down the stairs on his bottom. From Chapter 2 through the beginning of Chapter 5, his standard dress is a grey winding sheet, typical dress for the dead. In Chapter 4, in preparation to procure a headstone for Liza from among the living, Bod dons green-stained, over-large gardening jeans with rolled cuffs and twine to hold them on at the waist, and a brown working-man's jacket, which is his idea of fitting in, but which immediately draws Abanazer Bolger's attention because it is unusual. At the beginning of Chapter 5, Silas brings him a grey sweater, the same color as his winding sheet (presumably to help Bod avoid notice), jeans, underwear, and pale green sneakers so that he can go among the living for the Macabray and be clearly recognized as a living boy, not a dead boy (which identification the winding sheet might confound), and—it is implied, but not stated—to get him used to the clothes he will have to wear when he leaves the graveyard.

3. Bod interprets the conversation in terms of having a chance to ride a big, impressive horse, while it is actually about the fact that we all, one day, must die, and the opportunity to ride with the Lady on the Grey is an inevitable result of that fact.

4. In Chapter 5, Bod has not received overt permission to leave the graveyard, but since "all must dance the Macabray" and since Silas provides him the clothes so that for the first time he can go among the living as one of them, it is clear that he is "supposed to" leave the graveyard and join in the dance. In Chapter 3, he left because, feeling sorry for himself, he looked for friends in places where he shouldn't have, and was ghoulnapped as a result. In Chapter 4, he disobeys the injunction to stay within the safety of the graveyard and comes close to pulling the wrath of Jack down on his head, which would likely have ended in his death, had Liza not intervened.

5. Answers will vary because we do not know enough about Jack's connection with the card and Silas's knowledge of Jack to be sure. Possible responses: If Silas suspected Jack's supernatural ability to locate the card, he may have taken it somewhere far away and buried it (so Jack would find nothing of use), taken it to a place at which he prepared an ambush, should Jack come to find it, or destroyed it, but far away from the graveyard, so Jack could not follow it to Bod.

6. In Chapters 1, 3, and 4 there is a plot in which a strong desire forms the basis of the structure for most of the chapter: Chapter 1 - Mrs. Owens's and Silas's desire to save and protect Bod; Chapter 3 - Bod's desire to have a friend; Chapter 4 - Bod's desire to procure a headstone for Liza. Chapter 5 is more exploratory, with Bod doing what he can to learn about the Macabray, but it doesn't have the same challenges to his safety or danger of exposure that the other chapters have.

7. Both Silas and the Lady on the Grey guard Bod—Silas appears to be a detective and warrior, seeking clues and fighting battles to keep Bod safe. He is also Bod's chief educator. The Lady in Grey has a less hands-on role: aside from her intervention in Chapter 1, her interest is reserved and removed and calm, conducted at a distance. She will see him again, no matter what, for all must ride the grey, but Silas is trying to protect Bod's chance to fulfill his potential, make his own choices, and live his life.

8. Answers will vary. Students may suggest that it is a bittersweet experience: given that he has never danced it himself, it is heart-wrenching; given that he has helped protect Bod long enough that he has a chance to dance it as a living boy, it is heartwarming. Astute readers may add that for the first time since his entry into the graveyard—albeit in large part through Silas's own efforts—Silas sees Bod not as a resident of the graveyard but as a soon-to-be member of the community of the living, and implicit in this is their separation, which breaks Silas's heart.

9. Students descriptions should capture the lively, enticing, evocative, memory-inducing, and mysterious quality of the music.

10. Answers will vary. Possible response: It provides Bod with a window on how others of the living experience the Macabray, allowing him to participate it in it, but also to know that his experience is different because he lives among the dead and has the Freedom of the Graveyard.

11. In Chapter 5, Bod—as a living boy—is made to feel in a number of ways like an outsider to the graveyard community that has worked so hard to be his family. In Chapter 6, there are several reversals: Bod getting to spend time among the living for the first time; Bod shutting down Nick's and Mo's extortion racket, and Silas coming to understand Bod's need to be among his own kind and to learn what he will need to know as a living adult.

12. Students may note that *Macabray* seems like it might be a colloquial English pronunciation of the French *Macabre*—pronounced as if it were English (and much easier to rhyme, thus facilitating Gaiman's use of couplets throughout the chapter!).

13. Possible response: The Macabray is a mystery to those who cannot participate (Silas); it is forbidden to the

dead; it is forgotten by the living.

14. Answers will vary. Students may suggest that the two important plot points to cover are a confrontation between Bod and Jack and Bod's departure from the graveyard.

Chapter 7 Every Man Jack, page 47

1. His garb has the characteristics of a disguise—it is widely seen and pretty non-descript. He chooses to live in the house where Bod's family was murdered (return to the scene of the crime). Astute readers may notice that Frost's ostensible reason for being in the graveyard is nearly identical to Miss Lupescu's ostensible reason, and this may raise their suspicions. They may also be alerted when Frost adapts a saying that Mr. Dandy used ("Time and tide wait for no man" --> "Time, tide, and historical research wait for no man.")

2. Answers should include the following key points: Chapter 1: Jack hunts alone; Bod initially flees alone and innocently: he is not aware of the danger; once Bod and Jack reaches the graveyard, they both become passive, Bod because he is a baby, Jack because he is in Silas's power; the results of Chapter 1 are a temporary solution to a larger problem. Chapter 7: Jack is joined by other Jacks of All Trades; Bod initially flees with Scarlett and knows the danger they both are in; once Bod and Jack reach the graveyard, they both continue to be the main actors: Bod deploys troops, while Jack's companions follow their own paths; the results of Chapter 7 are a final solution to the problem of the Jacks—they are wiped out—and Bod may safely go out into the world of the living.

3. Yes—Bod finds his name, not by being told it but by declaring himself to be Nobody Owens, the name given to him by the people—living, dead, and otherwise—who claimed and owned him so that he could grow up and go out into the world. No—Trot advises Bod to risk Unfading to talk to Scarlett and that revenge "is a dish best served cold," but Scarlett can see Bod in his Faded state, and he serves his revenge hot.

4. Scarlett and her mother do not understand each other's challenges and dreams and this puts them at odds. They do not have the rules of civility, like those that govern the graveyard (for the most part), to keep things amiable in times of disagreement; they do not trust each other; they are not honest with each other.

5. Answers will vary. Possible responses: She acquired them from having known Bod as a child. Jack Frost was in some way able to give them to her. Silas (and the rest of the graveyard?) granted her a temporary Freedom of the Graveyard because they (Silas) could see her connection to Mr. Frost and understood that she would be important in unraveling things. It's a mystery—we don't know. It's a plot lapse: Gaiman wants Scarlett to be able to do and see certain things, and in order for that to happen, he must give her powers which there is no logical explanation for her to have.

6. Answers should include the following points: Bod's visit to the barrow with Scarlett in Chapter 2 gives him a place to hide her and gives her knowledge of where to go. Bod's further conversations with the Sleer (Chapter 4; Chapter 7) gives him the idea of how to dispose of Jack Frost. Bod's trip through the ghoul-gate (Chapter 3) gives him the knowledge to escort several Jacks through it. Bod's fall into Mr. Carstairs's grave (reported in Chapter 7, although it happened earlier) gives him another disposal area. Bod's securing Liza a headstone in Chapter 4 and his general good will and amicable relations with the rest of the graveyard folk, including his parents, provides the allies he needs in the battle.

7. Answers will vary. Students' reports should be in the style of a news story and objectively reported.

8. Through taking the wrong bus, Scarlett ends up as a tool used by Jack Frost to get to Bod. Jay Frost is Jack Frost in disguise.

9. Bod has to come to accept his departure from the graveyard, which up till now, he has been loathe to do, and then he has to actually leave.

10. Mrs. Owens is with Mr. Owens in Josiah Worthington's tomb and discussing Silas's absence. Josiah is leading the discussion of Silas's unexplained absence. While Mr. Owens emphasizes Silas's promise to be there for Bod, Mrs. Owens is torn between worrying about Silas and blaming him, and when the men begin to discuss the fact that there's money available for Bod to go out and purchase food if he needs to, she gets fed up with both of them, because his leaving the graveyard when neither Silas nor Miss Lupescu is present is not to be thought of. Leaving Josiah's tomb, she goes in search of Bod and finds him at the top of the hill looking at the town (where the living people live) and asks what he's thinking about. He replies that he's thinking about what is out in the world of the living and how they know that his family's murderer is still alive. Mrs. Owens replies that they have Silas's word. Bod protests that Silas hasn't filled in the picture any more than that. When Mrs. Owens doesn't answer, Bod asks her to confirm that she saw the man who killed his family. She nods. Bod asks what the man was like. Mrs. Owens confesses that she was mainly attending to Bod, but tells him that he was dark and frightening and appeared hungry and angry

and that Silas saw him out of the graveyard. Bod asks why Silas didn't just kill the man, and Mrs. Owens says, "He's not a monster" (presumably referring to Silas, but she doesn't say and the grammar isn't clear). Bod adds that if Silas had killed the man, then Bod would be free in the world. Mrs. Owens responds that Silas knows more about the situation and about life and death, and resolving the situation is not as easy as killing the murderer. Bod asks the man's name, and Mrs. Owens first obfuscates by saying that the man didn't say his name, and when Bod presses, she first tells him there's nothing he can do (as if she fears that he will try to avenge his family if he knows their murderer). Bod says he can learn everything he needs to know, and mentions some of what he's learned. Mrs. Owens touches Bod's shoulder and begins to speak, but pauses when she realizes that one day she will no longer be able to touch him. And then she seems to come to a decision and tells Bod the name, Jack. Bod asks when Silas will return, and Mrs. Owens's anger at Silas is gone. She tells Bod that she wishes she knew. Time passes. Mrs. Owens overhears Bod asking Mr. Owens about the change in Liza's behavior, and corrects Mr. Owens's story of their courtship. [We learn from Bod's conversation with Mr. Owens that he wants Mrs. Owens to take care of Scarlett if anything happens to him, but we don't get her perspective on this.]

Strategy 18: Engaging with a Text Through Imagery and Mapping, pages 48–49

1. Answers will vary. You may wish to invite a music teacher to co-teach musical imagery with you. Note that a) students reading the graphic novel do not even have a complete verse to work with (I would suggest giving them lyrics as they appear on page 26 of the US edition), and b) students have not yet read Chapter 8, so the words for the song are not yet complete: they should make educated guesses about the rhythm of the song's ending. They will have the opportunity to revise their work in the test that follows Chapter 8.

   Permission to reprint the music from the book was not granted for setting the words to the lullaby due to previous commitments, so I cannot provide a model answer, but this situation provides an excellent opportunity to teach students about copyright, derivative works, and what can be done with a book privately, as opposed to what is allowed in public, and freedoms allowed in the classroom that are not permitted outside of education. If you have questions about what is permissible in the classroom, please seek the advice of a music teacher colleague, a lawyer, or the literary agent for the author whose work you wish to use.

2. Answers will vary depending on the examples students pick. Possible responses: *Sight*: Scarlett's first view of the magpies and the church in the graveyard upon her return. *Smell*: the burning food that Scarlett smells when she returns home from the library *Touch*: the rain in Scarlett's hair as she tries to decide whether to take a ride from Mr. Frost. *Taste*: Jay Frost's description of the change that comes about in eating chips. *Hearing*: the sounds that carry Scarlett from sleeping to waking when she Dreamwalks.

3. Answers will vary depending on students' choices of what to record, the media they choose, and their level of skill with that media.

4. Answers will vary. The following should be true: The northwest wilderness is behind the Egyptian Wall and accessed through an arch. Within are the graves of Carstairs, Nehemiah Trot, and Alonso Jones. Beside the Egyptian Wall is the willow grove. To the west are Mother Slaughter's grave Liberty Roach's grave, and between Liberty and the apple tree, Harrison Westwood's grave. The apple tree extends over the fence that separates the graveyard proper from the Potter's Field. At the farthest end (north?) of the graveyard is the gardener's hut. At the top of the hill (which seems to be to the north) is Josiah's obelisk and the natural amphitheater. Fifty feet away (perhaps south) is the Frobisher Vault, in which is Ephraim Pettyfer's casket, behind which is the entrance to the barrow. The alley wall, over which Jack in Chapter 1 and the Jacks in Chapter 7 climb may be to the east. Presumably farther southeast are the front or main gate and, right beside it, the side or pedestrian gate. Ahead of the gate is the collection of broken gravestones where Mrs. Owens is when she first sees Bod. Perhaps to the left of the main gate (south) is the spired chapel, where Silas sleeps, with a bench in front and a crypt below. In the southwest, near the lightning tree, is the ghoulgate. The Owenses' tomb is "down," perhaps due south.

Writer's Forum 4: Writing a Short Research Report, page 50

1. Answers may vary somewhat, depending on sources.

| Handy spandy **Jack-a-dandy** Loves plum cake and sugar candy, He bought some at the grocers shop And out he came, hop, hop, hop | **Jack** be **nimble**, Jack be quick, Jack jump over The candlestick. | **Jack Frost:** personification of winter |
| | | **Jack Tar**: nickname for a sailor |

| **Jack Ketch**: Charles II's infamous executioner, who botched many jobs, with the result that his name is a synonym for Death |

Strategy 19: Drawing on a Source, Part III "Tiger! Tiger!", page 51

1. If you chose to have students stop reading the first section of *The Jungle Book* to avoid spoilers, they should finish it before part III, starting on p. 91 "Now you must be content to skip . . ."
   Parallels: With collaboration from those in his second home, the boy kills the one who meant to kill him; both successes lead to loss, but of different kinds.
   Differences: Bod is not cast out of his second home; Mowgli's prey has no colleagues (left); Mowgli has no one else to protect; Bod saves Scarlett's life, but loses her friendship; Mowgli restores Akela but loses his place in the village. Miss Lupescu dies fighting the Jacks.
2. Mowgli is more capable and bitter, less willing to put up with human foibles. Bod is more capable, strategic, and clever, able to apply what he's learned and pull together years' of education to new ends.
3. Kipling seems set on revealing the inhumanity of humans, while Gaiman focuses on their generosity and potential for good.
4. Reading Kipling shows how Gaiman has made the 'boy raised by strangers" trope his own, veering from Kipling and going his own way to his own ends.
5. Answers will vary. Students may be disappointed by Mowgli's rejection and Scarlett's memory wipe.

Chapter 8 Leavings and Partings, page 52

1. Mother Slaughter gives herself the prime role in speaking for Bod, diminishing Mrs. Owens and the Lady.
2. As Bod reaches maturity, he loses the gifts bestowed by Freedom of the Graveyard.
3. Possible answer: love.
4. Mrs. Owens repeats the lullaby and remembers the ending, framing the period during which Bod has been under her care and protection. Looking back, we can now see that the second stanza was foreshadowing, for during his time in the graveyard, Bod has kissed (or been kissed by) a lover, danced a measure, found his name, and found buried treasure. The lullaby makes sense of the story's ending (Bod setting off to live his life) via the third stanza, proclaiming, as it does, the wish for Bod to have exactly the opportunities that are now his to claim and enjoy. While the second stanza is, on the one hand, pertinent to Bod alone, it is phrased in a such a way that it might be a mother's wish for any child: to find love, enjoy life, establish identity, and find something that one prizes, and coupled with the third stanza, allows Bod to stand in for any child.
5. Bod no longer needs, and so loses, the powers that kept him safe in the graveyard. Silas displays more of the warm side of his personality, which is—in general—reserved and removed.
6. He accepts the identity bestowed on him by the people who raised him; he accepts his past.
7. Answers will vary. Students may be moved.
8. Answers will vary. Students may feel hopeful for Bod's experience of a long, satisfying life.
9. Mrs. Owens uses her last moments with her son to close the circle, completing her expression to him of exactly what she wished to give him when she chose to stand between him and the man who wished to murder him, and what is now his to claim. It is a poignant moment, but she accepts it.

Strategy 20: Rereading a Book, page 53

1. Students may report a fuller experience of the story, having already learned the vocabulary and sorted out any misunderstandings. They may also find that they are more aware of patterns and repetitions.
2. *Ancient Conspiracy*: Students may interpret either the Jacks of All Trades or both the Jacks of All Trades and the Honour Guard as ancient conspiracies—but the word *conspiracy* suggests harm to law and order: the Honour Guard is—within the moral stance of this book—a secret society, but not a conspiracy. Therefore, students should mention information about the Convocation, its members, its goals, its battles, and its

downfall, as reported in Chapter 1, the Interlude, Chapter 7, and Chapter 8. *Don't Fear the Reaper*: In *The Graveyard Book,* Death is represented not by the Grim Reaper, but by the kind, gentle, and generous Lady on the Grey, presenting a kinder, gentler image of the end of life and the transition to being dead. Students should cite evidence from Chapters 1, 5, and 8.

3. Students should mention the following: he has no reflection; he eats only one food, and it is not bananas (blood); he sleeps in a spire, and clambers down it headfirst (as a bat); he sleeps in a coffin-shaped steamer trunk when he's away from home; he is neither living nor dead, and if he is killed, he will simply cease to be; there are ways to kill him, but they do not involve cars; he avoids sunlight. Students with the UK version or the graphic novel may point out aspects of the illustrations showing Silas that are typical of vampire imagery.

4. Answers will vary depending on a student's initial hypotheses and whether the book has provided any evidence that has a bearing on it.

Writer's Forum 5: Composing a Book Review, page 54

1. Answers will vary. Reviews must include a summary and evaluation, though they can be intertwined. The evaluation should respond to the main parts of the story and be criteria-based.

Writer's Forum 6: Comparing Two Treatments, page 55

1. Answers will vary, depending on which two treatments of *The Graveyard Book* the students choose. Depending on their choices, they should focus on:
    • the differences in language and illustrations between the US and UK versions
    • what is left out of the text and added through images in the graphic novel
    • what is conveyed by voicing the characters in the audio version that is not conveyed (or is not as obvious) when reading silently,
    • how Gaiman's gestures and tone of voice add interpretation

Test: Chapters 7–8, page 56

Vocabulary
1. These are things that Bod wanted Alonso Jones to tell him about on his last day in the graveyard.
2. These words relate to the return of Scarlett and her mother to the Old Town.
3. These words appear in the newspaper article about the murder of Bod's family.
4. These words come from Silas's explantion and confession to Bod.
5. These words describe Jay Frost when Scarlett first meets him.
6. These words come from the description of Silas as Bod prepares to leave.
7. These words come from Jay Frost's reaction to there having been a murder in the house where he lives.
8. These words come from the moment when Bod realizes that Silas is leaving the graveyard.
9. These words describe Jack Frost as the Sleer takes him to be their master.
10. These words are from Bod's response to learning of Miss Lupescu's death.
11. These words are from the battle at Dragon's Den.
12. These words are from Liza's farewell to Bod.

Essay Topics
1. Bod remaining alive was essential to the overthrow of the entire Jacks of All Trades organization.
2. Students should mention Mrs. Owens, Miss Lupescu, Mother Slaughter, and Scarlett.
3. Arguably both his dealings with Mo and Nick and the exchange with the Perssons prove useful.
4. That Scarlett returns, is able to see Faded Bod, and Dreamwalks with him suggests romantic possibilities.
5. He secures the safety of all (himself included) from the Jacks and loses Scarlett's friendship.
6. Scarlett and Bod each feels that she/he is being used as bait: Bod chooses for himself, but Scarlett doesn't.
7. When Bod wishes Silas had killed Jack, Mrs. Owens says Silas is not a monster. Scarlett accuses Bod of being a monster for the way he treats Jack. Silas claims to have been a monster in the past. Silas met Jack before learning what was going on: killing him would have been premature, unjust. Scarlett does not understand the situation or what's at stake. Silas seems to be judging justly, but says, "People can change."
8. The members of the graveyard bring their memories and customs into the present through interactions.
9. *Macbeth*, I, i; spoken by the Second Witch. The reference is not appropriate and shows Trot's foolishness.
10. Possible response: Sad that she died, but glad she was willing to sacrifice herself to save Bod.
11. Bod attains his freedom and the ability to unlock his potential, but loses key relationships.

12. Crusoe, like Bod wants to find another living being; his footstep signifies making his mark on the world.
13. Students should include key elements from throughout the book, particularly Chapters 7 and 8.
14. Bod is often described as *grave*; Jay Frost says he usually *defrosts* his dinner.
15. See pages 48–49 and 84.
16. Students may suggest including what Bod and Silas do next and what happens to the last Jack.

Theme Page, page 57

Maturity and Adulthood
1. Maturity is the measure of Bod's need for parents and a guardian and for his ability to take on the Jacks.
2. The dead cannot become any more mature than they are, no matter the age at which they died.
3. His ability to avenge the deaths of his family, save Scarlett, apply everything he's learned, not follow advice slavishly, and collaborate with the graveyard residents testify to his maturity. The fact that he's not emotionally ready to leave the graveyard suggests he needs more development in this area.
4. Possible response: Fading with Liza's assistance.

Identity
1. Answers will vary. Possible response: Bod's community creates boundaries for adolescents' choices (laws and rules), provides training and information to help him learn skills and develop talents, and responds to his choices with evaluative feedback, both positive and negative. Within this structure, Bod is able to build and discover identity (though doubtless, he will continue this process in the world of the living).

Appearance vs. Reality
1. Lists should include misinformation, lies, invalid conclusions, and wishful thinking.
2. Answers will vary depending on the character chosen. Students who choose Silas may say that further information made his change more meaningful to them.
3. Answers will vary. Students may note a difference between withholding information and deceiving someone and between deception and allowing readers to use interpretive skills to draw conclusions.
4. The man Jack's deception of Scarlett and her mother in his guise as Jay Frost is key to his second attempt to kill Bod.

Education and Reading
1. Answers will vary. Students may suggest that education takes place anywhere a person is—if they're willing to learn, and that it includes some or all of the following: learning of skills, facts, methods, tools, strategies, modes, values, and development of the student's inherent gifts/talents. Students may suggest that while education may tend to increase maturity, there is not a simple, direct relationship.
2. Answers will vary. Students may contrast the quality of education in the graveyard vs. in the school.
3. Possible responses: Schools—convey a particular set of facts, no more and no less; Miss Lupescu, Mr. Pennyworth, and Silas: to provide Bod with the skills and understanding that will keep him safe (and possibly allow him to exact a fitting revenge when he is ready).
4. Reading is key to Bod's acquiring some of the things he needs to know to go among the living and understand what kind of life he wants for himself.
5. Answers will vary. Accept reasonable responses.

Civility and Manners
1. In the graveyard: using titles, greetings, and partings; apologizing for transgressions; asking after others' health and well-being. In town: limited use of titles; speech is generally less formal, with fewer civilities.
2. He does everything in 1 and does it in the manner and using the speech of the time that is apt for the person he is addressing.

Excerpts from The Jungle Book

Mowgli's Brothers

It was seven o'clock of a very warm evening in the Seeonee hills when Father Wolf woke up from his day's rest, scratched himself, yawned, and spread out his paws one after the other to get rid of the sleepy feeling in their tips. Mother Wolf lay with her big gray nose dropped across her four tumbling, squealing cubs, and the moon shone into the mouth of the cave where they all lived. "Augrh!" said Father Wolf. "It is time to hunt again." He was going to spring down hill when a little shadow with a bushy tail crossed the threshold and whined: "Good luck go with you, O Chief of the Wolves. And good luck and strong white teeth go with noble children that they may never forget the hungry in this world."

It was the jackal—Tabaqui, the Dish-licker—and the wolves of India despise Tabaqui because he runs about making mischief, and telling tales, and eating rags and pieces of leather from the village rubbish-heaps. But they are afraid of him too, because Tabaqui, more than anyone else in the jungle, is apt to go mad, and then he forgets that he was ever afraid of anyone, and runs through the forest biting everything in his way. Even the tiger runs and hides when little Tabaqui goes mad, for madness is the most disgraceful thing that can overtake a wild creature. We call it hydrophobia, but they call it dewanee—the madness—and run.

"Enter, then, and look," said Father Wolf stiffly, "but there is no food here."

"For a wolf, no," said Tabaqui, "but for so mean a person as myself a dry bone is a good feast. Who are we, the Gidur-log [the jackal people], to pick and choose?" He scuttled to the back of the cave, where he found the bone of a buck with some meat on it, and sat cracking the end merrily.

"All thanks for this good meal," he said, licking his lips. "How beautiful are the noble children! How large are their eyes! And so young too! Indeed, indeed, I might have remembered that the children of kings are men from the beginning."

Now, Tabaqui knew as well as anyone else that there is nothing so unlucky as to compliment children to their faces. It pleased him to see Mother and Father Wolf look uncomfortable.

Tabaqui sat still, rejoicing in the mischief that he had made, and then he said spitefully:

"Shere Khan, the Big One, has shifted his hunting grounds. He will hunt among these hills for the next moon, so he has told me."

Shere Khan was the tiger who lived near the Waingunga River, twenty miles away.

"He has no right!" Father Wolf began angrily—"By the Law of the Jungle he has no right to change his quarters without due warning. He will frighten every head of game within ten miles, and I—I have to kill for two, these days."

"His mother did not call him Lungri [the Lame One] for nothing," said Mother Wolf quietly. "He has been lame in one foot from his birth. That is why he has only killed cattle. Now the villagers of the Waingunga are angry with him, and he has come here to make our villagers angry. They will scour the jungle for him when he is far away, and we and our children must run when the grass is set alight. Indeed, we are very grateful to Shere Khan!"

"Shall I tell him of your gratitude?" said Tabaqui.

"Out!" snapped Father Wolf. "Out and hunt with thy master. Thou hast done harm enough for one night."

"I go," said Tabaqui quietly. "Ye can hear Shere Khan below in the thickets. I might have saved myself the message."

Father Wolf listened, and below in the valley that ran down to a little river he heard the dry, angry, snarly, singsong whine of a tiger who has caught nothing and does not care if all the jungle knows it.

"The fool!" said Father Wolf. "To begin a night's work with that noise! Does he think that our buck are like his fat Waingunga bullocks?"

"H'sh. It is neither bullock nor buck he hunts to-night," said Mother Wolf. "It is Man."

The whine had changed to a sort of humming purr that seemed to come from every quarter of the compass. It was the noise that bewilders woodcutters and gypsies sleeping in the open, and makes them run sometimes into the very mouth of the tiger.

"Man!" said Father Wolf, showing all his white teeth. "Faugh! Are there not enough beetles and frogs in the tanks that he must eat Man, and on our ground too!"

The Law of the Jungle, which never orders anything without a reason, forbids every beast to eat Man except when he is killing to show his children how to kill, and then he must hunt outside the hunting grounds of his pack or tribe. The real reason for this is that man-killing means, sooner or later, the arrival of white men on elephants, with guns, and hundreds of brown men with gongs and rockets and torches. Then everybody in the jungle suffers. The reason the beasts give among themselves is that Man is the weakest and most defenseless of all living things, and it is unsportsmanlike to touch him. They say too—and it is true—that man-eaters become mangy, and lose their teeth.

The purr grew louder, and ended in the full-throated "Aaarh!" of the tiger's charge.

Then there was a howl—an untigerish howl—from Shere Khan. "He has missed," said Mother Wolf. "What is it?"

Father Wolf ran out a few paces and heard Shere Khan muttering and mumbling savagely as he tumbled about in the scrub.

"The fool has had no more sense than to jump at a woodcutter's campfire, and has burned his feet," said Father Wolf with a grunt. "Tabaqui is with him."

"Something is coming uphill," said Mother Wolf, twitching one ear. "Get ready."

The bushes rustled a little in the thicket, and Father Wolf dropped with his haunches under him, ready for his leap. Then, if you had been watching, you would have seen the most wonderful thing in the world—the wolf checked in mid-spring. He made his bound before he saw what it was he was jumping at, and then he tried to stop himself. The result was that he shot up straight into the air for four or five feet, landing almost where he left ground.

"Man!" he snapped. "A man's cub. Look!"

Directly in front of him, holding on by a low branch, stood a naked brown baby who could just walk—as soft and as dimpled a little atom as ever came to a wolf's cave at night. He looked up into Father Wolf's face, and laughed.

"Is that a man's cub?" said Mother Wolf. "I have never seen one. Bring it here."

A Wolf accustomed to moving his own cubs can, if necessary, mouth an egg without breaking it, and though Father Wolf's jaws closed right on the child's back not a tooth even scratched the skin as he laid it down among the cubs.

"How little! How naked, and—how bold!" said Mother Wolf softly. The baby was pushing his way between the cubs to get close to the warm hide. "Ahai! He is taking his meal with the others. And so this is a man's cub. Now, was there ever a wolf that could boast of a man's cub among her children?"

"I have heard now and again of such a thing, but never in our Pack or in my time," said Father Wolf. "He is altogether without hair, and I could kill him with a touch of my foot. But see, he looks up and is not afraid."

The moonlight was blocked out of the mouth of the cave, for Shere Khan's great square head and shoulders were thrust into the entrance. Tabaqui, behind him, was squeaking: "My lord, my lord, it went in here!"

"Shere Khan does us great honor," said Father Wolf, but his eyes were very angry. "What does Shere Khan need?"

"My quarry. A man's cub went this way," said Shere Khan. "Its parents have run off. Give it to me."

Shere Khan had jumped at a woodcutter's campfire, as Father Wolf had said, and was furious from the pain of his burned feet. But Father Wolf knew that the mouth of the cave was too narrow for a tiger to come in by. Even where he was, Shere Khan's shoulders and forepaws were cramped for want of room, as a man's would be if he tried to fight in a barrel.

"The Wolves are a free people," said Father Wolf. "They take orders from the Head of the Pack, and not from any striped cattle-killer. The man's cub is ours—to kill if we choose."

"Ye choose and ye do not choose! What talk is this of choosing? By the bull that I killed, am I to stand nosing into your dog's den for my fair dues? It is I, Shere Khan, who speak!"

The tiger's roar filled the cave with thunder. Mother Wolf shook herself clear of the cubs and sprang forward, her eyes, like two green moons in the darkness, facing the blazing eyes of Shere Khan.

"And it is I, Raksha [The Demon], who answers. The man's cub is mine, Lungri—mine to me! He shall not be killed. He shall live to run with the Pack and to hunt with the Pack; and in the end, look you, hunter of little naked cubs—frog-eater—fish-killer—he shall hunt thee! Now get hence, or by the Sambhur that I killed (I eat no starved cattle), back thou goest to thy mother, burned beast of the jungle, lamer than ever thou camest into the world! Go!"

Father Wolf looked on amazed. He had almost forgotten the days when he won Mother Wolf in fair fight from five other wolves, when she ran in the Pack and was not called The Demon for compliment's sake. Shere Khan might have faced Father Wolf, but he could not stand up against Mother Wolf, for he knew that where he was she had all the advantage of the ground, and would fight to the death. So he backed out of the cave mouth growling, and when he was clear he shouted:

"Each dog barks in his own yard! We will see what the Pack will say to this fostering of man-cubs. The cub is mine, and to my teeth he will come in the end, O bush-tailed thieves!"

Mother Wolf threw herself down panting among the cubs, and Father Wolf said to her gravely:

"Shere Khan speaks this much truth. The cub must be shown to the Pack. Wilt thou still keep him, Mother?"

"Keep him!" she gasped. "He came naked, by night, alone and very hungry; yet he was not afraid! Look, he has pushed one of my babes to one side already. And that lame butcher would have killed him and would have run off to the Waingunga while the villagers here hunted through all our lairs in revenge! Keep him? Assuredly I will keep him. Lie still, little frog. O thou Mowgli—for Mowgli the Frog I will call thee—the time will come when thou wilt hunt Shere Khan as he has hunted thee."

"But what will our Pack say?" said Father Wolf.

The Law of the Jungle lays down very clearly that any wolf may, when he marries, withdraw from the Pack he belongs to. But as soon as his cubs are old enough to stand on their feet he must bring them to the Pack Council, which is generally held once a month at full moon, in order that the other wolves may identify them. After that inspection the cubs are free to run where they please, and until they have killed their first buck no excuse is accepted if a grown wolf of the Pack kills one of them. The punishment is death where the murderer can be found; and if you think for a minute you will see that this must be so.

Father Wolf waited till his cubs could run a little, and then on the night of the Pack Meeting took them and Mowgli and Mother Wolf to the Council Rock—a hilltop covered with stones and boulders where a hundred wolves could hide. Akela, the great gray Lone Wolf, who led all the Pack by strength and cunning, lay out at full length on his rock, and below him sat forty or more wolves of every size and color, from badger-colored veterans who could handle a buck alone to young black three-year-olds who thought they could. The Lone Wolf had led them for a year now. He had fallen twice into a wolf trap in his youth, and once he had been beaten and left for dead; so he knew the manners and customs of men. There was very little talking at the Rock. The cubs tumbled over each other in the center of the circle where their mothers and fathers sat, and now and again a senior wolf would go quietly up to a cub, look at him carefully, and return to his place on noiseless feet. Sometimes a mother would push her cub far out into the moonlight to be sure that he had not been overlooked. Akela from his rock would cry: "Ye know the Law—ye know the Law. Look well, O Wolves!" And the anxious mothers would take up the call: "Look—look well, O Wolves!"

At last—and Mother Wolf's neck bristles lifted as the time came—Father Wolf pushed "Mowgli the Frog," as they called him, into the center, where he sat laughing and playing with some pebbles that glistened in the moonlight.

Akela never raised his head from his paws, but went on with the monotonous cry: "Look well!" A muffled roar came up from behind the rocks—the voice of Shere Khan crying: "The cub is mine. Give him to me. What have the Free People to do with a man's cub?" Akela never even twitched his ears. All he said was: "Look well, O Wolves! What have the Free People to do with the orders of any save the Free People? Look well!"

There was a chorus of deep growls, and a young wolf in his fourth year flung back Shere Khan's question to Akela: "What have the Free People to do with a man's cub?" Now, the Law of the Jungle lays down that if there is any dispute as to the right of a cub to be accepted by the Pack, he must be spoken for by at least two members of the Pack who are not his father and mother.

"Who speaks for this cub?" said Akela. "Among the Free People who speaks?" There was no answer and Mother Wolf got ready for what she knew would be her last fight, if things came to fighting.

Then the only other creature who is allowed at the Pack Council—Baloo, the sleepy brown bear who teaches the wolf cubs the Law of the Jungle: old Baloo, who can come and go where he pleases because he eats only nuts and roots and honey—rose upon his hind quarters and grunted.

"The man's cub—the man's cub?" he said. "I speak for the man's cub. There is no harm in a man's cub. I have no gift of words, but I speak the truth. Let him run with the Pack, and be entered with the others. I myself will teach him."

"We need yet another," said Akela. "Baloo has spoken, and he is our teacher for the young cubs. Who speaks besides Baloo?"

A black shadow dropped down into the circle. It was Bagheera the Black Panther, inky black all over, but with the panther markings showing up in certain lights like the pattern of watered silk. Everybody knew Bagheera, and nobody cared to cross his path; for he was as cunning as Tabaqui, as bold as the wild buffalo, and as reckless as the wounded elephant. But he had a voice as soft as wild honey dripping from a tree, and a skin softer than down.

"O Akela, and ye the Free People," he purred, "I have no right in your assembly, but the Law of the Jungle says that if there is a doubt which is not a killing matter in regard to a new cub, the life of that cub may be bought at a price. And the Law does not say who may or may not pay that price. Am I right?"

"Good! Good!" said the young wolves, who are always hungry. "Listen to Bagheera. The cub can be bought for a price. It is the Law."

"Knowing that I have no right to speak here, I ask your leave."

"Speak then," cried twenty voices.

"To kill a naked cub is shame. Besides, he may make better sport for you when he is grown. Baloo has spoken in his behalf. Now to Baloo's word I will add one bull, and a fat one, newly killed, not half a mile from here, if ye will accept the man's cub according to the Law. Is it difficult?"

There was a clamor of scores of voices, saying: "What matter? He will die in the winter rains. He will scorch in the sun. What harm can a naked frog do us? Let him run with the Pack. Where is the bull, Bagheera? Let him be accepted." And then came Akela's deep bay, crying: "Look well—look well, O Wolves!"

Mowgli was still deeply interested in the pebbles, and he did not notice when the wolves came and looked at him one by one. At last they all went down the hill for the dead bull, and only Akela, Bagheera, Baloo, and Mowgli's own wolves were left. Shere Khan roared still in the night, for he was very angry that Mowgli had not been handed over to him.

"Ay, roar well," said Bagheera, under his whiskers, "for the time will come when this naked thing will make thee roar to another tune, or I know nothing of man."

"It was well done," said Akela. "Men and their cubs are very wise. He may be a help in time."

"Truly, a help in time of need; for none can hope to lead the Pack forever," said Bagheera.

Akela said nothing. He was thinking of the time that comes to every leader of every pack when his strength goes from him and he gets feebler and feebler, till at last he is killed by the wolves and a new leader comes up—to be killed in his turn.

"Take him away," he said to Father Wolf, "and train him as befits one of the Free People."

And that is how Mowgli was entered into the Seeonee Wolf Pack for the price of a bull and on Baloo's good word.

Now you must be content to skip ten or eleven whole years, and only guess at all the wonderful life that Mowgli led among the wolves, because if it were written out it would fill ever so many books. He grew up with the cubs, though they, of course, were grown wolves almost before he was a child. And Father Wolf taught him his business, and the meaning of things in the jungle, till every rustle in the grass, every breath of the warm night air, every note of the owls above his head, every scratch of a bat's claws as it roosted for a while in a tree, and every splash of every little fish jumping in a pool meant just as much to him as the work of his office means to a business man. When he was not learning he sat out in the sun and slept, and ate and went to sleep again. When he felt dirty or hot he swam in the forest pools; and when he wanted honey (Baloo told him that honey and nuts were just as pleasant to eat as raw meat) he climbed up for it, and that Bagheera showed him how to do. Bagheera would lie out on a branch and call, "Come along, Little Brother," and at first Mowgli would cling like the sloth, but afterward he would fling himself through the branches almost as boldly as the gray ape. He took his place at the Council Rock, too, when the Pack met, and there he discovered that if he stared hard at any wolf, the wolf would be forced to drop his eyes, and so he used to stare for fun. At other times he would pick the long thorns out of the pads of his friends, for wolves suffer terribly from thorns and burs in their coats. He would go down the hillside into the cultivated lands by night, and look very curiously at the villagers in their huts, but he had a mistrust of men because Bagheera showed him a square box with a drop gate so cunningly hidden in the jungle that he nearly walked into it, and told him that it was a trap. He loved better than anything else to go with Bagheera into the dark warm heart of the forest, to sleep all through the drowsy day, and at night see how Bagheera did his killing. Bagheera killed right and left as he felt hungry, and so did Mowgli—with one exception. As soon as he was old enough to understand things, Bagheera told him that he must never touch cattle because he had been bought into the Pack at the price of a bull's life. "All the jungle is thine," said Bagheera, "and thou canst kill everything that thou art strong enough to kill; but for the sake of the bull that bought thee thou must never kill or eat any cattle young or old. That is the Law of the Jungle." Mowgli obeyed faithfully.

And he grew and grew strong as a boy must grow who does not know that he is learning any lessons, and who has nothing in the world to think of except things to eat.

Mother Wolf told him once or twice that Shere Khan was not a creature to be trusted, and that some day he must kill Shere Khan. But though a young wolf would have remembered that advice every hour, Mowgli forgot it because he was only a boy—though he would have called himself a wolf if he had been able to speak in any human tongue.

Shere Khan was always crossing his path in the jungle, for as Akela grew older and feebler the lame tiger had come to be great friends with the younger wolves of the Pack, who followed him for scraps, a thing Akela would never have allowed if he had dared to push his authority to the proper bounds. Then Shere Khan would flatter them and wonder that such fine young hunters were content to be led by a dying wolf and a man's cub. "They tell me," Shere Khan would say, "that at Council ye dare not look him between the eyes." And the young wolves would growl and bristle.

Bagheera, who had eyes and ears everywhere, knew something of this, and once or twice he told Mowgli in so many words that Shere Khan would kill him some day. Mowgli would laugh and answer: "I have the Pack and I have thee; and Baloo, though he is so lazy, might strike a blow or two for my sake. Why should I be afraid?"

It was one very warm day that a new notion came to Bagheera—born of something that he had heard. Perhaps Ikki the Porcupine had told him; but he said to Mowgli when they were deep in the jungle, as the boy lay with his head on Bagheera's beautiful black skin, "Little Brother, how often have I told thee that Shere Khan is thy enemy?"

"As many times as there are nuts on that palm," said Mowgli, who, naturally, could not count. "What of it? I am sleepy, Bagheera, and Shere Khan is all long tail and loud talk—like Mao, the Peacock."

"But this is no time for sleeping. Baloo knows it; I know it; the Pack know it; and even the foolish, foolish deer know. Tabaqui has told thee too."

"Ho! ho!" said Mowgli. "Tabaqui came to me not long ago with some rude talk that I was a naked man's cub and not fit to dig pig-nuts. But I caught Tabaqui by the tail and swung him twice against a palm-tree to teach him better manners."

"That was foolishness, for though Tabaqui is a mischief-maker, he would have told thee of something that concerned thee closely. Open those eyes, Little Brother. Shere Khan dare not kill thee in the jungle. But remember, Akela is very old, and soon the day comes when he cannot kill his buck, and then he will be leader no more. Many of the wolves that looked thee over when thou wast brought to the Council first are old too, and the young wolves believe, as Shere Khan has taught them, that a man-cub has no place with the Pack. In a little time thou wilt be a man."

"And what is a man that he should not run with his brothers?" said Mowgli. "I was born in the jungle. I have obeyed the Law of the Jungle, and there is no wolf of ours from whose paws I have not pulled a thorn. Surely they are my brothers!"

Bagheera stretched himself at full length and half shut his eyes. "Little Brother," said he, "feel under my jaw."

Mowgli put up his strong brown hand, and just under Bagheera's silky chin, where the giant rolling muscles were all hid by the glossy hair, he came upon a little bald spot.

"There is no one in the jungle that knows that I, Bagheera, carry that mark—the mark of the collar; and yet, Little Brother, I was born among men, and it was among men that my mother died—in the cages of the king's palace at Oodeypore. It was because of this that I paid the price for thee at the Council when thou wast a little naked cub. Yes, I too was born among men. I had never seen the jungle. They fed me behind bars from an iron pan till one night I felt that I was Bagheera—the Panther—and no man's plaything, and I broke the silly lock with one blow of my paw and came away. And because I had learned the ways of men, I became more terrible in the jungle than Shere Khan. Is it not so?"

"Yes," said Mowgli, "all the jungle fear Bagheera—all except Mowgli."

"Oh, thou art a man's cub," said the Black Panther very tenderly. "And even as I returned to my jungle, so thou must go back to men at last—to the men who are thy brothers—if thou art not killed in the Council."

"But why—but why should any wish to kill me?" said Mowgli.

"Look at me," said Bagheera. And Mowgli looked at him steadily between the eyes. The big panther turned his head away in half a minute.

"That is why," he said, shifting his paw on the leaves. "Not even I can look thee between the eyes, and I was born among men, and I love thee, Little Brother. The others they hate thee because their eyes cannot meet thine; because thou art wise; because thou hast pulled out thorns from their feet—because thou art a man."

"I did not know these things," said Mowgli sullenly, and he frowned under his heavy black eyebrows.

"What is the Law of the Jungle? Strike first and then give tongue. By thy very carelessness they know that thou art a man. But be wise. It is in my heart that when Akela misses his next kill—and at each hunt it costs him more to pin the buck—the Pack will turn against him and against thee. They will hold a jungle Council at the Rock, and then—and then—I have it!" said Bagheera, leaping up. "Go thou down quickly to the men's huts in the valley, and take some of the Red Flower which they grow there, so that when the time comes thou mayest have even a stronger friend than I or Baloo or those of the Pack that love thee. Get the Red Flower."

By Red Flower Bagheera meant fire, only no creature in the jungle will call fire by its proper name. Every beast lives in deadly fear of it, and invents a hundred ways of describing it.

"The Red Flower?" said Mowgli. "That grows outside their huts in the twilight. I will get some."

"There speaks the man's cub," said Bagheera proudly. "Remember that it grows in little pots. Get one swiftly, and keep it by thee for time of need."

"Good!" said Mowgli. "I go. But art thou sure, O my Bagheera"—he slipped his arm around the splendid neck and looked deep into the big eyes—"art thou sure that all this is Shere Khan's doing?"

"By the Broken Lock that freed me, I am sure, Little Brother."

"Then, by the Bull that bought me, I will pay Shere Khan full tale for this, and it may be a little over," said Mowgli, and he bounded away.

"That is a man. That is all a man," said Bagheera to himself, lying down again. "Oh, Shere Khan, never was a blacker hunting than that frog-hunt of thine ten years ago!"

Mowgli was far and far through the forest, running hard, and his heart was hot in him. He came to the cave as the evening mist rose, and drew breath, and looked down the valley. The cubs were out, but Mother Wolf, at the back of the cave, knew by his breathing that something was troubling her frog.

"What is it, Son?" she said.

"Some bat's chatter of Shere Khan," he called back. "I hunt among the plowed fields tonight," and he plunged downward through the bushes, to the stream at the bottom of the valley. There he checked, for he heard the yell of the Pack hunting, heard the bellow of a hunted Sambhur, and the snort as the buck turned at bay. Then there were wicked, bitter howls from the young wolves: "Akela! Akela! Let the Lone Wolf show his strength. Room for the leader of the Pack! Spring, Akela!"

The Lone Wolf must have sprung and missed his hold, for Mowgli heard the snap of his teeth and then a yelp as the Sambhur knocked him over with his forefoot.

He did not wait for anything more, but dashed on; and the yells grew fainter behind him as he ran into the croplands where the villagers lived.

"Bagheera spoke truth," he panted, as he nestled down in some cattle fodder by the window of a hut. "To-morrow is one day both for Akela and for me."

Then he pressed his face close to the window and watched the fire on the hearth. He saw the husbandman's wife get up and feed it in the night with black lumps. And when the morning came and the mists were all white and cold, he saw the man's child pick up a wicker pot plastered inside with earth, fill it with lumps of red-hot charcoal, put it under his blanket, and go out to tend the cows in the byre.

"Is that all?" said Mowgli. "If a cub can do it, there is nothing to fear." So he strode round the corner and met the boy, took the pot from his hand, and disappeared into the mist while the boy howled with fear.

"They are very like me," said Mowgli, blowing into the pot as he had seen the woman do. "This thing will die if I do not give it things to eat"; and he dropped twigs and dried bark on the red stuff. Halfway up the hill he met Bagheera with the morning dew shining like moonstones on his coat.

"Akela has missed," said the Panther. "They would have killed him last night, but they needed thee also. They were looking for thee on the hill."

"I was among the plowed lands. I am ready. See!" Mowgli held up the fire-pot.

"Good! Now, I have seen men thrust a dry branch into that stuff, and presently the Red Flower blossomed at the end of it. Art thou not afraid?"

"No. Why should I fear? I remember now—if it is not a dream—how, before I was a Wolf, I lay beside the Red Flower, and it was warm and pleasant."

All that day Mowgli sat in the cave tending his fire pot and dipping dry branches into it to see how they looked. He found a branch that satisfied him, and in the evening when Tabaqui came to the cave and told him rudely enough that he was wanted at the Council Rock, he laughed till Tabaqui ran away. Then Mowgli went to the Council, still laughing.

Akela the Lone Wolf lay by the side of his rock as a sign that the leadership of the Pack was open, and Shere Khan with his following of scrap-fed wolves walked to and fro openly being flattered. Bagheera lay close to Mowgli, and the fire pot was between Mowgli's knees. When they were all gathered together, Shere Khan began to speak—a thing he would never have dared to do when Akela was in his prime.

"He has no right," whispered Bagheera. "Say so. He is a dog's son. He will be frightened."

Mowgli sprang to his feet. "Free People," he cried, "does Shere Khan lead the Pack? What has a tiger to do with our leadership?"

"Seeing that the leadership is yet open, and being asked to speak—" Shere Khan began.

"By whom?" said Mowgli. "Are we all jackals, to fawn on this cattle butcher? The leadership of the Pack is with the Pack alone."

There were yells of "Silence, thou man's cub!" "Let him speak. He has kept our Law"; and at last the seniors of the Pack thundered: "Let the Dead Wolf speak." When a leader of the Pack has missed his kill, he is called the Dead Wolf as long as he lives, which is not long.

Akela raised his old head wearily:—

"Free People, and ye too, jackals of Shere Khan, for twelve seasons I have led ye to and from the kill, and in all that time not one has been trapped or maimed. Now I have missed my kill. Ye know how that plot was made. Ye know how ye brought me up to an untried buck to make my weakness known. It was cleverly done. Your right is to kill me here on the Council Rock, now. Therefore, I ask, who comes to make an end of the Lone Wolf? For it is my right, by the Law of the Jungle, that ye come one by one."

There was a long hush, for no single wolf cared to fight Akela to the death. Then Shere Khan roared: "Bah! What have we to do with this toothless fool? He is doomed to die! It is the man-cub who has lived too long. Free People, he was my meat from the first. Give him to me. I am weary of this man-wolf folly. He has troubled the jungle for ten seasons. Give me the man-cub, or I will hunt here always, and not give you one bone. He is a man, a man's child, and from the marrow of my bones I hate him!"

Then more than half the Pack yelled: "A man! A man! What has a man to do with us? Let him go to his own place."

"And turn all the people of the villages against us?" clamored Shere Khan. "No, give him to me. He is a man, and none of us can look him between the eyes."

Akela lifted his head again and said, "He has eaten our food. He has slept with us. He has driven game for us. He has broken no word of the Law of the Jungle."

"Also, I paid for him with a bull when he was accepted. The worth of a bull is little, but Bagheera's honor is something that he will perhaps fight for," said Bagheera in his gentlest voice.

"A bull paid ten years ago!" the Pack snarled. "What do we care for bones ten years old?"

"Or for a pledge?" said Bagheera, his white teeth bared under his lip. "Well are ye called the Free People!"

"No man's cub can run with the people of the jungle," howled Shere Khan. "Give him to me!"

"He is our brother in all but blood," Akela went on, "and ye would kill him here! In truth, I have lived too long. Some of ye are eaters of cattle, and of others I have heard that, under Shere Khan's teaching, ye go by dark night and snatch children from the villager's doorstep. Therefore I know ye to be cowards, and it is to cowards I speak. It is certain that I must die, and my life is of no worth, or I would offer that in the man-cub's place. But for the sake of the Honor of the Pack,—a little matter that by being without a leader ye have forgotten,—I promise that if ye let the man-cub go to his own place, I will not, when my time comes to die, bare one tooth against ye. I will die without fighting. That will at least save the Pack three lives. More I cannot do; but if ye will, I can save ye the shame that comes of killing a brother against whom there is no fault—a brother spoken for and bought into the Pack according to the Law of the Jungle."

"He is a man—a man—a man!" snarled the Pack. And most of the wolves began to gather round Shere Khan, whose tail was beginning to switch.

"Now the business is in thy hands," said Bagheera to Mowgli. "We can do no more except fight."

Mowgli stood upright—the fire pot in his hands. Then he stretched out his arms, and yawned in the face of the Council; but he was furious with rage and sorrow, for, wolflike, the wolves had never told him how they hated him. "Listen you!" he cried. "There is no need for this dog's jabber. Ye have told me so often tonight that I am a man (and indeed I would have been a wolf with you to my life's end) that I feel your words are true. So I do not call ye my brothers any more, but sag [dogs], as a man should. What ye will do, and what ye will not do, is not yours to say. That matter is with me; and that we may see the matter more plainly, I, the man, have brought here a little of the Red Flower which ye, dogs, fear."

He flung the fire pot on the ground, and some of the red coals lit a tuft of dried moss that flared up, as all the Council drew back in terror before the leaping flames.

Mowgli thrust his dead branch into the fire till the twigs lit and crackled, and whirled it above his head among the cowering wolves.

"Thou art the master," said Bagheera in an undertone. "Save Akela from the death. He was ever thy friend."

Akela, the grim old wolf who had never asked for mercy in his life, gave one piteous look at Mowgli as the boy stood all naked, his long black hair tossing over his shoulders in the light of the blazing branch that made the shadows jump and quiver.

"Good!" said Mowgli, staring round slowly. "I see that ye are dogs. I go from you to my own people—if they be my own people. The jungle is shut to me, and I must forget your talk and your companionship. But I will be more merciful than ye are. Because I was all but your brother in blood, I promise that when I am a man among men I will not betray ye to men as ye have betrayed me." He kicked the fire with his foot, and the sparks flew up. "There shall be no war between any of us in the Pack. But here is a debt to pay before I go." He strode forward to where Shere Khan sat blinking stupidly at the flames, and caught him by the tuft on his chin. Bagheera followed in case of accidents. "Up, dog!" Mowgli cried. "Up, when a man speaks, or I will set that coat ablaze!"

Shere Khan's ears lay flat back on his head, and he shut his eyes, for the blazing branch was very near.

"This cattle-killer said he would kill me in the Council because he had not killed me when I was a cub. Thus and thus, then, do we beat dogs when we are men. Stir a whisker, Lungri, and I ram the Red Flower down thy gullet!" He beat Shere Khan over the head with the branch, and the tiger whimpered and whined in an agony of fear.

"Pah! Singed jungle cat—go now! But remember when next I come to the Council Rock, as a man should come, it will be with Shere Khan's hide on my head. For the rest, Akela goes free to live as he pleases. Ye will not kill him, because that is not my will. Nor do I think that ye will sit here any longer, lolling out your tongues as though ye were somebodies, instead of dogs whom I drive out—thus! Go!" The fire was burning furiously at the end of the branch, and Mowgli struck right and left round the circle, and the wolves ran howling with the sparks burning their fur. At last there were only Akela, Bagheera, and perhaps ten wolves that had taken Mowgli's part. Then something began to hurt Mowgli inside him, as he had never been hurt in his life before, and he caught his breath and sobbed, and the tears ran down his face.

"What is it? What is it?" he said. "I do not wish to leave the jungle, and I do not know what this is. Am I dying, Bagheera?"

"No, Little Brother. That is only tears such as men use," said Bagheera. "Now I know thou art a man, and a man's cub no longer. The jungle is shut indeed to thee henceforward. Let them fall, Mowgli. They are only tears." So Mowgli sat and cried as though his heart would break; and he had never cried in all his life before.

"Now," he said, "I will go to men. But first I must say farewell to my mother." And he went to the cave where she lived with Father Wolf, and he cried on her coat, while the four cubs howled miserably.

"Ye will not forget me?" said Mowgli.

"Never while we can follow a trail," said the cubs. "Come to the foot of the hill when thou art a man, and we will talk to thee; and we will come into the croplands to play with thee by night."

"Come soon!" said Father Wolf. "Oh, wise little frog, come again soon; for we be old, thy mother and I."

"Come soon," said Mother Wolf, "little naked son of mine. For, listen, child of man, I loved thee more than ever I loved my cubs."

"I will surely come," said Mowgli. "And when I come it will be to lay out Shere Khan's hide upon the Council Rock. Do not forget me! Tell them in the jungle never to forget me!"

The dawn was beginning to break when Mowgli went down the hillside alone, to meet those mysterious things that are called men.

Kaa's Hunting

All that is told here happened some time before Mowgli was turned out of the Seeonee Wolf Pack, or revenged himself on Shere Khan the tiger. It was in the days when Baloo was teaching him the Law of the Jungle. The big, serious, old brown bear was delighted to have so quick a pupil, for the young wolves will only learn as much of the Law of the Jungle as applies to their own pack and tribe, and run away as soon as they can repeat the Hunting Verse—"Feet that make no noise; eyes that can see in the dark; ears that can hear the winds in their lairs, and sharp white teeth, all these things are the marks of our brothers except Tabaqui the Jackal and the Hyaena whom we hate." But Mowgli, as a man-cub, had to learn a great deal more than this. Sometimes Bagheera the Black Panther would come lounging through the jungle to see how his pet was getting on, and would purr with his head against a tree while Mowgli recited the day's lesson to Baloo. The boy could climb almost as well as he could swim, and swim almost as well as he could run. So Baloo, the Teacher of the Law, taught him the Wood and Water Laws: how to tell a rotten branch from a sound one; how to speak politely to the wild bees when he came upon a hive of them fifty feet above ground; what to say to Mang the Bat when he disturbed him in the branches at midday; and how to warn the water-snakes in the pools before he splashed down among them. None of the Jungle People like being disturbed, and all are very ready to fly at an intruder. Then, too, Mowgli was taught the Strangers' Hunting Call, which must be repeated aloud till it is answered, whenever one of the Jungle-People hunts outside his own grounds. It means, translated, "Give me leave to hunt here because I am hungry." And the answer is, "Hunt then for food, but not for pleasure."

All this will show you how much Mowgli had to learn by heart, and he grew very tired of saying the same thing over a hundred times. But, as Baloo said to Bagheera, one day when Mowgli had been cuffed and run off in a temper, "A man's cub is a man's cub, and he must learn all the Law of the Jungle."

"But think how small he is," said the Black Panther, who would have spoiled Mowgli if he had had his own way. "How can his little head carry all thy long talk?"

"Is there anything in the jungle too little to be killed? No. That is why I teach him these things, and that is why I hit him, very softly, when he forgets."

"Softly! What dost thou know of softness, old Iron-feet?" Bagheera grunted. "His face is all bruised today by thy—softness. Ugh."

"Better he should be bruised from head to foot by me who love him than that he should come to harm through ignorance," Baloo answered very earnestly. "I am now teaching him the Master Words of the Jungle that shall protect him with the birds and the Snake People, and all that hunt on four feet, except his own pack. He can now claim protection, if he will only remember the words, from all in the jungle. Is not that worth a little beating?"

"Well, look to it then that thou dost not kill the man-cub. He is no tree trunk to sharpen thy blunt claws upon. But what are those Master Words? I am more likely to give help than to ask it"—Bagheera stretched out one paw and admired the steel-blue, ripping-chisel talons at the end of it—"still I should like to know."

"I will call Mowgli and he shall say them—if he will. Come, Little Brother!"

"My head is ringing like a bee tree," said a sullen little voice over their heads, and Mowgli slid down a tree trunk very angry and indignant, adding as he reached the ground: "I come for Bagheera and not for thee, fat old Baloo!"

"That is all one to me," said Baloo, though he was hurt and grieved. "Tell Bagheera, then, the Master Words of the Jungle that I have taught thee this day."

"Master Words for which people?" said Mowgli, delighted to show off. "The jungle has many tongues. I know them all."

"A little thou knowest, but not much. See, O Bagheera, they never thank their teacher. Not one small wolfling has ever come back to thank old Baloo for his teachings. Say the word for the Hunting-People, then—great scholar."

"We be of one blood, ye and I," said Mowgli, giving the words the Bear accent which all the Hunting People use.

"Good. Now for the birds."

Mowgli repeated, with the Kite's whistle at the end of the sentence.

"Now for the Snake-People," said Bagheera.

The answer was a perfectly indescribable hiss, and Mowgli kicked up his feet behind, clapped his hands together to applaud himself, and jumped on to Bagheera's back, where he sat sideways, drumming with his heels on the glossy skin and making the worst faces he could think of at Baloo.

"There—there! That was worth a little bruise," said the brown bear tenderly. "Some day thou wilt remember me." Then he turned aside to tell Bagheera how he had begged the Master Words from Hathi the Wild Elephant, who knows all about these things, and how Hathi had taken Mowgli down to a pool to get the Snake Word from a water-snake, because Baloo could not pronounce it, and how Mowgli was now reasonably safe against all accidents in the jungle, because neither snake, bird, nor beast would hurt him.

"No one then is to be feared," Baloo wound up, patting his big furry stomach with pride.

"Except his own tribe," said Bagheera, under his breath; and then aloud to Mowgli, "Have a care for my ribs, Little Brother! What is all this dancing up and down?"

Mowgli had been trying to make himself heard by pulling at Bagheera's shoulder fur and kicking hard. When the two listened to him he was shouting at the top of his voice, "And so I shall have a tribe of my own, and lead them through the branches all day long."

"What is this new folly, little dreamer of dreams?" said Bagheera.

"Yes, and throw branches and dirt at old Baloo," Mowgli went on. "They have promised me this. Ah!"

"Whoof!" Baloo's big paw scooped Mowgli off Bagheera's back, and as the boy lay between the big forepaws he could see the Bear was angry.

"Mowgli," said Baloo, "thou hast been talking with the Bandar-log—the Monkey People."

Mowgli looked at Bagheera to see if the Panther was angry too, and Bagheera's eyes were as hard as jade stones.

"Thou hast been with the Monkey People—the gray apes—the people without a law—the eaters of everything. That is great shame."

"When Baloo hurt my head," said Mowgli (he was still on his back), "I went away, and the gray apes came down from the trees and had pity on me. No one else cared." He snuffled a little.

"The pity of the Monkey People!" Baloo snorted. "The stillness of the mountain stream! The cool of the summer sun! And then, man-cub?"

"And then, and then, they gave me nuts and pleasant things to eat, and they—they carried me in their arms up to the top of the trees and said I was their blood brother except that I had no tail, and should be their leader some day."

"They have no leader," said Bagheera. "They lie. They have always lied."

"They were very kind and bade me come again. Why have I never been taken among the Monkey People? They stand on their feet as I do. They do not hit me with their hard paws. They play all day. Let me get up! Bad Baloo, let me up! I will play with them again."

"Listen, man-cub," said the Bear, and his voice rumbled like thunder on a hot night. "I have taught thee all the Law of the Jungle for all the peoples of the jungle—except the Monkey-Folk who live in the trees. They have no law. They are outcasts. They have no speech of their own, but use the stolen words which they overhear when they listen, and peep, and wait up above in the branches. Their way is not our way. They are without leaders. They have no remembrance. They boast and chatter and pretend that they are a great people about to do great affairs in the jungle, but the falling of a nut turns their minds to laughter and all is forgotten. We of the jungle have no dealings with them. We do not drink where the monkeys drink; we do not go where the monkeys go; we do not hunt where they hunt; we do not die where they die. Hast thou ever heard me speak of the Bandar-log till today?"

"No," said Mowgli in a whisper, for the forest was very still now Baloo had finished.

"The Jungle-People put them out of their mouths and out of their minds. They are very many, evil, dirty, shameless, and they desire, if they have any fixed desire, to be noticed by the Jungle People. But we do not notice them even when they throw nuts and filth on our heads."

He had hardly spoken when a shower of nuts and twigs spattered down through the branches; and they could hear coughings and howlings and angry jumpings high up in the air among the thin branches.

"The Monkey-People are forbidden," said Baloo, "forbidden to the Jungle-People. Remember."

"Forbidden," said Bagheera, "but I still think Baloo should have warned thee against them."

"I—I? How was I to guess he would play with such dirt. The Monkey People! Faugh!"

A fresh shower came down on their heads and the two trotted away, taking Mowgli with them. What Baloo had said about the monkeys was perfectly true. They belonged to the tree-tops, and as beasts very seldom look up, there was no occasion for the monkeys and the Jungle-People to cross each other's path. But whenever they found a sick wolf, or a wounded tiger, or bear, the monkeys would torment him, and would throw sticks and nuts at any beast for fun and in the hope of being noticed. Then they would howl and shriek senseless songs, and invite the Jungle-People to climb up their trees and fight them, or would start furious battles over nothing among themselves, and leave the dead monkeys where the Jungle-People could see them. They were always just going to have a leader, and laws and customs of their own, but they never did, because their memories would not hold over from day to day, and so they compromised things by making up a saying, "What the Bandar-log think now the jungle will think later," and that comforted them a great deal. None of the beasts could reach them, but on the other hand none of the beasts would notice them, and that was why they were so pleased when Mowgli came to play with them, and they heard how angry Baloo was.

They never meant to do any more—the Bandar-log never mean anything at all; but one of them invented what seemed to him a brilliant idea, and he told all the others that Mowgli would be a useful person to keep in the tribe, because he could weave sticks together for protection from the wind; so, if they caught him, they could make him teach them. Of course Mowgli, as a woodcutter's child, inherited all sorts of instincts, and used to make little huts of fallen branches without thinking how he came to do it. The Monkey-People, watching in the trees, considered his play most wonderful. This time, they said, they were really going to have a leader and become the wisest people in the jungle—so wise that everyone else would notice and envy them. Therefore they followed Baloo and Bagheera and Mowgli through the jungle very quietly till it was time for the midday nap, and Mowgli, who was very much ashamed of himself, slept between the Panther and the Bear, resolving to have no more to do with the Monkey People.

The next thing he remembered was feeling hands on his legs and arms—hard, strong, little hands—and then a swash of branches in his face, and then he was staring down through the swaying boughs as Baloo woke the jungle with his deep cries and Bagheera bounded up the trunk with every tooth bared. The Bandar-log howled with triumph and scuffled away to the upper branches where Bagheera dared not follow, shouting: "He has noticed us! Bagheera has noticed us. All the Jungle-People admire us for our skill and our cunning." Then they began their flight; and the flight of the Monkey-People through tree-land is one of the things nobody can describe. They have their regular roads and crossroads, up hills and down hills, all laid out from fifty to seventy or a hundred feet above ground, and by these they can travel even at night if necessary. Two of the strongest monkeys caught Mowgli under the arms and swung off with him through the treetops, twenty feet at a bound. Had they been alone they could have gone twice as fast, but the boy's weight held them back. Sick and giddy as Mowgli was he could not help enjoying the wild rush, though the glimpses of earth far down below frightened him, and the terrible check and jerk at the end of the swing over nothing but empty air brought his heart between his teeth. His escort would rush him up a tree till he felt the thinnest topmost branches crackle and bend under them, and then with a cough and a whoop would fling themselves into the air outward and downward, and bring up, hanging by their hands or their feet to the lower limbs of the next tree. Sometimes he could see for miles and miles across the still green jungle, as a man on the top of a mast can see for miles across the sea, and then the branches and leaves would lash him across the face, and he and his two guards would be almost down to earth again. So, bounding and crashing and whooping and yelling, the whole tribe of Bandar-log swept along the tree-roads with Mowgli their prisoner.

For a time he was afraid of being dropped. Then he grew angry but knew better than to struggle, and then he began to think. The first thing was to send back word to Baloo and Bagheera, for, at the pace the monkeys were going, he knew his friends would be left far behind. It was useless to look down, for he could only see the topsides of the branches, so he stared upward and saw, far away in the blue, Rann the Kite balancing and wheeling as he kept watch over the jungle waiting for things to die. Rann saw that the monkeys were carrying something, and dropped a few hundred yards to find out whether their load was good to eat. He whistled with surprise when he saw Mowgli being dragged up to a treetop and heard him give the Kite call for—"We be of one blood, thou and I." The waves of the branches closed over the boy, but Rann balanced away to the next tree in time to see the little brown face come up again. "Mark my trail!" Mowgli shouted. "Tell Baloo of the Seeonee Pack and Bagheera of the Council Rock."

"In whose name, Brother?" Rann had never seen Mowgli before, though of course he had heard of him.

"Mowgli, the Frog. Man-cub they call me! Mark my trail!"

The last words were shrieked as he was being swung through the air, but Rann nodded and rose up till he looked no bigger than a speck of dust, and there he hung, watching with his telescope eyes the swaying of the treetops as Mowgli's escort whirled along.

"They never go far," he said with a chuckle. "They never do what they set out to do. Always pecking at new things are the Bandar-log. This time, if I have any eye-sight, they have pecked down trouble for themselves, for Baloo is no fledgling and Bagheera can, as I know, kill more than goats."

So he rocked on his wings, his feet gathered up under him, and waited.

Meantime, Baloo and Bagheera were furious with rage and grief. Bagheera climbed as he had never climbed before, but the thin branches broke beneath his weight, and he slipped down, his claws full of bark.

"Why didst thou not warn the man-cub?" he roared to poor Baloo, who had set off at a clumsy trot in the hope of overtaking the monkeys. "What was the use of half slaying him with blows if thou didst not warn him?"

"Haste! O haste! We—we may catch them yet!" Baloo panted.

"At that speed! It would not tire a wounded cow. Teacher of the Law—cub-beater—a mile of that rolling to and fro would burst thee open. Sit still and think! Make a plan. This is no time for chasing. They may drop him if we follow too close."

"Arrula! Whoo! They may have dropped him already, being tired of carrying him. Who can trust the Bandar-log? Put dead bats on my head! Give me black bones to eat! Roll me into the hives of the wild bees that I may be stung to death, and bury me with the Hyaena, for I am most miserable of bears! Arulala! Wahooa! O Mowgli, Mowgli! Why did I not warn thee against the Monkey-Folk instead of breaking thy head? Now perhaps I may have knocked the day's lesson out of his mind, and he will be alone in the jungle without the Master Words."

Baloo clasped his paws over his ears and rolled to and fro moaning.

"At least he gave me all the Words correctly a little time ago," said Bagheera impatiently. "Baloo, thou hast neither memory nor respect. What would the jungle think if I, the Black Panther, curled myself up like Ikki the Porcupine, and howled?"

"What do I care what the jungle thinks? He may be dead by now."

"Unless and until they drop him from the branches in sport, or kill him out of idleness, I have no fear for the man-cub. He is wise and well taught, and above all he has the eyes that make the Jungle-People afraid. But (and it is a great evil) he is in the power of the Bandar-log, and they, because they live in trees, have no fear of any of our people." Bagheera licked one forepaw thoughtfully.

"Fool that I am! Oh, fat, brown, root-digging fool that I am," said Baloo, uncoiling himself with a jerk, "it is true what Hathi the Wild Elephant says: `To each his own fear'; and they, the Bandar-log, fear Kaa the Rock Snake. He can climb as well as they can. He steals the young monkeys in the night. The whisper of his name makes their wicked tails cold. Let us go to Kaa."

"What will he do for us? He is not of our tribe, being footless—and with most evil eyes," said Bagheera.

"He is very old and very cunning. Above all, he is always hungry," said Baloo hopefully. "Promise him many goats."

"He sleeps for a full month after he has once eaten. He may be asleep now, and even were he awake what if he would rather kill his own goats?" Bagheera, who did not know much about Kaa, was naturally suspicious.

"Then in that case, thou and I together, old hunter, might make him see reason." Here Baloo rubbed his faded brown shoulder against the Panther, and they went off to look for Kaa the Rock Python.

They found him stretched out on a warm ledge in the afternoon sun, admiring his beautiful new coat, for he had been in retirement for the last ten days changing his skin, and now he was very splendid—darting his big blunt-nosed head along the ground, and twisting the thirty feet of his body into fantastic knots and curves, and licking his lips as he thought of his dinner to come.

"He has not eaten," said Baloo, with a grunt of relief, as soon as he saw the beautifully mottled brown and yellow jacket. "Be careful, Bagheera! He is always a little blind after he has changed his skin, and very quick to strike."

Kaa was not a poison snake—in fact he rather despised the poison snakes as cowards—but his strength lay in his hug, and when he had once lapped his huge coils round anybody there was no more to be said. "Good hunting!" cried Baloo, sitting up on his haunches. Like all snakes of his breed Kaa was rather deaf, and did not hear the call at first. Then he curled up ready for any accident, his head lowered.

"Good hunting for us all," he answered. "Oho, Baloo, what dost thou do here? Good hunting, Bagheera. One of us at least needs food. Is there any news of game afoot? A doe now, or even a young buck? I am as empty as a dried well."

"We are hunting," said Baloo carelessly. He knew that you must not hurry Kaa. He is too big.

"Give me permission to come with you," said Kaa. "A blow more or less is nothing to thee, Bagheera or Baloo, but I—I have to wait and wait for days in a wood-path and climb half a night on the mere chance of a young ape. Psshaw! The branches are not what they were when I was young. Rotten twigs and dry boughs are they all."

"Maybe thy great weight has something to do with the matter," said Baloo.

"I am a fair length—a fair length," said Kaa with a little pride. "But for all that, it is the fault of this new-grown timber. I came very near to falling on my last hunt—very near indeed—and the noise of my slipping, for my tail was not tight wrapped around the tree, waked the Bandar-log, and they called me most evil names."

"Footless, yellow earth-worm," said Bagheera under his whiskers, as though he were trying to remember something.

"Sssss! Have they ever called me that?" said Kaa.

"Something of that kind it was that they shouted to us last moon, but we never noticed them. They will say anything—even that thou hast lost all thy teeth, and wilt not face anything bigger than a kid, because (they are indeed shameless, these Bandar-log)—because thou art afraid of the he-goat's horns," Bagheera went on sweetly.

Now a snake, especially a wary old python like Kaa, very seldom shows that he is angry, but Baloo and Bagheera could see the big swallowing muscles on either side of Kaa's throat ripple and bulge.

"The Bandar-log have shifted their grounds," he said quietly. "When I came up into the sun today I heard them whooping among the tree-tops."

"It—it is the Bandar-log that we follow now," said Baloo, but the words stuck in his throat, for that was the first time in his memory that one of the Jungle-People had owned to being interested in the doings of the monkeys.

"Beyond doubt then it is no small thing that takes two such hunters—leaders in their own jungle I am certain—on the trail of the Bandar-log," Kaa replied courteously, as he swelled with curiosity.

"Indeed," Baloo began, "I am no more than the old and sometimes very foolish Teacher of the Law to the Seeonee wolf-cubs, and Bagheera here—"

"Is Bagheera," said the Black Panther, and his jaws shut with a snap, for he did not believe in being humble. "The trouble is this, Kaa. Those nut-stealers and pickers of palm leaves have stolen away our man-cub of whom thou hast perhaps heard."

"I heard some news from Ikki (his quills make him presumptuous) of a man-thing that was entered into a wolf pack, but I did not believe. Ikki is full of stories half heard and very badly told."

"But it is true. He is such a man-cub as never was," said Baloo. "The best and wisest and boldest of man-cubs—my own pupil, who shall make the name of Baloo famous through all the jungles; and besides, I—we—love him, Kaa."

"Ts! Ts!" said Kaa, weaving his head to and fro. "I also have known what love is. There are tales I could tell that—"

"That need a clear night when we are all well fed to praise properly," said Bagheera quickly. "Our man-cub is in the hands of the Bandar-log now, and we know that of all the Jungle-People they fear Kaa alone."

"They fear me alone. They have good reason," said Kaa. "Chattering, foolish, vain—vain, foolish, and chattering, are the monkeys. But a man-thing in their hands is in no good luck. They grow tired of the nuts they pick, and throw them down. They carry a branch half a day, meaning to do great things with it, and then they snap it in two. That man-thing is not to be envied. They called me also—`yellow fish' was it not?"

"Worm—worm—earth-worm," said Bagheera, "as well as other things which I cannot now say for shame."

"We must remind them to speak well of their master. Aaa-ssp! We must help their wandering memories. Now, whither went they with the cub?"

"The jungle alone knows. Toward the sunset, I believe," said Baloo. "We had thought that thou wouldst know, Kaa."

"I? How? I take them when they come in my way, but I do not hunt the Bandar-log, or frogs—or green scum on a water-hole, for that matter."

"Up, Up! Up, Up! Hillo! Illo! Illo, look up, Baloo of the Seeonee Wolf Pack!"

Baloo looked up to see where the voice came from, and there was Rann the Kite, sweeping down with the sun shining on the upturned flanges of his wings. It was near Rann's bedtime, but he had ranged all over the jungle looking for the Bear and had missed him in the thick foliage.

"What is it?" said Baloo.

"I have seen Mowgli among the Bandar-log. He bade me tell you. I watched. The Bandar-log have taken him beyond the river to the monkey city—to the Cold Lairs. They may stay there for a night, or ten nights, or an hour. I have told the bats to watch through the dark time. That is my message. Good hunting, all you below!"

"Full gorge and a deep sleep to you, Rann," cried Bagheera. "I will remember thee in my next kill, and put aside the head for thee alone, O best of kites!"

"It is nothing. It is nothing. The boy held the Master Word. I could have done no less," and Rann circled up again to his roost.

"He has not forgotten to use his tongue," said Baloo with a chuckle of pride. "To think of one so young remembering the Master Word for the birds too while he was being pulled across trees!"

"It was most firmly driven into him," said Bagheera. "But I am proud of him, and now we must go to the Cold Lairs."

They all knew where that place was, but few of the Jungle People ever went there, because what they called the Cold Lairs was an old deserted city, lost and buried in the jungle, and beasts seldom use a place that men have once used. The wild boar will, but the hunting tribes do not. Besides, the monkeys lived there as much as they could be said to live anywhere, and no self-respecting animal would come within eyeshot of it except in times of drought, when the half-ruined tanks and reservoirs held a little water.

"It is half a night's journey—at full speed," said Bagheera, and Baloo looked very serious. "I will go as fast as I can," he said anxiously.

"We dare not wait for thee. Follow, Baloo. We must go on the quick-foot—Kaa and I."

"Feet or no feet, I can keep abreast of all thy four," said Kaa shortly. Baloo made one effort to hurry, but had to sit down panting, and so they left him to come on later, while Bagheera hurried forward, at the quick panther-canter. Kaa said nothing, but, strive as Bagheera might, the huge Rock-python held level with him. When they came to a hill stream, Bagheera gained, because he bounded across while Kaa swam, his head and two feet of his neck clearing the water, but on level ground Kaa made up the distance.

"By the Broken Lock that freed me," said Bagheera, when twilight had fallen, "thou art no slow goer!"

"I am hungry," said Kaa. "Besides, they called me speckled frog."

"Worm—earth-worm, and yellow to boot."

"All one. Let us go on," and Kaa seemed to pour himself along the ground, finding the shortest road with his steady eyes, and keeping to it.

In the Cold Lairs the Monkey-People were not thinking of Mowgli's friends at all. They had brought the boy to the Lost City, and were very much pleased with themselves for the time. Mowgli had never seen an Indian city before, and though this was almost a heap of ruins it seemed very wonderful and splendid. Some king had built it long ago on a little hill. You could still trace the stone causeways that led up to the ruined gates where the last splinters of wood hung to the worn, rusted hinges. Trees had grown into and out of the walls; the battlements were tumbled down and decayed, and wild creepers hung out of the windows of the towers on the walls in bushy hanging clumps.

A great roofless palace crowned the hill, and the marble of the courtyards and the fountains was split, and stained with red and green, and the very cobblestones in the courtyard where the king's elephants used to live had been thrust up and apart by grasses and young trees. From the palace you could see the rows and rows of roofless houses that made up the city looking like empty honeycombs filled with blackness; the shapeless block of stone that had been an idol in the square where four roads met; the pits and dimples at street corners where the public wells once stood, and the shattered domes of temples with wild figs sprouting on their sides. The monkeys called the place their city, and pretended to despise the Jungle-People because they lived in the forest. And yet they never knew what the buildings were made for nor how to use them. They would sit in circles on the hall of the king's council chamber, and scratch for fleas and pretend to be men; or they would run in and out of the roofless houses and collect pieces of plaster and old bricks in a corner, and forget where they had hidden them, and fight and cry in scuffling crowds, and then break off to play up and down the terraces of the king's garden, where they would shake the rose trees and the oranges in sport to see the fruit and flowers fall. They explored all the passages and dark tunnels in the palace and the hundreds of little dark rooms, but they never remembered what they had seen and what they had not; and so drifted about in ones and twos or crowds telling each other that they were doing as men did. They drank at the tanks and made the water all muddy, and then they fought over it, and then they would all rush together in mobs and shout: "There is no one in the jungle so wise and good and clever and strong and gentle as the Bandar-log." Then all would begin again till they grew tired of the city and went back to the tree-tops, hoping the Jungle-People would notice them.

Mowgli, who had been trained under the Law of the Jungle, did not like or understand this kind of life.

The monkeys dragged him into the Cold Lairs late in the afternoon, and instead of going to sleep, as Mowgli would have done after a long journey, they joined hands and danced about and sang their foolish songs. One of the monkeys made a speech and told his companions that Mowgli's capture marked a new thing in the history of the Bandar-log, for Mowgli was going to show them how to weave sticks and canes together as a protection against rain and cold. Mowgli picked up some creepers and began to work them in and out, and the monkeys tried to imitate; but in a very few minutes they lost interest and began to pull their friends' tails or jump up and down on all fours, coughing.

"I wish to eat," said Mowgli. "I am a stranger in this part of the jungle. Bring me food, or give me leave to hunt here."

Twenty or thirty monkeys bounded away to bring him nuts and wild pawpaws. But they fell to fighting on the road, and it was too much trouble to go back with what was left of the fruit. Mowgli was sore and angry as well as hungry, and he roamed through the empty city giving the Strangers' Hunting Call from time to time, but no one answered him, and Mowgli felt that he had reached a very bad place indeed. "All that Baloo has said about the Bandar-log is true," he thought to himself. "They have no Law, no Hunting Call, and no leaders—nothing but foolish words and little picking thievish hands. So if I am starved or killed here, it will be all my own fault. But I must try to return to my own jungle. Baloo will surely beat me, but that is better than chasing silly rose leaves with the Bandar-log."

No sooner had he walked to the city wall than the monkeys pulled him back, telling him that he did not know how happy he was, and pinching him to make him grateful. He set his teeth and said nothing, but went with the shouting monkeys to a terrace above the red sandstone reservoirs that were half-full of rain water. There was a ruined summer-house of white marble in the center of the terrace, built for queens dead a hundred years ago. The domed roof had half fallen in and blocked up the underground passage from the palace by which the queens used to enter. But the walls were made of screens of marble tracery—beautiful milk-white fretwork, set with agates and cornelians and jasper and lapis lazuli, and as the moon came up behind the hill it shone through the open work, casting shadows on the ground like black velvet embroidery. Sore, sleepy, and hungry as he was, Mowgli could not help laughing when the Bandar-log began, twenty at a time, to tell him how great and wise and strong and gentle they were, and how foolish he was to wish to leave them. "We are great. We are free. We are wonderful. We are the most wonderful people in all the jungle! We all say so, and so it must be true," they shouted. "Now as you are a new listener and can carry our words back to the Jungle-People so that they may notice us in future, we will tell you all about our most excellent selves." Mowgli made no objection, and the monkeys gathered by hundreds and hundreds on the terrace to listen to their own speakers singing the praises of the Bandar-log, and whenever a speaker stopped for want of breath they would all shout together: "This is true; we all say so." Mowgli nodded and blinked, and said "Yes" when they asked him a question, and his head spun with the noise. "Tabaqui the Jackal must have bitten all these people," he said to himself, "and now they have madness. Certainly this is dewanee, the madness. Do they never go to sleep? Now there is a cloud coming to cover that moon. If it were only a big enough cloud I might try to run away in the darkness. But I am tired."

That same cloud was being watched by two good friends in the ruined ditch below the city wall, for Bagheera and Kaa, knowing well how dangerous the Monkey-People were in large numbers, did not wish to run any risks. The monkeys never fight unless they are a hundred to one, and few in the jungle care for those odds.

"I will go to the west wall," Kaa whispered, "and come down swiftly with the slope of the ground in my favor. They will not throw themselves upon my back in their hundreds, but—"

"I know it," said Bagheera. "Would that Baloo were here, but we must do what we can. When that cloud covers the moon I shall go to the terrace. They hold some sort of council there over the boy."

"Good hunting," said Kaa grimly, and glided away to the west wall. That happened to be the least ruined of any, and the big snake was delayed awhile before he could find a way up the stones. The cloud hid the moon, and as Mowgli wondered what would come next he heard Bagheera's light feet on the terrace. The Black Panther had raced up the slope almost without a sound and was striking—he knew better than to waste time in biting—right and left among the monkeys, who were seated round Mowgli in circles fifty and sixty deep. There was a howl of fright and rage, and then as Bagheera tripped on the rolling kicking bodies beneath him, a monkey shouted: "There is only one here! Kill him! Kill." A scuffling mass of monkeys, biting, scratching, tearing, and pulling, closed over Bagheera, while five or six laid hold of Mowgli, dragged him up the wall of the summerhouse and pushed him through the hole of the broken dome. A man-trained boy would have been badly bruised, for the fall was a good fifteen feet, but Mowgli fell as Baloo had taught him to fall, and landed on his feet.

"Stay there," shouted the monkeys, "till we have killed thy friends, and later we will play with thee—if the Poison-People leave thee alive."

"We be of one blood, ye and I," said Mowgli, quickly giving the Snake's Call. He could hear rustling and hissing in the rubbish all round him and gave the Call a second time, to make sure.

"Even ssso! Down hoods all!" said half a dozen low voices (every ruin in India becomes sooner or later a dwelling place of snakes, and the old summerhouse was alive with cobras). "Stand still, Little Brother, for thy feet may do us harm."

Mowgli stood as quietly as he could, peering through the open work and listening to the furious din of the fight round the Black Panther—the yells and chatterings and scufflings, and Bagheera's deep, hoarse cough as he backed and bucked and twisted and plunged under the heaps of his enemies. For the first time since he was born, Bagheera was fighting for his life.

"Baloo must be at hand; Bagheera would not have come alone," Mowgli thought. And then he called aloud: "To the tank, Bagheera. Roll to the water tanks. Roll and plunge! Get to the water!"

Bagheera heard, and the cry that told him Mowgli was safe gave him new courage. He worked his way desperately, inch by inch, straight for the reservoirs, halting in silence. Then from the ruined wall nearest the jungle rose up the rumbling war-shout of Baloo. The old Bear had done his best, but he could not come before. "Bagheera," he shouted, "I am here. I climb! I haste! Ahuwora! The stones slip under my feet! Wait my coming, O most infamous Bandar-log!" He panted up the terrace only to disappear to the head in a wave of monkeys, but he threw himself squarely on his haunches, and, spreading out his forepaws, hugged as many as he could hold, and then began to hit with a regular bat-bat-bat, like the flipping strokes of a paddle wheel. A crash and a splash told Mowgli that Bagheera had fought his way to the tank where the monkeys could not follow. The Panther lay gasping for breath, his head just out of the water, while the monkeys stood three deep on the red steps, dancing up and down with rage, ready to spring upon him from all sides if he came out to help Baloo. It was then that Bagheera lifted up his dripping chin, and in despair gave the Snake's Call for protection—"We be of one blood, ye and I"—for he believed that Kaa had turned tail at the last minute. Even Baloo, half smothered under the monkeys on the edge of the terrace, could not help chuckling as he heard the Black Panther asking for help.

Kaa had only just worked his way over the west wall, landing with a wrench that dislodged a coping stone into the ditch. He had no intention of losing any advantage of the ground, and coiled and uncoiled himself once or twice, to be sure that every foot of his long body was in working order. All that while the fight with Baloo went on, and the monkeys yelled in the tank round Bagheera, and Mang the Bat, flying to and fro, carried the news of the great battle over the jungle, till even Hathi the Wild Elephant trumpeted, and, far away, scattered bands of the Monkey-Folk woke and came leaping along the tree-roads to help their comrades in the Cold Lairs, and the noise of the fight roused all the day birds for miles round. Then Kaa came straight, quickly, and anxious to kill. The fighting strength of a python is in the driving blow of his head backed by all the strength and weight of his body. If you can imagine a lance, or a battering ram, or a hammer weighing nearly half a ton driven by a cool, quiet mind living in the handle of it, you can roughly imagine what Kaa was like when he fought. A python four or five feet long can knock a man down if he hits him fairly in the chest, and Kaa was thirty feet long, as you know. His first stroke was delivered into the heart of the crowd round Baloo. It was sent home with shut mouth in silence, and there was no need of a second. The monkeys scattered with cries of—"Kaa! It is Kaa! Run! Run!"

Generations of monkeys had been scared into good behavior by the stories their elders told them of Kaa, the night thief, who could slip along the branches as quietly as moss grows, and steal away the strongest monkey that ever lived; of old Kaa, who could make himself look so like a dead branch or a rotten stump that the wisest were deceived, till the branch caught them. Kaa was everything that the monkeys feared in the jungle, for none of them knew the limits of his power, none of them could look him in the face, and none had ever come alive out of his hug. And so they ran, stammering with terror, to the walls and the roofs of the houses, and Baloo drew a deep breath of relief. His fur was much thicker than Bagheera's, but he had suffered sorely in the fight. Then Kaa opened his mouth for the first time and spoke one long hissing word, and the far-away monkeys, hurrying to the defense of the Cold Lairs, stayed where they were, cowering, till the loaded branches bent and crackled under them. The monkeys on the walls and the empty houses stopped their cries, and in the stillness that fell upon the city Mowgli heard Bagheera shaking his wet sides as he came up from the tank. Then the clamor broke out again. The monkeys leaped higher up the walls. They clung around the necks of the big stone idols and shrieked as they skipped along the battlements, while Mowgli, dancing in the summerhouse, put his eye to the screenwork and hooted owl-fashion between his front teeth, to show his derision and contempt.

"Get the man-cub out of that trap; I can do no more," Bagheera gasped. "Let us take the man-cub and go. They may attack again."

"They will not move till I order them. Stay you sssso!" Kaa hissed, and the city was silent once more. "I could not come before, Brother, but I think I heard thee call"—this was to Bagheera.

"I—I may have cried out in the battle," Bagheera answered. "Baloo, art thou hurt?"

"I am not sure that they did not pull me into a hundred little bearlings," said Baloo, gravely shaking one leg after the other. "Wow! I am sore. Kaa, we owe thee, I think, our lives—Bagheera and I."

"No matter. Where is the manling?"

"Here, in a trap. I cannot climb out," cried Mowgli. The curve of the broken dome was above his head.

"Take him away. He dances like Mao the Peacock. He will crush our young," said the cobras inside.

"Hah!" said Kaa with a chuckle, "he has friends everywhere, this manling. Stand back, manling. And hide you, O Poison People. I break down the wall."

Kaa looked carefully till he found a discolored crack in the marble tracery showing a weak spot, made two or three light taps with his head to get the distance, and then lifting up six feet of his body clear of the ground, sent home half a dozen full-power smashing blows, nose-first. The screen-work broke and fell away in a cloud of dust and rubbish, and Mowgli leaped through the opening and flung himself between Baloo and Bagheera—an arm around each big neck.

"Art thou hurt?" said Baloo, hugging him softly.

"I am sore, hungry, and not a little bruised. But, oh, they have handled ye grievously, my Brothers! Ye bleed."

"Others also," said Bagheera, licking his lips and looking at the monkey-dead on the terrace and round the tank.

"It is nothing, it is nothing, if thou art safe, oh, my pride of all little frogs!" whimpered Baloo.

"Of that we shall judge later," said Bagheera, in a dry voice that Mowgli did not at all like. "But here is Kaa to whom we owe the battle and thou owest thy life. Thank him according to our customs, Mowgli."

Mowgli turned and saw the great Python's head swaying a foot above his own.

"So this is the manling," said Kaa. "Very soft is his skin, and he is not unlike the Bandar-log. Have a care, manling, that I do not mistake thee for a monkey some twilight when I have newly changed my coat."

"We be one blood, thou and I," Mowgli answered. "I take my life from thee tonight. My kill shall be thy kill if ever thou art hungry, O Kaa."

"All thanks, Little Brother," said Kaa, though his eyes twinkled. "And what may so bold a hunter kill? I ask that I may follow when next he goes abroad."

"I kill nothing,—I am too little,—but I drive goats toward such as can use them. When thou art empty come to me and see if I speak the truth. I have some skill in these [he held out his hands], and if ever thou art in a trap, I may pay the debt which I owe to thee, to Bagheera, and to Baloo, here. Good hunting to ye all, my masters."

"Well said," growled Baloo, for Mowgli had returned thanks very prettily. The Python dropped his head lightly for a minute on Mowgli's shoulder. "A brave heart and a courteous tongue," said he. "They shall carry thee far through the jungle, manling. But now go hence quickly with thy friends. Go and sleep, for the moon sets, and what follows it is not well that thou shouldst see."

The moon was sinking behind the hills and the lines of trembling monkeys huddled together on the walls and battlements looked like ragged shaky fringes of things. Baloo went down to the tank for a drink and Bagheera began to put his fur in order, as Kaa glided out into the center of the terrace and brought his jaws together with a ringing snap that drew all the monkeys' eyes upon him.

"The moon sets," he said. "Is there yet light enough to see?"

From the walls came a moan like the wind in the tree-tops—"We see, O Kaa."

"Good. Begins now the dance—the Dance of the Hunger of Kaa. Sit still and watch."

He turned twice or thrice in a big circle, weaving his head from right to left. Then he began making loops and figures of eight with his body, and soft, oozy triangles that melted into squares and five-sided figures, and coiled mounds, never resting, never hurrying, and never stopping his low humming song. It grew darker and darker, till at last the dragging, shifting coils disappeared, but they could hear the rustle of the scales.

Baloo and Bagheera stood still as stone, growling in their throats, their neck hair bristling, and Mowgli watched and wondered.

"Bandar-log," said the voice of Kaa at last, "can ye stir foot or hand without my order? Speak!"

"Without thy order we cannot stir foot or hand, O Kaa!"

"Good! Come all one pace nearer to me."

The lines of the monkeys swayed forward helplessly, and Baloo and Bagheera took one stiff step forward with them.

"Nearer!" hissed Kaa, and they all moved again.

Mowgli laid his hands on Baloo and Bagheera to get them away, and the two great beasts started as though they had been waked from a dream.

"Keep thy hand on my shoulder," Bagheera whispered. "Keep it there, or I must go back—must go back to Kaa. Aah!"

"It is only old Kaa making circles on the dust," said Mowgli. "Let us go." And the three slipped off through a gap in the walls to the jungle.

"Whoof!" said Baloo, when he stood under the still trees again. "Never more will I make an ally of Kaa," and he shook himself all over.

"He knows more than we," said Bagheera, trembling. "In a little time, had I stayed, I should have walked down his throat."

"Many will walk by that road before the moon rises again," said Baloo. "He will have good hunting—after his own fashion."

"But what was the meaning of it all?" said Mowgli, who did not know anything of a python's powers of fascination. "I saw no more than a big snake making foolish circles till the dark came. And his nose was all sore. Ho! Ho!"

"Mowgli," said Bagheera angrily, "his nose was sore on thy account, as my ears and sides and paws, and Baloo's neck and shoulders are bitten on thy account. Neither Baloo nor Bagheera will be able to hunt with pleasure for many days."

"It is nothing," said Baloo; "we have the man-cub again."

"True, but he has cost us heavily in time which might have been spent in good hunting, in wounds, in hair—I am half plucked along my back—and last of all, in honor. For, remember, Mowgli, I, who am the Black Panther, was forced to call upon Kaa for protection, and Baloo and I were both made stupid as little birds by the Hunger Dance. All this, man-cub, came of thy playing with the Bandar-log."

"True, it is true," said Mowgli sorrowfully. "I am an evil man-cub, and my stomach is sad in me."

"Mf! What says the Law of the Jungle, Baloo?"

Baloo did not wish to bring Mowgli into any more trouble, but he could not tamper with the Law, so he mumbled: "Sorrow never stays punishment. But remember, Bagheera, he is very little."

"I will remember. But he has done mischief, and blows must be dealt now. Mowgli, hast thou anything to say?"

"Nothing. I did wrong. Baloo and thou are wounded. It is just."

Bagheera gave him half a dozen love-taps from a panther's point of view (they would hardly have waked one of his own cubs), but for a seven-year-old boy they amounted to as severe a beating as you could wish to avoid. When it was all over Mowgli sneezed, and picked himself up without a word.

"Now," said Bagheera, "jump on my back, Little Brother, and we will go home."

One of the beauties of Jungle Law is that punishment settles all scores. There is no nagging afterward.

Mowgli laid his head down on Bagheera's back and slept so deeply that he never waked when he was put down in the home-cave.

"Tiger! Tiger!"

Now we must go back to the first tale. When Mowgli left the wolf's cave after the fight with the Pack at the Council Rock, he went down to the plowed lands where the villagers lived, but he would not stop there because it was too near to the jungle, and he knew that he had made at least one bad enemy at the Council. So he hurried on, keeping to the rough road that ran down the valley, and followed it at a steady jog-trot for nearly twenty miles, till he came to a country that he did not know. The valley opened out into a great plain dotted over with rocks and cut up by ravines. At one end stood a little village, and at the other the thick jungle came down in a sweep to the grazing-grounds, and stopped there as though it had been cut off with a hoe. All over the plain, cattle and buffaloes were grazing, and when the little boys in charge of the herds saw Mowgli they shouted and ran away, and the yellow pariah dogs that hang about every Indian village barked. Mowgli walked on, for he was feeling hungry, and when he came to the village gate he saw the big thorn-bush that was drawn up before the gate at twilight, pushed to one side.

"Umph!" he said, for he had come across more than one such barricade in his night rambles after things to eat. "So men are afraid of the People of the Jungle here also." He sat down by the gate, and when a man came out he stood up, opened his mouth, and pointed down it to show that he wanted food. The man stared, and ran back up the one street of the village shouting for the priest, who was a big, fat man dressed in white, with a red and yellow mark on his forehead. The priest came to the gate, and with him at least a hundred people, who stared and talked and shouted and pointed at Mowgli.

"They have no manners, these Men Folk," said Mowgli to himself. "Only the gray ape would behave as they do." So he threw back his long hair and frowned at the crowd.

"What is there to be afraid of?" said the priest. "Look at the marks on his arms and legs. They are the bites of wolves. He is but a wolf-child run away from the jungle."

Of course, in playing together, the cubs had often nipped Mowgli harder than they intended, and there were white scars all over his arms and legs. But he would have been the last person in the world to call these bites, for he knew what real biting meant.

"Arre! Arre!" said two or three women together. "To be bitten by wolves, poor child! He is a handsome boy. He has eyes like red fire. By my honor, Messua, he is not unlike thy boy that was taken by the tiger."

"Let me look," said a woman with heavy copper rings on her wrists and ankles, and she peered at Mowgli under the palm of her hand. "Indeed he is not. He is thinner, but he has the very look of my boy."

The priest was a clever man, and he knew that Messua was wife to the richest villager in the place. So he looked up at the sky for a minute and said solemnly: "What the jungle has taken the jungle has restored. Take the boy into thy house, my sister, and forget not to honor the priest who sees so far into the lives of men."

"By the Bull that bought me," said Mowgli to himself, "but all this talking is like another looking-over by the Pack! Well, if I am a man, a man I must become."

The crowd parted as the woman beckoned Mowgli to her hut, where there was a red lacquered bedstead, a great earthen grain chest with funny raised patterns on it, half a dozen copper cooking pots, an image of a Hindu god in a little alcove, and on the wall a real looking glass, such as they sell at the country fairs.

She gave him a long drink of milk and some bread, and then she laid her hand on his head and looked into his eyes; for she thought perhaps that he might be her real son come back from the jungle where the tiger had taken him. So she said, "Nathoo, O Nathoo!" Mowgli did not show that he knew the name. "Dost thou not remember the day when I gave thee thy new shoes?" She touched his foot, and it was almost as hard as horn. "No," she said sorrowfully, "those feet have never worn shoes, but thou art very like my Nathoo, and thou shalt be my son."

Mowgli was uneasy, because he had never been under a roof before. But as he looked at the thatch, he saw that he could tear it out any time if he wanted to get away, and that the window had no fastenings. "What is the good of a man," he said to himself at last, "if he does not understand man's talk? Now I am as silly and dumb as a man would be with us in the jungle. I must speak their talk."

It was not for fun that he had learned while he was with the wolves to imitate the challenge of bucks in the jungle and the grunt of the little wild pig. So, as soon as Messua pronounced a word Mowgli would imitate it almost perfectly, and before dark he had learned the names of many things in the hut.

There was a difficulty at bedtime, because Mowgli would not sleep under anything that looked so like a panther trap as that hut, and when they shut the door he went through the window. "Give him his will," said Messua's husband. "Remember he can never till now have slept on a bed. If he is indeed sent in the place of our son he will not run away."

So Mowgli stretched himself in some long, clean grass at the edge of the field, but before he had closed his eyes a soft gray nose poked him under the chin.

"Phew!" said Gray Brother (he was the eldest of Mother Wolf's cubs). "This is a poor reward for following thee twenty miles. Thou smellest of wood smoke and cattle—altogether like a man already. Wake, Little Brother; I bring news."

"Are all well in the jungle?" said Mowgli, hugging him.

"All except the wolves that were burned with the Red Flower. Now, listen. Shere Khan has gone away to hunt far off till his coat grows again, for he is badly singed. When he returns he swears that he will lay thy bones in the Waingunga."

"There are two words to that. I also have made a little promise. But news is always good. I am tired to-night,—very tired with new things, Gray Brother,—but bring me the news always."

"Thou wilt not forget that thou art a wolf? Men will not make thee forget?" said Gray Brother anxiously.

"Never. I will always remember that I love thee and all in our cave. But also I will always remember that I have been cast out of the Pack."

"And that thou mayest be cast out of another pack. Men are only men, Little Brother, and their talk is like the talk of frogs in a pond. When I come down here again, I will wait for thee in the bamboos at the edge of the grazing-ground."

For three months after that night Mowgli hardly ever left the village gate, he was so busy learning the ways and customs of men. First he had to wear a cloth round him, which annoyed him horribly; and then he had to learn about money, which he did not in the least understand, and about plowing, of which he did not see the use. Then the little children in the village made him very angry. Luckily, the Law of the Jungle had taught him to keep his temper, for in the jungle life and food depend on keeping your temper; but when they made fun of him because he would not play games or fly kites, or because he mispronounced some word, only the knowledge that it was unsportsmanlike to kill little naked cubs kept him from picking them up and breaking them in two.

He did not know his own strength in the least. In the jungle he knew he was weak compared with the beasts, but in the village people said that he was as strong as a bull.

And Mowgli had not the faintest idea of the difference that caste makes between man and man. When the potter's donkey slipped in the clay pit, Mowgli hauled it out by the tail, and helped to stack the pots for their journey to the market at Khanhiwara. That was very shocking, too, for the potter is a low-caste man, and his donkey is worse. When the priest scolded him, Mowgli threatened to put him on the donkey too, and the priest told Messua's husband that Mowgli had better be set to work as soon as possible; and the village head-man told Mowgli that he would have to go out with the buffaloes next day, and herd them while they grazed. No one was more pleased than Mowgli; and that night, because he had been appointed a servant of the village, as it were, he went off to a circle that met every evening on a masonry platform under a great fig-tree. It was the village club, and the head-man and the watchman and the barber, who knew all the gossip of the village, and old Buldeo, the village hunter, who had a Tower musket, met and smoked. The monkeys sat and talked in the upper branches, and there was a hole under the platform where a cobra lived, and he had his little platter of milk every night because he was sacred; and the old men sat around the tree and talked, and pulled at the big huqas (the water-pipes) till far into the night. They told wonderful tales of gods and men and ghosts; and Buldeo told even more wonderful ones of the ways of beasts in the jungle, till the eyes of the children sitting outside the circle bulged out of their heads. Most of the tales were about animals, for the jungle was always at their door. The deer and the wild pig grubbed up their crops, and now and again the tiger carried off a man at twilight, within sight of the village gates.

Mowgli, who naturally knew something about what they were talking of, had to cover his face not to show that he was laughing, while Buldeo, the Tower musket across his knees, climbed on from one wonderful story to another, and Mowgli's shoulders shook.

Buldeo was explaining how the tiger that had carried away Messua's son was a ghost-tiger, and his body was inhabited by the ghost of a wicked, old money-lender, who had died some years ago. "And I know that this is true," he said, "because Purun Dass always limped from the blow that he got in a riot when his account books were burned, and the tiger that I speak of he limps, too, for the tracks of his pads are unequal."

"True, true, that must be the truth," said the gray-beards, nodding together.

"Are all these tales such cobwebs and moon talk?" said Mowgli. "That tiger limps because he was born lame, as everyone knows. To talk of the soul of a money-lender in a beast that never had the courage of a jackal is child's talk."

Buldeo was speechless with surprise for a moment, and the head-man stared.

"Oho! It is the jungle brat, is it?" said Buldeo. "If thou art so wise, better bring his hide to Khanhiwara, for the Government has set a hundred rupees on his life. Better still, talk not when thy elders speak."

Mowgli rose to go. "All the evening I have lain here listening," he called back over his shoulder, "and, except once or twice, Buldeo has not said one word of truth concerning the jungle, which is at his very doors. How, then, shall I believe the tales of ghosts and gods and goblins which he says he has seen?"

"It is full time that boy went to herding," said the head-man, while Buldeo puffed and snorted at Mowgli's impertinence.

The custom of most Indian villages is for a few boys to take the cattle and buffaloes out to graze in the early morning, and bring them back at night. The very cattle that would trample a white man to death allow themselves to be banged and bullied and shouted at by children that hardly come up to their noses. So long as the boys keep with the herds they are safe, for not even the tiger will charge a mob of cattle. But if they straggle to pick flowers or hunt lizards, they are sometimes carried off. Mowgli went through the village street in the dawn, sitting on the back of Rama, the great herd bull. The slaty-blue buffaloes, with their long, backward-sweeping horns and savage eyes, rose out their byres, one by one, and followed him, and Mowgli made it very clear to the children with him that he was the master. He beat the buffaloes with a long, polished bamboo, and told Kamya, one of the boys, to graze the cattle by themselves, while he went on with the buffaloes, and to be very careful not to stray away from the herd.

An Indian grazing ground is all rocks and scrub and tussocks and little ravines, among which the herds scatter and disappear. The buffaloes generally keep to the pools and muddy places, where they lie wallowing or basking in the warm mud for hours. Mowgli drove them on to the edge of the plain where the Waingunga came out of the jungle; then he dropped from Rama's neck, trotted off to a bamboo clump, and found Gray Brother. "Ah," said Gray Brother, "I have waited here very many days. What is the meaning of this cattle-herding work?"

"It is an order," said Mowgli. "I am a village herd for a while. What news of Shere Khan?"

"He has come back to this country, and has waited here a long time for thee. Now he has gone off again, for the game is scarce. But he means to kill thee."

"Very good," said Mowgli. "So long as he is away do thou or one of the four brothers sit on that rock, so that I can see thee as I come out of the village. When he comes back wait for me in the ravine by the dhak tree in the center of the plain. We need not walk into Shere Khan's mouth."

Then Mowgli picked out a shady place, and lay down and slept while the buffaloes grazed round him. Herding in India is one of the laziest things in the world. The cattle move and crunch, and lie down, and move on again, and they do not even low. They only grunt, and the buffaloes very seldom say anything, but get down into the muddy pools one after another, and work their way into the mud till only their noses and staring china-blue eyes show above the surface, and then they lie like logs. The sun makes the rocks dance in the heat, and the herd children hear one kite (never any more) whistling almost out of sight overhead, and they know that if they died, or a cow died, that kite would sweep down, and the next kite miles away would see him drop and follow, and the next, and the next, and almost before they were dead there would be a score of hungry kites come out of nowhere. Then they sleep and wake and sleep again, and weave little baskets of dried grass and put grasshoppers in them; or catch two praying mantises and make them fight; or string a necklace of red and black jungle nuts; or watch a lizard basking on a rock, or a snake hunting a frog near the wallows. Then they sing long, long songs with odd native quavers at the end of them, and the day seems longer than most people's whole lives, and perhaps they make a mud castle with mud figures of men and horses and buffaloes, and put reeds into the men's hands, and pretend that they are kings and the figures are their armies, or that they are gods to be worshiped. Then evening comes and the children call, and the buffaloes lumber up out of the sticky mud with noises like gunshots going off one after the other, and they all string across the gray plain back to the twinkling village lights.

Day after day Mowgli would lead the buffaloes out to their wallows, and day after day he would see Gray Brother's back a mile and a half away across the plain (so he knew that Shere Khan had not come back), and day after day he would lie on the grass listening to the noises round him, and dreaming of old days in the jungle. If Shere Khan had made a false step with his lame paw up in the jungles by the Waingunga, Mowgli would have heard him in those long, still mornings.

At last a day came when he did not see Gray Brother at the signal place, and he laughed and headed the buffaloes for the ravine by the dhk tree, which was all covered with golden-red flowers. There sat Gray Brother, every bristle on his back lifted.

"He has hidden for a month to throw thee off thy guard. He crossed the ranges last night with Tabaqui, hot-foot on thy trail," said the Wolf, panting.

Mowgli frowned. "I am not afraid of Shere Khan, but Tabaqui is very cunning."

"Have no fear," said Gray Brother, licking his lips a little. "I met Tabaqui in the dawn. Now he is telling all his wisdom to the kites, but he told me everything before I broke his back. Shere Khan's plan is to wait for thee at the village gate this evening—for thee and for no one else. He is lying up now, in the big dry ravine of the Waingunga."

"Has he eaten today, or does he hunt empty?" said Mowgli, for the answer meant life and death to him.

"He killed at dawn,—a pig,—and he has drunk too. Remember, Shere Khan could never fast, even for the sake of revenge."

"Oh! Fool, fool! What a cub's cub it is! Eaten and drunk too, and he thinks that I shall wait till he has slept! Now, where does he lie up? If there were but ten of us we might pull him down as he lies. These buffaloes will not charge unless they wind him, and I cannot speak their language. Can we get behind his track so that they may smell it?"

"He swam far down the Waingunga to cut that off," said Gray Brother.

"Tabaqui told him that, I know. He would never have thought of it alone." Mowgli stood with his finger in his mouth, thinking. "The big ravine of the Waingunga. That opens out on the plain not half a mile from here. I can take the herd round through the jungle to the head of the ravine and then sweep down—but he would slink out at the foot. We must block that end. Gray Brother, canst thou cut the herd in two for me?"

"Not I, perhaps—but I have brought a wise helper." Gray Brother trotted off and dropped into a hole. Then there lifted up a huge gray head that Mowgli knew well, and the hot air was filled with the most desolate cry of all the jungle—the hunting howl of a wolf at midday.

"Akela! Akela!" said Mowgli, clapping his hands. "I might have known that thou wouldst not forget me. We have a big work in hand. Cut the herd in two, Akela. Keep the cows and calves together, and the bulls and the plow buffaloes by themselves."

The two wolves ran, ladies'-chain fashion, in and out of the herd, which snorted and threw up its head, and separated into two clumps. In one, the cow-buffaloes stood with their calves in the center, and glared and pawed, ready, if a wolf would only stay still, to charge down and trample the life out of him. In the other, the bulls and the young bulls snorted and stamped, but though they looked more imposing they were much less dangerous, for they had no calves to protect. No six men could have divided the herd so neatly.

"What orders!" panted Akela. "They are trying to join again."

Mowgli slipped on to Rama's back. "Drive the bulls away to the left, Akela. Gray Brother, when we are gone, hold the cows together, and drive them into the foot of the ravine."

"How far?" said Gray Brother, panting and snapping.

"Till the sides are higher than Shere Khan can jump," shouted Mowgli. "Keep them there till we come down." The bulls swept off as Akela bayed, and Gray Brother stopped in front of the cows. They charged down on him, and he ran just before them to the foot of the ravine, as Akela drove the bulls far to the left.

"Well done! Another charge and they are fairly started. Careful, now—careful, Akela. A snap too much and the bulls will charge. Hujah! This is wilder work than driving black-buck. Didst thou think these creatures could move so swiftly?" Mowgli called.

"I have—have hunted these too in my time," gasped Akela in the dust. "Shall I turn them into the jungle?"

"Ay! Turn. Swiftly turn them! Rama is mad with rage. Oh, if I could only tell him what I need of him to-day."

The bulls were turned, to the right this time, and crashed into the standing thicket. The other herd children, watching with the cattle half a mile away, hurried to the village as fast as their legs could carry them, crying that the buffaloes had gone mad and run away.

But Mowgli's plan was simple enough. All he wanted to do was to make a big circle uphill and get at the head of the ravine, and then take the bulls down it and catch Shere Khan between the bulls and the cows; for he knew that after a meal and a full drink Shere Khan would not be in any condition to fight or to clamber up the sides of the ravine. He was soothing the buffaloes now by voice, and Akela had dropped far to the rear, only whimpering once or twice to hurry the rear-guard. It was a long, long circle, for they did not wish to get too near the ravine and give Shere Khan warning. At last Mowgli rounded up the bewildered herd at the head of the ravine on a grassy patch that sloped steeply down to the ravine itself. From that height you could see across the tops of the trees down to the plain below; but what Mowgli looked at was the sides of the ravine, and he saw with a great deal of satisfaction that they ran nearly straight up and down, while the vines and creepers that hung over them would give no foothold to a tiger who wanted to get out.

"Let them breathe, Akela," he said, holding up his hand. "They have not winded him yet. Let them breathe. I must tell Shere Khan who comes. We have him in the trap."

He put his hands to his mouth and shouted down the ravine—it was almost like shouting down a tunnel—and the echoes jumped from rock to rock.

After a long time there came back the drawling, sleepy snarl of a full-fed tiger just wakened.

"Who calls?" said Shere Khan, and a splendid peacock fluttered up out of the ravine screeching.

"I, Mowgli. Cattle thief, it is time to come to the Council Rock! Down—hurry them down, Akela! Down, Rama, down!"

The herd paused for an instant at the edge of the slope, but Akela gave tongue in the full hunting-yell, and they pitched over one after the other, just as steamers shoot rapids, the sand and stones spurting up round them. Once started, there was no chance of stopping, and before they were fairly in the bed of the ravine Rama winded Shere Khan and bellowed.

"Ha! Ha!" said Mowgli, on his back. "Now thou knowest!" and the torrent of black horns, foaming muzzles, and staring eyes whirled down the ravine just as boulders go down in floodtime; the weaker buffaloes being shouldered out to the sides of the ravine where they tore through the creepers. They knew what the business was before them—the terrible charge of the buffalo herd against which no tiger can hope to stand. Shere Khan heard the thunder of their hoofs, picked himself up, and lumbered down the ravine, looking from side to side for some way of escape, but the walls of the ravine were straight and he had to hold on, heavy with his dinner and his drink, willing to do anything rather than fight. The herd splashed through the pool he had just left, bellowing till the narrow cut rang. Mowgli heard an answering bellow from the foot of the ravine, saw Shere Khan turn (the tiger knew if the worst came to the worst it was better to meet the bulls than the cows with their calves), and then Rama tripped, stumbled, and went on again over something soft, and, with the bulls at his heels, crashed full into the other herd, while the weaker buffaloes were lifted clean off their feet by the shock of the meeting. That charge carried both herds out into the plain, goring and stamping and snorting. Mowgli watched his time, and slipped off Rama's neck, laying about him right and left with his stick.

"Quick, Akela! Break them up. Scatter them, or they will be fighting one another. Drive them away, Akela. Hai, Rama! Hai, hai, hai! my children. Softly now, softly! It is all over."

Akela and Gray Brother ran to and fro nipping the buffaloes' legs, and though the herd wheeled once to charge up the ravine again, Mowgli managed to turn Rama, and the others followed him to the wallows.

Shere Khan needed no more trampling. He was dead, and the kites were coming for him already.

"Brothers, that was a dog's death," said Mowgli, feeling for the knife he always carried in a sheath round his neck now that he lived with men. "But he would never have shown fight. His hide will look well on the Council Rock. We must get to work swiftly."

A boy trained among men would never have dreamed of skinning a ten-foot tiger alone, but Mowgli knew better than anyone else how an animal's skin is fitted on, and how it can be taken off. But it was hard work, and Mowgli slashed and tore and grunted for an hour, while the wolves lolled out their tongues, or came forward and tugged as he ordered them. Presently a hand fell on his shoulder, and looking up he saw Buldeo with the Tower musket. The children had told the village about the buffalo stampede, and Buldeo went out angrily, only too anxious to correct Mowgli for not taking better care of the herd. The wolves dropped out of sight as soon as they saw the man coming.

"What is this folly?" said Buldeo angrily. "To think that thou canst skin a tiger! Where did the buffaloes kill him? It is the Lame Tiger too, and there is a hundred rupees on his head. Well, well, we will overlook thy letting the herd run off, and perhaps I will give thee one of the rupees of the reward when I have taken the skin to Khanhiwara." He fumbled in his waist cloth for flint and steel, and stooped down to singe Shere Khan's whiskers. Most native hunters always singe a tiger's whiskers to prevent his ghost from haunting them.

"Hum!" said Mowgli, half to himself as he ripped back the skin of a forepaw. "So thou wilt take the hide to Khanhiwara for the reward, and perhaps give me one rupee? Now it is in my mind that I need the skin for my own use. Heh! Old man, take away that fire!"

"What talk is this to the chief hunter of the village? Thy luck and the stupidity of thy buffaloes have helped thee to this kill. The tiger has just fed, or he would have gone twenty miles by this time. Thou canst not even skin him properly, little beggar brat, and forsooth I, Buldeo, must be told not to singe his whiskers. Mowgli, I will not give thee one anna of the reward, but only a very big beating. Leave the carcass!"

"By the Bull that bought me," said Mowgli, who was trying to get at the shoulder, "must I stay babbling to an old ape all noon? Here, Akela, this man plagues me."

Buldeo, who was still stooping over Shere Khan's head, found himself sprawling on the grass, with a gray wolf standing over him, while Mowgli went on skinning as though he were alone in all India.

"Ye-es," he said, between his teeth. "Thou art altogether right, Buldeo. Thou wilt never give me one anna of the reward. There is an old war between this lame tiger and myself—a very old war, and—I have won."

To do Buldeo justice, if he had been ten years younger he would have taken his chance with Akela had he met the wolf in the woods, but a wolf who obeyed the orders of this boy who had private wars with man-eating tigers was not a common animal. It was sorcery, magic of the worst kind, thought Buldeo, and he wondered whether the amulet round his neck would protect him. He lay as still as still, expecting every minute to see Mowgli turn into a tiger too.

"Maharaj! Great King," he said at last in a husky whisper.

"Yes," said Mowgli, without turning his head, chuckling a little.

"I am an old man. I did not know that thou wast anything more than a herdsboy. May I rise up and go away, or will thy servant tear me to pieces?"

"Go, and peace go with thee. Only, another time do not meddle with my game. Let him go, Akela."

Buldeo hobbled away to the village as fast as he could, looking back over his shoulder in case Mowgli should change into something terrible. When he got to the village he told a tale of magic and enchantment and sorcery that made the priest look very grave.

Mowgli went on with his work, but it was nearly twilight before he and the wolves had drawn the great gay skin clear of the body.

"Now we must hide this and take the buffaloes home! Help me to herd them, Akela."

The herd rounded up in the misty twilight, and when they got near the village Mowgli saw lights, and heard the conches and bells in the temple blowing and banging. Half the village seemed to be waiting for him by the gate. "That is because I have killed Shere Khan," he said to himself. But a shower of stones whistled about his ears, and the villagers shouted: "Sorcerer! Wolf's brat! Jungle demon! Go away! Get hence quickly or the priest will turn thee into a wolf again. Shoot, Buldeo, shoot!"

The old Tower musket went off with a bang, and a young buffalo bellowed in pain.

"More sorcery!" shouted the villagers. "He can turn bullets. Buldeo, that was thy buffalo."

"Now what is this?" said Mowgli, bewildered, as the stones flew thicker.

"They are not unlike the Pack, these brothers of thine," said Akela, sitting down composedly. "It is in my head that, if bullets mean anything, they would cast thee out."

"Wolf! Wolf's cub! Go away!" shouted the priest, waving a sprig of the sacred tulsi plant.

"Again? Last time it was because I was a man. This time it is because I am a wolf. Let us go, Akela."

A woman—it was Messua—ran across to the herd, and cried: "Oh, my son, my son! They say thou art a sorcerer who can turn himself into a beast at will. I do not believe, but go away or they will kill thee. Buldeo says thou art a wizard, but I know thou hast avenged Nathoo's death."

"Come back, Messua!" shouted the crowd. "Come back, or we will stone thee."

Mowgli laughed a little short ugly laugh, for a stone had hit him in the mouth. "Run back, Messua. This is one of the foolish tales they tell under the big tree at dusk. I have at least paid for thy son's life. Farewell; and run quickly, for I shall send the herd in more swiftly than their brickbats. I am no wizard, Messua. Farewell!"

"Now, once more, Akela," he cried. "Bring the herd in."

The buffaloes were anxious enough to get to the village. They hardly needed Akela's yell, but charged through the gate like a whirlwind, scattering the crowd right and left.

"Keep count!" shouted Mowgli scornfully. "It may be that I have stolen one of them. Keep count, for I will do your herding no more. Fare you well, children of men, and thank Messua that I do not come in with my wolves and hunt you up and down your street."

He turned on his heel and walked away with the Lone Wolf, and as he looked up at the stars he felt happy. "No more sleeping in traps for me, Akela. Let us get Shere Khan's skin and go away. No, we will not hurt the village, for Messua was kind to me."

When the moon rose over the plain, making it look all milky, the horrified villagers saw Mowgli, with two wolves at his heels and a bundle on his head, trotting across at the steady wolf's trot that eats up the long miles like fire. Then they banged the temple bells and blew the conches louder than ever. And Messua cried, and Buldeo embroidered the story of his adventures in the jungle, till he ended by saying that Akela stood up on his hind legs and talked like a man.

The moon was just going down when Mowgli and the two wolves came to the hill of the Council Rock, and they stopped at Mother Wolf's cave.

"They have cast me out from the Man-Pack, Mother," shouted Mowgli, "but I come with the hide of Shere Khan to keep my word."

Mother Wolf walked stiffly from the cave with the cubs behind her, and her eyes glowed as she saw the skin.

"I told him on that day, when he crammed his head and shoulders into this cave, hunting for thy life, Little Frog—I told him that the hunter would be the hunted. It is well done."

"Little Brother, it is well done," said a deep voice in the thicket. "We were lonely in the jungle without thee," and Bagheera came running to Mowgli's bare feet. They clambered up the Council Rock together, and Mowgli spread the skin out on the flat stone where Akela used to sit, and pegged it down with four slivers of bamboo, and Akela lay down upon it, and called the old call to the Council, "Look—look well, O Wolves," exactly as he had called when Mowgli was first brought there.

Ever since Akela had been deposed, the Pack had been without a leader, hunting and fighting at their own pleasure. But they answered the call from habit; and some of them were lame from the traps they had fallen into, and some limped from shot wounds, and some were mangy from eating bad food, and many were missing. But they came to the Council Rock, all that were left of them, and saw Shere Khan's striped hide on the rock, and the huge claws dangling at the end of the empty dangling feet. It was then that Mowgli made up a song that came up into his throat all by itself, and he shouted it aloud, leaping up and down on the rattling skin, and beating time with his heels till he had no more breath left, while Gray Brother and Akela howled between the verses.

"Look well, O Wolves. Have I kept my word?" said Mowgli. And the wolves bayed "Yes," and one tattered wolf howled:

"Lead us again, O Akela. Lead us again, O Man-cub, for we be sick of this lawlessness, and we would be the Free People once more."

"Nay," purred Bagheera, "that may not be. When ye are full-fed, the madness may come upon you again. Not for nothing are ye called the Free People. Ye fought for freedom, and it is yours. Eat it, O Wolves."

"Man-Pack and Wolf-Pack have cast me out," said Mowgli. "Now I will hunt alone in the jungle."

"And we will hunt with thee," said the four cubs.

So Mowgli went away and hunted with the four cubs in the jungle from that day on. But he was not always alone, because, years afterward, he became a man and married.

But that is a story for grown-ups.